THE RECORD OF THE PAPER

THE RECORD OF THE PAPER

How the *New York Times* Misreports US Foreign Policy

◆

HOWARD FRIEL AND **RICHARD FALK**

V

VERSO

London · New York

First published by Verso 2004
© Howard Friel and Richard Falk 2004
This paperback edition published by Verso 2007
© Howard Friel and Richard Falk 2007
All rights reserved
The moral rights of the authors have been asserted

1 3 5 7 9 10 8 6 4 2

Verso
UK: 6 Meard Street, London W1F OEG
USA: 180 Varick Street, New York NY 10014-4606
www.versobooks.com

Verso is the imprint of New Left Books

ISBN 978-1-84467-583-8

British Library Cataloguing in Publication Data
A catalogue record for this book is available from the British Library

Library of Congress Cataloging-in-Publication Data
Friel, Howard, 1955–
    The record of the paper : how the New York Times
misreports US foreign policy / Howard Friel and Richard Falk.
        p. cm.
Includes bibliographical references and index.
    ISBN 1-84467-019-8 (hardcover : alk. paper)
    1. New York Times. 2. United States–Foreign relations–2001–3.
3. Newspapers–Objectivity. 4. Iraq War, 2003–Press coverage–
United States.
I. Falk, Richard A. II. Title.
    PN4899.N42T544 2004
    071'471–dc22

                                                    2004017357

Printed and bound in the USA by Quebecor World/Fairfield

For my wife, Michelle, our two daughters, Espi and
Maggie, and my parents, Anna and Howard.
—Howard Friel

For Deb, who combines courage and *joie de vivre* as no other.
—Richard Falk

CONTENTS

ACKNOWLEDGMENTS

I would like to thank Michael Brooks, Francis Burch, John Burroughs, Thomas Butera, Noam Chomsky, Brian D'Agostino, Dominic D'Angelo, Bob D'Avela, Charlie Donahue, Rick Fantasia, Edward S Herman, David Krieger, Arn Krugman, Harvey Lederman, Greg Levey, Brian Levin, Marc Raskin, Peter Weiss, and Burns Weston for their friendship, encouragement, and assistance throughout various stages of this project, and Tariq Ali, Amy Scholder, Jane Hindle, Tim Clark, Niels Hooper, Andrea Woodman, and Gavin Browning at Verso for their support and extraordinary skill and dedication. I would like also to extend my very special gratitude to Richard Falk, whose uncommon generosity and decency is deeply embedded not only in this book but in our hope of a better world for all its citizens. Finally, I would like to thank Michelle Joffroy for making room in her sabbatical year for a second book, and for her expert and ruthless readings of the manuscript throughout.

Howard Friel

As for so many of my generation, especially those of us growing up in New York City, reading the *New York Times* assumed the status of a sacred ritual, engendering unqualified trust and respect for its treatment of the news. In my case, it took the long decade of the Vietnam War to begin the gradual, and somewhat painful, process of demystification. Along the way, I am deeply indebted to three inspirational friends who cleared the path: Noam Chomsky, Gloria Emerson, and Edward Said. This book can be read as a testament to their pioneering efforts to get closer to the truth than *Times'* journalism often permits.

I would like, above all, to thank Howard Friel for conceiving of this project and inviting me to take part. He deserves the overwhelming credit for the result. Along the way, I wish to express my deep appreciation to Amy Scholder for her display of editorial excellence, and to the Verso staff generally for helping us so much to bring this book to publication on such a tight schedule. I would also thank my wife, Hilal, who, while skeptical of my collaborations, was the mainstay of support and love, especially during times of pressure associated with meeting firm deadlines disruptive of our normal serenity.

Richard Falk

INTRODUCTION

It is the major premise of this book that international law presents clear and authoritative standards with respect to the use of force and recourse to war that should be followed by *all* states. Given the power and influence of the United States, its behavior with respect to international law is of particular importance in setting the tone and substance of world politics. It is only under *exceptional* circumstances that principled departures from international law can be made to address *urgent* requirements of defensive and humanitarian necessity, but in such instances a heavy burden of persuasion is on the state claiming the exception.

It is our judgment, supported by a consensus of international law experts from around the world, that the United States government has repeatedly violated international law with respect to its war-making over the past half-century or so, resulting in unjustifiable death and destruction, as well as diminishing the quality of world order.[1]

This American disposition to pursue foreign policy free from the constraints of international law has grown dramatically since September 11, and presents a serious threat of a series of illegal wars that would undermine international law in relation to its most important undertaking—war prevention. This militaristic disposition, accentuated by the Bush presidency but by no means limited to a single leadership or political party, lends urgency to the existence of an informed citizenry that believes in the need for its government to respect international law, especially when it comes to matters of war and peace. Such a vigilant citizenry depends on appropriate public education and awareness. It is here that the news media in the United States bear such a heavy responsibility, which it has shirked to date. We focus our criticism particularly on the *New York Times*, not because it is more at fault than other influential media outlets, but because it occupies such an exalted place in the political and moral imagination of influential Americans and others as the most authoritative source of information and guidance on issues of public policy. It is on this basis that the *Times* has acquired its special status as the newspaper of record in the United States, a trusted media source that supposedly is dedicated to truthfulness and objectivity, regardless of political consequences.[2]

Accordingly, we are critical of the *Times* for its persistent refusal to consider international law arguments opposing recourse to and the conduct of war by American political leaders, and by this refusal allowing the citizenry to overlook this essential dimension of controversial foreign-policy decisions. This refusal reinforces an increasingly passive US Congress that has been derelict in upholding its constitutional role in the area of war and peace; mainly, its responsibility to ensure that all wars fought under an American flag have been authorized by a proper congressional declaration of war in accordance with Article I, section 8 of the US Constitution. Ignoring this legal requirement in recent American constitutional practice has greatly compromised the intended essential role of Congress in sustaining the system of checks and balances that was supposed to guard the country, and now the world, precisely against wars embarked upon solely on the basis of executive initiative. Such a fundamental obligation is supplemented by the directive under Article VI, section 2 of the Constitution to regard ratified treaties as part of the "supreme law of the land." As we will explain later, a proper reading of the UN Charter, a validly ratified treaty, would require Congress to refuse a requested declaration of war if the proposed war was not reconcilable with international law. Under modern international law, such a reconciliation is only possible if the proposed war is to be undertaken as a matter of self-defense *in response to an armed attack*, or if mandated by decision of the UN Security Council. It is ironic that the founders of our republic were so much more sensitive to the dangers of an ill-considered recourse to war than our elected representatives have been for the last several decades.

We are convinced of the actual and potential importance of the *New York Times* as an authoritative voice with respect to controversial issues of policy facing the nation, and affecting the world. Many citizens depend on this newspaper, and a few others, to shape their understanding of important events, because they believe that the *Times* publishes reliable information and presents relevant considerations that help shape an informed and enlightened approach to complex foreign-policy decisions.

In discussing the *Times* it may be useful to understand in an elementary way how the *Times* is structured: (a) news pages report the news through various bureaus or desks, including the foreign, national, and city (or metropolitan) bureaus, and also include business and science news, the arts, and technology; (b) the editorial page expresses the opinions and positions of the paper about these and other contemporary news topics; (c) the "op-ed page" ("opposite-the-editorial page") features staff columnists on a regular basis who as a group represent a fairly wide range of opinion;* (d) additional op-ed page commentary from guest contributors; (e) letters to the editor, which allow readers to respond to news and commentary published in the *Times*; (f) and the magazine and book review. Our coverage in this volume is focused on the *Times* news pages, editorial page, op-ed page, and the Sunday magazine because most of the paper's foreign-policy content is published in these sections.

We argue that, despite this diverse layout of news and commentary, there is a discernible, and disturbing, editorial policy at the *Times* that applies generally to each of these sections. The approach taken by the *Times* over the course of the last half-century or so to issues involving international law in circumstances of severe international conflict is particularly disturbing. Our experience with past wars, especially the Vietnam War, suggests that policy makers in successive presidential administrations and the Congress can make terrible mistakes over long periods, and that when the news media do not act with diligence to challenge these errors in a timely manner by pointing out weaknesses and failures as the policy unfolds, it becomes that much more difficult for the leaders to change course, thereby allowing a failed and futile policy to persist, sometimes for years.

These concerns have deep and varied roots, but they have been strongly activated recently by the *Times*' failure to raise in its news, editorial, and op-ed pages the major objections under international law to the Iraq war in the months leading up to its initiation, or for that matter during the first months of its bloody aftermath. It was clear from

---

*   Current op-ed page columnists are David Brooks, Maureen Dowd, Thomas Friedman, Bob Herbert, Nicholas Kristof, Paul Krugman, and William Safire.

the depth of anti-war activism that the mobilization for this war was being challenged from the outset by many Americans and by the citizenry of almost every liberal democracy in the world. It was also clear that these sentiments opposing the war were based, to a significant degree, on opposition to embarking upon an illegal war, especially so in the absence of a mandate from the UN Security Council. Under these circumstances, the unilateral initiation of a non-defensive war against Iraq was also directed at undermining the authority of international law and the United Nations. From this perspective, the US invasion of Iraq established a dangerous and destructive precedent for the future that other states, following the precedent, could invoke at times of their choosing.

Opposition to the Iraq war, especially abroad, was also reinforced by suspicions that the real motivations for the war were undisclosed by Washington. In effect, the reasons given, emphasizing the threat of Iraqi weapons of mass destruction (WMD) and Iraq's links to Al Qaeda, were widely regarded as smokescreens designed to hide the greed for Iraqi oil, a strategic interest in establishing regional military bases, a readiness to carry out Israel's security agenda, and the American pursuit of world domination. When the WMD failed to materialize, these suspicions were confirmed for many skeptics, both in the United States and around the world.

It is particularly striking that, despite a great deal of published commentary in the *Times* supporting the war, and commentary opposing it, no space was accorded to the broad array of international law and world-order arguments opposing the war. This exclusion becomes more disturbing, given that the only references to US-based international law opinion in the *Times* news pages were to a few unrepresentative specialists, with close past and present ties to the government, who supported the war. How can this pro-war partisanship be explained in this setting, an aspect of which was the weakness of the international law case for the war? Is it part of a broader pattern that applies to any legal argument that is critical of US foreign policy and national security initiatives? Even a brief scan of the literature dealing with the international law perspective would inform the most casual observer that there were many qualified high-profile opponents of the Iraq war who based their opposition on international law, including individuals who in the past have been reluctant to criticize controversial uses of force by the United States.[3]

The *Times* also did not mention or challenge British Prime Minister

Tony Blair's serious though confused justification for the Iraq war, which included an insistence that since current international law might well stand in the way of such wars of choice, the law should be changed so as to enlarge the discretion of states to wage war.[4] We reject such an analysis, but it at least acknowledges the fundamental relevance of international law as generally understood to controversies over recourse to war.

We do not intend to suggest that this exclusion of international law from the *Times*' coverage and commentary represents a sly embrace of the neoconservative view that since international law does not matter in world affairs, it should not be allowed to muddy the discernment of national interests.[5] We doubt also that the exclusion betrays an acceptance of the view that when it comes to foreign policy there are no practical checks on the exercise of power by the executive branch, and doubt even less that the *Times* now endorses the related neoconservative view that international treaties are worthless in relation to global problems, especially with respect to national security policy.

The *Times* in fact is vigorous in its denunciation of global adversaries of the United States who contemplate aggressive wars or engage in hostile acts against American citizens that violate their rights under international law. Editorials and columnists display no reluctance to invoke international law in support of their condemnation of such behavior by enemies of the United States. The newspaper also almost always supports the ratification of international treaties in the area of arms control that are designed to reduce the dangers and costs of war, and in the area of environmental protection. And the editorial outlook of the newspaper appears comfortable with the indictment and criminal punishment of foreign leaders, such as Slobodan Miloševic, Augusto Pinochet, and Saddam Hussein, who have abused their power by committing crimes under international law.

It is our view that if the *Times* were to discharge its public responsibilities properly with respect to international law, it would make at least four major adjustments. First, the editorial page would frame its assessments of a proposed use of international force and recourse to war by all states, including the United States, by referencing the clearly articulated guidelines of international law as set forth in the United Nations Charter and elsewhere. On the basis of precedents, there are almost no occasions on which it is or has been justifiable to depart from these international law guidelines. Second, in exceptional circumstances, where anomalous or asymmetrical challenges arise that do not readily correspond to settled rules and principles of international law, the editorial page should consult responsible international law opinion and thereafter give its own judgment as a product of those consultations, bearing all the while a high burden of persuasion and principled opinion. Third, the op-ed page, the book review, and the Sunday magazine should provide ample and roughly equal space to the major international law positions that argue for and against a given policy, exposing readers to the best thinking available on both sides of a given issue. The purpose here is not to turn the *Times* into a scholarly journal, but to vet complicated issues of national policy in ways that enable citizens to reach informed conclusions. Fourth, the *Times* news pages should apply a rigorous standard of analysis to official factual assertions seeking to justify a use of force. It should also assess the international law implications of official claims that cannot be immediately confirmed or corroborated, given that such claims in the past—including that US ships were attacked in the Gulf of Tonkin on August 4 1964, that the Nicaraguan Sandinista government was shipping weapons to Salvadoran insurgents, and that Iraq possessed prohibited weapons of mass destruction—would not in any event have justified a US use of force under international law even upon confirmation.

Part of the explanation for the exclusion of international law from the policy debate seems to lie in an unacknowledged legacy of the general liberal view that American legalism and moralism in the 1930s contributed to the American reluctance to recognize and meet the threat posed by the rise of Hitler and European fascism. Highly influential public intellectuals such as George Kennan and Hans Morgenthau helped build a foreign-policy consensus after World War II that persisted throughout the cold war to the effect that peace and order in world affairs depended not on rights under international law, but on countervailing power, as reinforced by such doctrines as "containment" and "deterrence."[6] This "realist" compass for foreign policy is widely credited with a generally successful strategic diplomacy during the cold war, avoiding a third world war that likely would have produced a nuclear catastrophe, while effectively containing the Soviet Union within its borders. Other observers, including many who served in high office during this period, are far more skeptical about such realist claims, arguing that we were lucky to have avoided a catastrophic nuclear war, narrowly escaping this outcome in a series of international crises and near accidents. Robert McNamara offers such a view based on his understanding of the Cuban missile crisis of 1962, during which time he was secretary of defense.[7]

Of course, as critics of American foreign policy during the period since 1945 have often pointed out, this preoccupation with power represented a dangerous and destructive over-correction to earlier concerns about legalism and moralism as diversions from the true challenges of foreign policy, which concern the adequacy of military capabilities to deter an attack or, if necessary, to win a war.[8] Throughout the cold war the United States frequently disregarded international law while mounting overt and covert interventions against an array of Third World countries, most prominently, of course, in more than a decade of struggle over the future of Vietnam. Ironically, Kennan and Morgenthau, both arch-realists, were relatively early critics of Washington's approach to Vietnam, but, as might be expected, they based their criticism on "national-interest" grounds, and the proper deployment of available power, rather than on deviations from international legal obligations governing the use of force. This bipartisan triumph of realist thought in the inner circles of governmental policy-making undoubtedly affected the approach taken by the *Times*. This dismissal of the relevance of international law also reflected the American consensus that the closed nature of Soviet society and Moscow's own ultra-realist approach to foreign policy made it foolhardy for Washington to take international law more seriously than its geopolitical counterpart.

With the end of the cold war, one might have expected a greater receptivity at the *Times* to the regulatory role of international law. The distribution of power among leading states did not seem to matter nearly so much in this new era of world politics. There was no significant strategic rivalry among major states. The spread of marketized approaches to global economic policy was producing a new epoch that came to be widely known by the label "globalization." Policies governing the use of international force seemed to matter less in such a global setting of peaceful relations among sovereign states. Instead, the most significant claims to the use of force in the 1990s tended to involve interventions to deal with such matters as "failed states," responses to transnational terrorist acts, and humanitarian undertakings to prevent "ethnic cleansing" and genocide. The *Times* failed to notice that with the collapse of the Soviet Union there were no longer any "realist" checks on the exercise of American military power. Under these new global conditions international law would seem, at the very least, to offer a beneficial and pragmatic reinforcement of self-restraint, as well as providing a necessary framework of limits with regard to the use of force to carry out international policy.

The debate occasioned by the Iraqi invasion of Kuwait in 1990 was expressed in terms of how to respond to "aggression," and the response at the level of legality was fashioned within the collective security framework of the United Nations. As such, the United States suddenly presented itself as an ardent champion of the UN Charter and international law, dutifully awaiting a Security Council mandate to restore Kuwaiti sovereignty rather than acting on its own initiative. That mandate was given, but the unilateralist manner in which the US carried it out in the Gulf war occasioned serious concerns at the UN about allowing the world's most powerful state to appropriate the mantle of UN legitimacy to pursue what became a war controlled in all its operational aspects from Washington, not New York. Such a role of self-marginalization by the UN as occurred in the Gulf war seemed deeply at odds with what the drafters of the UN Charter had intended by way of "collective security," and contradicted the vision of an alternative to war that Woodrow Wilson had championed in the aftermath of World War I.

Even more dubious from the perspective of international law were the American-led moves toward war over Kosovo. Unlike the Gulf war, the UN Security Council was unwilling to give its blessing, and the war went forward in 1999 under American leadership beneath the purportedly legitimizing mantle of the NATO alliance. Unlike the invasion of Iraq in 2003, at least most of the regional neighbors of the former Yugoslavia supported humanitarian intervention, and there existed an imminent humanitarian catastrophe associated with recent Serb atrocities, the credible menace of an "ethnic cleansing" campaign seeking to drive Albanian Kosovars out of the country, the heavy flow of refugees, and the memory of the Srebrenica massacre in 1995. The actuality of the Kosovo war was hardly if ever discussed in the pages of the *Times* by reference to issues of legality, but only in terms of the failure of diplomacy and the humanitarian case for intervention.

The most significant challenges to the relevance of international law to the conduct of American foreign policy came after the September 11 attacks, especially given the character of the US response. The United States had been attacked out of the blue, with major symbolic and substantive damage, which initially put the US in a position to act in "self-defense," however unspecified that claim may have been since no sovereign state was evidently responsible for the attack. The novel character of the apparent attacker raised questions about its location and identity. It seemed reasonable, at first, to hold the Taliban regime in Afghanistan co-responsible with Al Qaeda because it had given sanctuary and operational freedom to Al Qaeda's leadership, allowing extensive training camps and a strong para-military presence within its territory. International law it appeared could be stretched to extend a somewhat exceptional right of self-defense to cover the Afghanistan war.

On closer inspection, however, there were legal difficulties with this attribution of responsibility for the September 11 attacks to the Taliban regime in Kabul. For one thing, the Taliban leadership in the days following the attacks indicated its willingness to cooperate with Washington in apprehending and extraditing the Al Qaeda leadership, including Osama Bin Laden, as well as in negotiating a peaceful resolution of the crisis. Of course, there is no way of assessing whether the Taliban would have followed through or whether an agreement avoiding war was negotiable. For the White House to reject, however, any apparent consideration to negotiate along these lines was to opt for war with a zeal that was not required by practical considerations of defensive necessity and was not allowed by international law. The United States in its rush to war against Afghanistan had thus violated a basic understanding of the UN approach to a valid claim of self-defense, which was to regard war as a last resort after the exhaustion of diplomatic alternatives.

In retrospect, such a law-enforcement approach to addressing the Al Qaeda challenge should have been considered by political leaders and the citizenry for both principled and pragmatic reasons. It would have exhibited an American reluctance to solve global security problems by reliance on war, and it might have eliminated the suspicion that the US government was using "anti-terrorism" as a pretext for the pursuit of a wider, pre-existing agenda. There are many reasons at this point to think that a law-enforcement approach might have proved to be a far more effective way to address the Al Qaeda challenge. It would have encouraged other governments to cooperate, given the shared interest in a more orderly world without non-state actors relying on transnational violence to attain their goals. But doctrinally and otherwise, the Bush administration immediately transposed the justification for war against the Taliban, based on its harboring of terrorists, into a totally distinct argument for regime change in Baghdad, extrapolating the war model of conflict-resolution to a context in which it lacked any basis whatsoever in international law.

What is clear beyond doubt is that the *Times'* failure to even consider the Bush administration's post-September 11 response within the context of international law was an inexcusable lapse, to the extent that the role of the newspaper is to contribute to informed debate on issues vital to the security and liberty of the United States and its citizenry, and to the wider world. This disregard shielded policies of controversial legality and propriety, which have been destructive of world order and have contributed to the serious deterioration of the republican character of American democracy.[9]

Our objections to the exclusion of international law from the news media's coverage of US foreign policy and global security issues rests on several assumptions that are not particularly controversial. International law provides guidelines for government policy that have been agreed upon over the course of a century or more by national leaders, including our own. These rules have been embodied in validly ratified international treaties that, from an American constitutional perspective, are "the supreme law of the land." The failure to respect these rules in the past and present has inclined the country toward an "imperial presidency" of unchecked executive power, and has undermined the Congress' constitutional role in maintaining a system of "checks and balances," especially in the setting of recourse to war.

The failure to restrain war-making to limits prescribed by international law has also contributed to the militarization of American foreign policy. US military expenditures projected for fiscal year 2005 are over $400 billion. That is 40 percent of total world military expenditures, more than twenty-eight times the amount spent by so-called "rogue states," and eight times what Russia, with the second-largest military budget after the United States, spends. This disproportionate budgetary allocation to the Pentagon exerts an enormous militarizing influence throughout American society, including on the economy and public opinion, giving substance to President Dwight Eisenhower's warnings about the menace to American security of "the military-industrial complex."

The point here is not to argue about the content of international law, but to confirm the centrality and clarity of the prohibition on aggressive war-making as the foundation of the post-1945 world order. The postwar American government was the chief architect of this prohibi-

tion, and proud of its contribution. It is our judgment that this commitment to refrain from aggressive war-making remains valid and
beneficial under current world conditions.

The centrality of this commitment to war prevention was memorably
expressed in the famous opening words of the Preamble to the UN
Charter: "We the peoples of the United Nations determined to save
succeeding generations from the scourge of war, which twice in our
lifetime has brought untold sorrow to mankind." In an important
respect our argument can be reduced to the complaint that the *Times'*
approach to American war-making has proceeded as if those words were
never written. Or that they do not, or no longer, apply to the actions of
the United States government. The *Times* shows no current signs of
abandoning this way of handling international law, despite its recent
acknowledgement of mistakes with respect to its coverage of the Iraq
policy debate.[10]

The self-proclaimed goal of the *Times* is to provide readers with "all the
news that's fit to print," in the words of its familiar slogan. Such a goal
combined with the affirmation of the ethos of democracy, an unspoken
premise of any major newspaper in a free society, would suggest that the
international law dimensions of important policies involving such life-
and-death matters as recourse to war would be fully covered. The
American hope at the United States' moment of founding was to avoid
the bloody reality of war as "the sport of kings," and subject any
recourse to war to the full discipline of the basic constitutional functions
of "checks and balances," "separation of powers," and the rigors of
debate by elected representatives followed by a declaration of war. The
fact that American practice strayed from these constitutional ideals early
in its history does not explain the neglect of international law in the
course of the last half-century or so by either the press or the Congress
when the authority of law became increasingly relevant to diplomatic
practice, especially as applied to matters of war and peace.

Up until World War II it could be argued that international law was
not part of the constitutional picture. True, the Kellogg–Briand Pact did
draw a red line around recourse to aggressive war, which was understood to mean *any* war that could not be justified convincingly as a war
of self-defense, or as a war of defensive necessity. But the failure of states
to agree on what was meant by aggression, or for that matter self-
defense, rendered this agreement almost meaningless as a guide to
behavior in the specific circumstances of national policy. The vagueness

of the prohibition, however, did not prevent the judges at Nuremberg from relying on this legal standard to determine that Germany had been guilty of waging aggressive wars, and its leaders criminally responsible for perpetrating "crimes against peace."[11]

The UN General Assembly accepted by unanimous vote the outcome of the Nuremberg Judgment, and the UN Charter delimited the idea of self-defense in a manner that made it more awkward in most circumstances for governments to manipulate its application. And the UN finally agreed as well on a broad definition of "aggression," which, while not very satisfactory from a guidance viewpoint, does reinforce the commitment of all states to restrict recourse to war by reference to international law.[12]

The United States government was a leading party in this process of the international legalization of limits on the use of force by sovereign states, and these developments could not have taken place without official US support. As diplomacy during the cold war confirmed, the United States treated border-crossing "aggression" as a challenge to the whole world, and was careful to formulate its alliance treaty commitments in the language of collective self-defense, reinforced by a reference to the overriding authority of the UN Charter. It is then particularly disturbing that the *Times* did not envisage its responsibilities as extending to the consideration of international law objections to American foreign policy initiatives involving international uses of force.

It is true that the inability among states to agree upon an operationally useful definition of aggression has made governments reluctant to include this crime in the list of offenses for which political leaders can be held criminally accountable. But such limitations with respect to the application of international criminal law do not touch upon whether a state should adhere to the UN Charter and international law when parties resort to force in international disputes. The World Court settled these issues in the minds of many when it determined by a sizable majority in 1986, with reference to the US efforts in Nicaragua to overthrow the Sandinista government, that the American justifications for the use of force did not qualify as individual or collective self-defense in the absence of a prior armed attack, and were therefore legally unacceptable (see chapter 7).[13]

International law is also an important consideration when one takes into account recent revelations about the extent to which American political leaders have mobilized the country for war by deception and disinformation. Historical studies show that governments even in liberal democratic societies cannot be relied upon to disclose the truth about events and policies even to their own citizens.[14] Serious newspapers, including the *Times,* do purport to investigate such behavior, but in fact the major challenges directed at official versions of historic events have generally received scant exposure.

In view of this disposition to whitewash, democratic governance needs the "check" of international law. It is possible to consider the contested legality of proposed international action in a manner that does not draw into question the internal trustworthiness of the political system. International law can be considered as an alternative discourse for deciding whether policies should be adopted or rejected. Its relevance is partly a matter of principle: in a globalized world the rule of law needs also to be globalized, above all with respect to global security. Its relevance is also pragmatic: adherence to the guidelines of international law, periodically adjusted in response to exceptional circumstances, would tend to avoid policies of dubious merit.[15]

The extensive reliance by the US government on secret information and intelligence reports to shape national security policy lends additional impetus to a search for an understanding of purported threats from the perspective of international law. In this sense, the complementary disappointment with the *Times* has been its willingness to reinforce editorially, rather than critically challenge, government deception relevant to ongoing policy discussions. The argument as to legal doctrine, with respect to the adoption of what even supportive observers regard as "the most dramatic policy shift since the Cold War," is partly about the abandonment of the UN criterion of self-defense in response to an armed attack, and partly about the factual context that allegedly justified the initiation of war.[16] News media coverage, for instance, could emphasize the need of a state to sustain a burden of proof that an armed attack is imminent before it resorts to force. Colin Powell failed to meet this test in his heralded appearance before the UN Security Council in February 2003, even assuming the accuracy of his factual presentation with respect to Iraq's WMD and its deception efforts.

We believe that the country and the world are poised at the most dangerous crossroads since the end of the cold war. In one direction is a further slide into repression at home and a regime of global dominance overseas, a course of action certain to provoke violent resistance and continuous warfare. In the other direction is a historic effort to construct a form of global governance that rests on principles of law and justice, drawing on the cooperative capacities of leading governments, and building a more robust set of international institutions centered on the United Nations. We believe that only the second course of action will produce tolerable levels of security at home and in the world, but it will depend on an unprecedented willingness of the United States, as the most powerful global actor, to adjust its program accordingly: to subject its foreign policy to the discipline of international law and to use its diplomatic muscle to satisfy the legitimate grievances that are connected with its past policies, starting with working toward a solution to the Israel–Palestine conflict that is fair for both sides, and with acting to reduce the inequities of economic globalization.

To move toward such a hopeful future is the greatest challenge the American people have ever faced. If that challenge is to have any reasonable chance of being met it will depend on the mainstream media pursuing a course of action that is more responsible and educative than in the past. The purpose of our book is to underscore the importance of meeting this challenge with respect to international law as it applies to the use of international force.

The chapters that follow demonstrate the failure at the *New York Times* to incorporate international law into its coverage of US foreign policy, and thus show that the pretensions of the *Times*, in particular, to its skillful coverage of foreign policy are deeply misleading, and are inconsistent with the well-being of the American citizenry, the rule of law in the United States and the world, and the burden of public trust that the *Times* has inherited.

I

WITHOUT FACTS OR LAW: THE US INVADES IRAQ

On March 20 2003 the United States initiated a military invasion of Iraq. This attack followed numerous prior threats from the Bush administration that it would attack Iraq. Despite the fact that an invasion of one country by another implicates the most fundamental aspects of the UN Charter and international law, the *New York Times* editorial page never mentioned the words "UN Charter" or "international law" in any of its seventy editorials on Iraq from September 11 2001 to March 21 2003, nor has it cited international law to date with respect to the invasion or occupation after March 21.* Thus, the leading editorial voice in the United States simply declined to consider in print whether a major US military invasion and occupation of another country violated international law.

The broader political context clearly required the *Times* to state its position with respect to the legality of a US invasion of Iraq. The heads of state of important US allies, as well as their foreign ministers, UN ambassadors, and other officials argued that an invasion of Iraq without UN Security Council approval would violate the UN Charter—the foundation of modern international law. Millions of people around the world marched against the threatened US attack, many citing international law as the basis of their opposition. And fundamental rules of the UN Charter, which prohibit a state to use force without Security

---

* It was not until May 2004 that the *Times* used the words "international law," in the context of the abuse and torture revelations, in its editorials about the invasion and occupation of Iraq. See "The Abu Ghraib Spin," *New York Times*, May 12 2004; "The Wrong Direction," *New York Times*, May 14 2004.

Council authorization except in response to an armed attack, disallowed an invasion in this instance.

Despite this powerful convergence of mandates to oppose an invasion of Iraq on international law grounds, or, at a minimum, to invoke international law as a standard of analysis whether it viewed a resort to force in this case as legal or not, the *Times* editorial page showed that it would not hold President Bush accountable to the rule of law in his conduct of foreign policy. By failing to do so, the editorial page showed that it would not engage the legitimate concerns of the rest of the world about the legality and global legitimacy of an Iraq invasion.

Even while Bush administration officials cited the invasion as the front-line event of its global "preventive-war" doctrine—a doctrine with no support in international law—the *Times* editorial page declined in general to cite international law in assessing the doctrine. When the president and senior cabinet members said on several occasions that they were prepared to invade Iraq whether the Security Council authorized an invasion or not, the editorial page in response never mentioned the UN Charter's prohibition against the threat and use of force. And when the administration actually invaded Iraq without Security Council authorization, the *Times* editorial page simply ignored this violation of international law.

While declining to invoke international law, the editorial page also declined to cite the US Constitution's limitation on the legal authority of the president or Congress to authorize an invasion of another country that has not attacked the United States, or to act in any other way that violates the UN Charter. Article VI, section 2 of the Constitution says that "all treaties made, or which shall be made, under the authority of the United States, shall be the supreme law of the land." In 1967 a group of distinguished US legal scholars[1] wrote "the US Constitution considers ratified treaties to be the supreme law of the land and therefore considers any violation of such a treaty a violation also of the Constitution." Because, the lawyers argued, US "war actions [in Vietnam] violate the Charter of the United Nations," and

> because these actions violate the supreme law of the land, the question as to which branch of the Government may authorize them, or whether one branch of the Government may delegate to another branch legal powers to authorize them, becomes irrelevant. No branch of Government is permitted directly or indirectly (by delegation) to violate the Constitution.[2]

Furthermore, in an interview with *ABC News* following the Iraq invasion, US Supreme Court Justice Sandra Day O'Connor reaffirmed what the Constitution says, that US-ratified treaties, in her words (and the Constitution's), are "the supreme law of the land."[3] Thus, the US invasion of Iraq, by violating the UN Charter, also violated the US Constitution, whether President Bush alone ordered the invasion or did so with the approval of the Congress.

Even if the *Times* editorial page did not view the legality of the invasion in this light, it had an obligation as the most influential newspaper in the United States to publish its opinion about the legal status of the invasion under both the Charter and the Constitution, which it failed to do. In fact, the editorial page at times endorsed a unilateral US invasion of Iraq in violation of the Charter, and, by extension, the Constitution. The grim fact is there was no discernible effort by the *Times* editorial page to hold the Bush administration's threats and use of force against Iraq accountable to any law.

One implication of ignoring international law with respect to US foreign policy is that it becomes nearly impossible to report a category of related facts, and facts related to those facts, and so on. For example, the *Times* editorial page never reported that the US threats and use of force against Iraq in 2002–03 violated the UN Charter's prohibition against the threat and use of force—a fact widely reported by foreign news media. But the *Times'* Iraq coverage in this regard was not unusual— ignoring international law when it applies to US foreign policy is a fifty-year-old practice at the *Times* editorial page, which has rarely acknowledged US violations of the UN Charter since the Charter's founding. This record of coverage of US foreign policy over the past half-century, from the 1954 Geneva Accords on Vietnam to the recent Iraq invasion and its aftermath, will be discussed and documented throughout this volume.

An American threat and use of force in violation of international law is a fact of enormous global significance that is reported as such by much of the world's news media. When, in turn, the US news media ignore US violations of international law, an imbalance of knowledge develops between the United States and the rest of the world. This makes it relatively easy for US political leaders to manipulate US public opinion against foreign critics, while also increasing the supply of anti-American terrorists for reasons that escape public comprehension in the United States.

Because terrorism targeting the United States is often provoked by

US and US-sponsored violations of international law, a rational counterterrorism policy would include an effort to minimize political and
legal grievances against the United States. This is difficult to do, however, when the leading editorial page in the United States, in addition to
every other major US news organization, won't discuss or even mention
international law or the UN Charter as a constraint on US foreign policy.

By neglecting international law, the *Times* editorial page also
neglected to consider whether Iraqi WMD possession—even if Iraq had
weapons of mass destruction as charged by the Bush administration—constituted a *casus belli* against Iraq. (A *casus belli* is an act or
condition that justifies in turn the use of force or recourse to war under
international law.) This was a highly relevant issue to consider for
anyone publishing serious commentary at the time, given that the
administration repeatedly cited Iraqi WMD possession as a justification
for invading Iraq. In fact, elementary legal analysis of the WMD charge
against Iraq would have effectively undermined the administration's
legal arguments for attacking Iraq—insofar as it even made such arguments—and could have downgraded the pre-invasion status of the
WMD issue ideologically, shifting it from being a sacred cow that could
not be questioned to a more technical issue permitting closer scrutiny of
its underlying factual status. Conforming to its custom, therefore, the
Times editorial page not only ignored international law but, by extension, also failed to report related facts, presented below, about the
administration's policy toward Iraq either before or after the invasion
launch in March 2003:

- Two permanent members of the UN Security Council, the United
  States of America and the United Kingdom of Great Britain and
  Northern Ireland, repeatedly threatened the use of force against a
  United Nations member state, Iraq, without Security Council
  authorization in violation of United Nations Charter Article 2,
  paragraph 4, which stipulates, "All members shall refrain in their
  international relations from the threat or use of force against the
  territorial integrity or political independence of any state, or in any
  manner inconsistent with the Purposes of the United Nations."

- No Security Council resolution issued since 1991 has authorized
  the threat or use of force against Iraq.

- The claim that Security Council resolution 1441 (2002) authorized the automatic use of force against Iraq on the basis of its

renewed warning that Iraq "will face serious consequences as a result of its continued violations of its obligations" is unsupported by the resolution's drafting history (*travaux préparatoires*), inconsistent with the plain and natural meaning of the warning's text (cast in recollective rather than directive terms and making no mention of the use of armed force *per se*), and, in any event, contradicted by the post-adoption interpretive practice of a majority of the Security Council, including three-fifths of its permanent members.

- Iraq has not attacked any state since 1990; it has never attacked or threatened to attack either the United States or the United Kingdom, and possesses no military capability to engage in an armed attack on either the United States or the United Kingdom.

- Claims that Iraq intended to attack the United States or any state with weapons of mass destruction indirectly by providing such weapons to an international terrorist network were speculative and self-serving and lacked credible evidence.

- The American and British resort to a "preventive" use of force, including an armed attack against Iraq, as a response to a speculative, prospective terrorist threat from Iraq violated the United Nations Charter and fundamental principles of international law with respect to the prohibition of the use of force.

- While state practice may authorize a "preemptive" use of force to offset an immediate and severe short-term threat, this claim is at best controversial and, in any event, there is no international law precedent justifying a "preventive" use of force against a long-term threat, least of all a speculative one.

- United Nations Charter Article 51 stipulates that states are permitted to threaten or use force only "if an armed attack occurs" and "only until the Security Council has taken measures necessary to maintain international peace and security"; in this context, American and British claims that Iraq's failure to comply with its disarmament obligations as stipulated in a series of Security Council resolutions constituted a *casus belli* were inconsistent with the United Nations Charter or customary principles of international law with respect to the use of force.

- No Security Council resolution with respect to Iraq has identified Iraq's failure to comply with its disarmament obligations to
  the United Nations as a *casus belli*.

- The resort to force in the absence of Security Council authorization and any credible evidence of an imminent threat of armed
  attack violated not only the United Nations Charter; it also
  constituted a war of aggression and, thus, a crime against peace
  under the Nuremberg precedent.

- The United Nations had achieved considerably more disarmament success in Iraq than the governments of the United States
  and the United Kingdom had claimed, as reported by the United
  Nations Monitoring, Verification and Inspection Commission
  (UNMOVIC), the International Atomic Energy Agency (IAEA),
  and the Amorim Panel report (March 1999), which concluded,
  "The bulk of Iraq's proscribed weapons programme has been
  eliminated."[4]

The *Times* editorial page failed to report any of these legal and factual
findings, which were central to an evaluation of the administration's case
for war.

By ignoring international law, the *Times* editorial page essentially
granted itself a permit to ignore important facts—from WMD-related
facts to important details about UN Security Council resolutions. In
doing so, it neglected to exercise any serious journalistic oversight of the
illegal US threats and use of force against Iraq. Even more broadly, the
editorial page's coverage of the Iraq issue demonstrated that the *New
York Times* has no editorial policy in place that incorporates international
law when it applies to US foreign policy, and that would help ensure
that it reports and evaluates relevant facts and law in the context of any
future use of force by the United States.

Because the United States, historically, has justified illegal military
interventions with factual and legal deceptions, for example, against
Nicaragua in the 1980s and Vietnam in the 1960s, and because the *Times*
has seldom if ever accurately adjudicated the facts and law in these
instances, it is also clear there never has been an editorial policy in place
at the *Times* that would have enabled it to cover such military episodes
with the facts and law accurately recorded. The result is a record of
misleading, inaccurate, and incomplete reporting at the *New York Times*,

beginning at least since 1954, when it misrepresented the terms of the Geneva Accords on Vietnam, to 1964, when it misreported the facts and law pertaining to the Tonkin Gulf incidents and the illegal US reprisal bombings of North Vietnam that ensued, and to other such bombings, paramilitary interventions, invasions, threats, and war plans, up to the recent invasion of Iraq in March 2003, as well as its violent aftermath.

Incorporating international law into editorial policy would properly utilize two essential legal instruments—the UN Charter and the US Constitution—to consult when an American president claims a right to attack or invade another country. This would (a) introduce foundational legal principles to American journalism as evaluative criteria of US foreign policy, (b) replace the misguided go-along patriotism of long-standing editorial policy that has permitted a succession of presidents to lie and deceive to justify the use of force in violation of law, (c) help enforce the law of the land in the United States by identifying American policies that violate it, and (d) give the American citizenry the facts and law it needs to genuinely participate in policy making as the Constitution and modern First Amendment jurisprudence have intended. The editorial policy of the *New York Times*, contemporary and historical, upholds none of these principles.

In fact, the implementation of editorial policy at the *Times* presents a much worse picture than simply that of a neglect of international law and a failure to report important facts. It includes a history of complicity with official lies and illegal policies, and an inward institutional focus that prioritizes the interests of the newspaper over the nation, including an apparent obsession with what it regards as its neutral political positioning, irrespective of what the facts and law, or the condition of the country, might be. This is falsely represented as journalistic "objectivity," is widely perceived as an exemplary editorial policy, and is thus imitated by most other major newspapers and news organizations in the United States. In contrast, incorporating international law into editorial policy would lead to a superior journalistic product at the *Times* and contribute to a wiser US foreign policy, enhanced US national security, a more vigorous American democracy and a well-guarded Constitution, in addition to contributing to a more peaceful world order capable of addressing the threats to civilization confronting every nation and person today.

Whether Iraq had any WMD was hardly posed as a question by the *Times* editorial page. Using no obvious evidentiary standard, exercising no journalistic checks and balances of the government's "intelligence consensus" on Iraqi WMD, and apparently happy to accept the Bush administration's WMD charges against Iraq at face value, the editorial page persistently presented the notion of Iraqi WMD possession as an established fact, as these editorial-page excerpts indicate:

- Iraq already possesses biological and chemical weapons, and Mr. Hussein would probably not hesitate to use them in a desperate effort to prevent the dissolution of his regime. ("Steps Before War," *New York Times*, August 11 2002.)

- Iraq, with its storehouses of biological toxins, its advanced nuclear weapons program, its defiance of international sanctions and its ambitiously malignant dictator, is precisely the kind of threat that the United Nations was established to deal with. ("The Iraq Test," *New York Times*, September 13 2002.)

- The combination of Saddam Hussein's weapons programs, especially his effort to produce nuclear weapons, and Iraq's brazen defiance of the Security Council represent a serious threat to international order. ("A Measured Pace on Iraq," *New York Times*, September 14 2002.)

- That makes it all the more important to clarify what really counts in this conflict. The answer is the destruction of Iraq's unconventional weapons and the dismantling of its program to develop nuclear weapons. ("A Road Map For Iraq," *New York Times*, September 18 2002.)

- No further debate is needed to establish that Saddam Hussein is an evil dictator whose continued effort to build unconventional weapons in defiance of clear United Nations prohibitions threatens the Middle East and beyond. ("A Time For Debate and Reflection," *New York Times*, October 3 2002.)

- As inspections resumed yesterday after four years, the two men leading the effort, Hans Blix and Mohamed ElBaradei, have adopted an appropriately tough tone. Iraq's statements, however, continue to be disturbingly evasive, including a brazen assertion that Baghdad has no unconventional weapons programs. ... Although the Iraqis have promised to cooperate with the U.N., Baghdad's implausible claim to be weapons-free suggests that Saddam Hussein may have different plans. ("Inspecting Iraq," *New York Times*, November 28 2002.)

- Baghdad has not provided convincing documentation to back up its dubious claim to have eliminated all its illegal biological, chemical, nuclear and missile programs. The report [Iraq's WMD declaration to the UN Security Council] also omitted data on biological programs that had been disclosed previously and pointed to new violations of restrictions on chemical production and missile tests. In the nuclear area, Iraq failed to explain satisfactorily its recent purchase of aluminum tubes that can be used to enrich uranium for bomb-making. These are not trivial omissions. ("Iraqi Stonewalling," *New York Times*, December 20 2002.)

- While Iraq is ostensibly cooperating with U.N. weapons inspectors, Baghdad's overall accounting of its unconventional arms programs has been circumscribed at best and deceptive at worst. The failure to provide a full description of its nuclear weapons projects is especially troubling. ("The Exercise of American Power," *New York Times*, January 2 2003.)

- Saddam Hussein is obviously a brutal dictator who deserves toppling. No one who knows his history can doubt that he is secretly trying to develop weapons of mass destruction. ("The Race to War," *New York Times*, January 26 2003.)

- Secretary of State Colin Powell presented the United Nations and a global television audience yesterday with the most powerful case to date that Saddam Hussein stands in defiance of Security Council resolutions and has no intention of revealing or surrendering whatever unconventional weapons he may have. ("The Case Against Iraq," *New York Times*, February 6 2003.)

- It's up to the Council members—especially the veto-wielding quintet of the United States, Britain, France, Russia, and China—to decide whether Iraq is disarming. In our judgment, Iraq is not. ("Disarming Iraq," *New York Times*, February 15 2003.)

- The United States wants a new resolution reaffirming the conclusion that Iraq has failed to disarm, effectively opening the way to war sanctioned by the U.N. France, supported by Germany and Russia, prefers to give Hans Blix and his inspectors more time to see if they can disarm Iraq. The American resolution, introduced by Britain, deserves the Security Council's support. ("Facing Down Iraq," *New York Times*, February 25 2003.)

- Baghdad is still a very long way from living up to the Security Council's demand for it to give up its unconventional weapons. ("A Fractured Security Council," *New York Times*, March 8 2003.)

- America is on its way to war. President Bush has told Saddam Hussein to depart or face attack. For Mr. Hussein, getting rid of weapons of mass destruction is no longer an option. ("War in the Ruins of Democracy," *New York Times*, March 18 2003.)

While skepticism toward Iraq's disarmament claims was warranted up to a point, due to a number of unresolved verification issues and its history of concealing its WMD programs from UN inspectors in the early 1990s, the evidentiary record up to that point would have compelled any objective commentator to begin questioning the accuracy of the Bush administration's WMD claims against Iraq. However, while asserting Iraqi WMD possession as an established fact, the *Times* editorial page apparently felt unburdened by the absence of evidence pointing to Iraqi WMD, and ignored key findings and facts that clashed with the Bush administration's WMD claims with respect to Iraq.

One such finding was included in the March 1999 Amorim Panel report to the UN Security Council (a special panel appointed by the Council in December 1998 to assess the status of Iraqi WMD), which, even after highlighting the unresolved verification issues, concluded that "the bulk of Iraq's proscribed weapons programme has been eliminated."

The *Times* editorial page also ignored the Amorim Panel's more specific findings with respect to the destruction of Iraq's nuclear-weapons program in the 1990s by the International Atomic Energy Agency:

> Most of the IAEA activities involving the destruction, removal and rendering harmless of the components of Iraq's nuclear weapons programme, which to date have been revealed and destroyed, were completed by the end of 1992. In February 1994, the IAEA completed the removal from Iraq of all weapon-usable nuclear material, essentially reactor fuel. On the basis of its findings, the Agency [IAEA] is able to state that there is no indication that Iraq possesses nuclear weapons or any meaningful amounts of weapon-usable nuclear material or that Iraq has retained any practical capability (facilities or hardware) for the production of such material.[5]

The findings of the Amorim Panel were significant because they were among the last official assessments of the status of Iraq's WMD prior to the return of UN inspectors in November 2002. Furthermore, the IAEA itself, pursuant to Security Council resolutions 687 (1991) and 1051

(1996), published over sixty reports from 1991 to 2003 that documented its successful effort to dismantle and destroy Iraq's nuclear weapons program.[6] The *Times* editorial page ignored these reports, even as it asserted on many occasions that Iraq had a nuclear-weapons program that threatened the United States and was reason enough to invade Iraq.

In a report dated January 27 2003—its first substantive report on Iraq's nuclear-weapons program since 1998—the IAEA reaffirmed the findings of the 1999 Amorim Panel report and the IAEA's own prior reports, and concluded that the status of Iraq's nuclear-weapons program in 1998 as defunct had not changed during the absence of UN inspectors from late 1998 to late 2002:

> In September 1991, the IAEA seized documents in Iraq that demonstrated the extent of its nuclear weapons programme. By the end of 1991, we had largely destroyed, removed or rendered harmless all Iraqi facilities and equipment relevant to nuclear weapons production. We confiscated Iraq's nuclear weapons usable material—high enriched uranium and plutonium—and by early 1994 we had removed it from the country. By December 1998—when the inspections were brought to a halt with a military strike imminent—we were confident that we had not missed any significant component of Iraq's nuclear programme. ... To conclude, we have to date found no evidence that Iraq has revived its nuclear weapons programme since the elimination of the programme in the 1990s.[7]

In an editorial the next day, while citing the report, the *Times* editorial page ignored these central findings, noting only that the IAEA's director, Mohamed ElBaradei, "pointed to important unanswered questions" about Iraq's nuclear-weapons program.[8] This misrepresented ElBaradei's report on two counts: it ignored his confirmation that Iraq's dismantled nuclear-weapons program had not been revived, and it highlighted "important unanswered questions" that were not actually indicated as such in ElBaradei's report with respect to the issue of Iraq's nuclear disarmament. ElBaradei reported the only specific unanswered question as follows:

> The Iraqi [WMD] declaration [of December 7 2002] was consistent with our existing understanding of Iraq's pre-1991 nuclear program; however, it did not provide any new information relevant to certain questions that have been outstanding since 1998—in particular regarding Iraq's progress prior to 1991 related to weapons design and centrifuge development. While these questions do not constitute unresolved disarmament issues, they nevertheless need further clarification.

Thus, this unresolved area of investigation by the IAEA—which in particular pre-dated 1991 and was relevant to ongoing monitoring and verification, but not to the fundamental question of Iraqi disarmament—would hardly trump the finding that Iraq had no nuclear-weapons program since 1994. Yet this was how the *Times* editorial page on January 28 chose to represent the content of ElBaradei's January 27 report.

ElBaradei also listed five areas of "focus," but these were not identified or depicted as "unanswered questions" as the *Times* editorial page reported. These areas were:

(a) The inspection of "all of those buildings and facilities that were identified [by the United States and Britain] through satellite imagery, as having been modified or constructed over the past four years." ElBaradei reported that "I.A.E.A. inspectors have been able to gain ready access and to clarify the nature of the activities currently being conducted in these facilities. No prohibited nuclear activities have been identified during these inspections";

(b) "A particular issue of focus," ElBaradei reported, "has been the attempted procurement by Iraq of high strength aluminum tubes, and the question of whether these tubes, if acquired, could be used for the manufacture of nuclear centrifuges." ElBaradei reported that, while "the attempt [by Iraq] to acquire such tubes is prohibited under Security Council Resolution 687 ... it appears that the aluminum tubes would be consistent with the purpose stated by Iraq and, unless modified, would not be suitable for manufacturing centrifuges; however, we are still investigating this issue";

(c) "Another area of focus," ElBaradei continued, "has been to determine how certain dual-use materials have been relocated or used—that is, materials that could be used in nuclear weapons production but also have other legitimate uses." ElBaradei noted that "a good example is the Iraqi declaration concerning the high explosive H.M.X., which states that, out of the H.M.X. under I.A.E.A. seals in Iraq at the end of 1998, some had been supplied to cement plants as an industrial explosive for mining." HMX is a high explosive that could be used to detonate a nuclear device. ElBaradei reported "the whereabouts and final use of the removed material are matters that will require further investigation—although it will be difficult to verify the disposition of the H.M.X. that is declared to have been used";

(d) "A fourth focal point," ElBaradei reported, "has been the investigation of reports of Iraqi efforts to import uranium after 1991." With respect to this question, ElBaradei reported "at this stage, however, we do not have enough information, and we would appreciate receiving more"; and

(e) with regard to the fifth area of focus, ElBaradei simply stated: "We are also making progress on a number of other issues, related, for example, to the attempted importation of a magnet production facility."

Thus, other possible "unanswered questions" cited by the *Times* editorial page conceivably could have related to dual-use materials (including HMX, which Iraq had in fact declared in its December 7 WMD declaration to the United Nations and about which ElBaradei expressed no specific concern), or to Iraq's alleged post-1991 efforts to import uranium, or to US allegations that Iraq had sought to import aluminum tubes in order to make enriched uranium to make nuclear weapons. While these issues needed to be cited and investigated at the time in the interest of verification and ongoing monitoring, they clearly did not subvert ElBaradei's principal finding that Iraq had no nuclear-weapons program. Given the overall content of ElBaradei's January 27 report, it's hard to imagine that the *Times* editorial page characterized the report in good faith by citing only "unanswered questions" in its January 28 editorial.

Furthermore, after ignoring ElBaradei's central finding in the January 27 report that Iraq had no nuclear-weapons program, and exaggerating the significance of the unresolved issues mentioned in the report, the editorial page also ignored ElBaradei's central finding in his February 14 2003 report, which stated:

> The IAEA concluded, by December 1998, that it had neutralized Iraq's past nuclear programme and that, therefore, there were no unresolved disarmament issues left at that time. Hence, our focus since the resumption of our inspections in Iraq, two and a half months ago, has been verifying whether Iraq revived its nuclear programme in the intervening years. We have to date found no evidence of ongoing prohibited nuclear or nuclear related activities in Iraq.[9]

So the IAEA on February 14 2003 reported that it "found no evidence of ongoing prohibited nuclear or nuclear-related activities in Iraq." The next day (February 15), the *Times* editorial page, while neglecting to mention this finding, stated: "It's up to the [Security] Council members . . . to decide whether Iraq is disarming. In our judgment, it is not."[10] What evidence did the editorial page give to support its claim that Iraq was not disarming? It gave no evidence. By this point the editorial page had simply adopted the Bush administration's claims about Iraqi WMD as accurate and factual.

In the same spirit, the same February 15 *New York Times* editorial also stated:

> What should not be missed is that the positive aspects of the reports [from Blix and ElBaradei] dealt largely with secondary matters like process and access. On the essential issue of active Iraqi cooperation in the disclosure and destruction of prohibited unconventional weapons, the inspectors [Blix and ElBaradei] could find little encouraging to say.

To repeat: The February 15 *Times* editorial said that Blix and ElBaradei "could find little encouraging to say" about Iraqi cooperation. Continuing to focus for the moment on the IAEA's January 27 report, here is what ElBaradei had to say in that report about Iraqi cooperation and the destruction of prohibited weapons:

> In support of the I.A.E.A. inspections to date, the Iraqi authorities have provided access to all facilities visited—including presidential compounds and private residences—without conditions and without delay. The Iraqi authorities also have been cooperative in making available additional original documentation, in response to requests by I.A.E.A. inspectors."

Two weeks later, ElBaradei's February 14 report, with respect to Iraqi cooperation, stated:

> Since our January report, the I.A.E.A. has conducted an additional 38 inspections at 19 locations, for a total of 177 inspections at 125 locations. Iraq has continued to provide immediate access to all locations.[12]

Given what the IAEA's reports of January 27 2003 and February 14 2003 had confirmed with respect to Iraqi cooperation, the *Times* editorial page on February 15 either consciously misrepresented what the IAEA had reported about Iraqi cooperation, or it had simply accepted at face value what the Bush administration had claimed about Iraqi cooperation, without bothering to read the reports of the UN inspectors.

Furthermore, on January 24, three days before ElBaradei's January 27 report, the *Associated Press* reported that ElBaradei was planning to give Iraq a grade of "B" on the issue of cooperation:

The head of the UN nuclear agency will tell the Security Council next week that his inspectors need more time in Iraq, but that Saddam Hussein gets a "B" for his cooperation, an agency spokesman said Friday.

International Atomic Energy Agency director Mohamed ElBaradei, due to brief the council in New York on Monday along with chief UN inspector Hans Blix, will give Iraq "quite satisfactory" grades despite the need for improvement, spokesman Mark Gwozdecky said.

"Their report card will be a 'B,' " he told The Associated Press. Gwozdecky said ElBaradei will tell the Security Council that Saddam's government has provided good access to inspectors searching for weapons of mass destruction.

"Access and cooperation are good," he said. "We've been getting where and when we want to get, and we've been generally successful in getting what we need."[13]

On January 25, the day after this *AP* report, the *New York Times* news pages reported that the Bush administration, upon learning of ElBaradei's intention to give the Iraqi government a "B" on cooperation, sought to pressure ElBaradei to delete this evaluation from his upcoming report to the UN:

A bit of doubt was thrown into what the Blix report would say after a spokesman for Mr. ElBaradei said in Vienna that Mr. Hussein would get a "quite satisfactory" grade for cooperating with nuclear inspectors. The spokesman, Mark Gwozdecky, told The Associated Press that "their report card will be a 'B'—quite satisfactory." White House officials were reported to be furious about this comment and pressing the Atomic Energy Agency to rescind it, officials said.[14]

While ElBaradei never did give Iraq a "B" in his January 27 report, he nevertheless did give it good marks. However, the *Times* editorial page took a worst-case view of Iraqi cooperation, and noted only "the superficial cooperation Iraq has provided and its lack of cooperation on the core matter of what it has done with its weapons programs since the last round of inspections ended in 1998."[15]

The *Times* editorial page also ignored important aspects of the disarmament reports issued by UNMOVIC's executive chairman, Hans Blix, who, for example, reported to the UN Security Council on December 19 2002 that "in most cases, the issues are outstanding not because there is information that contradicts Iraq's account [that it has no WMD], but simply because there is a lack of supporting evidence,"[16] such as complete documentation, testimony, and physical evidence that

Iraq had disarmed as it had claimed. Thus, while unresolved verification issues were grounds for additional inspections and ongoing monitoring, they did not by themselves constitute evidence that Iraq had prohibited weapons.

On January 9 2003 Blix also reported to the Security Council: "I have not asserted on behalf of UNMOVIC that proscribed items or activities exist in Iraq."[17] As of that date, then, the UN's chief weapons inspector in Iraq had essentially reported that he had no specific evidence of Iraqi WMD. But this statement, and others like them, were neither reported nor apparently considered at the *Times* editorial page. (Blix immediately followed this statement by arguing, as he often did, that if Iraq had prohibited weapons, it "should present them and eliminate them in our presence," a difficult command to follow if in fact there was nothing or very little for Iraq to present.)

Even Blix's most negative assessment of Iraqi disarmament progress—the January 27 2003 report to the Security Council—included indications that Iraq may have already been disarmed by the United Nations. In his January 27 statement, Blix reported "Iraq appears not to have come to genuine acceptance—not even today—of the disarmament which was demanded of it and which it needs to carry out to win the confidence of the world and live in peace."[18]

The next day's front-page headlines in the *New York Times* (January 28) read: "U.N. Weapons Inspector Criticizes Iraq's Cooperation: Finds No Proof Hussein Has Disarmed." This article quoted Blix's statement cited above, and a number of other statements where Blix was critical of Iraq's accounting of its reported former stocks of VX, anthrax, and growth media relevant to biological weapons, as well as Blix's charge that the range of Iraq's Al-Samoud 2 and Fatah ballistic missiles exceeded the 150 km (90 mile) range limit set by Security Council resolutions. While these issues were a legitimate subject of focus by UNMOVIC's inspectors, they did not by themselves constitute evidence of Iraq's possession of prohibited weapons. In fact, Blix made several other substantive remarks in his January 27 report, including the one below, that received no coverage at all in the *Times*:

> The implementation of [Security Council] resolution 687 (1991) nevertheless brought about considerable disarmament results. It has been recognized that more weapons of mass destruction [in Iraq] were destroyed under this resolution than were destroyed during the [1991] Gulf War. Large quantities of chemical weapons were destroyed under UNSCOM

supervision before 1994. While Iraq claims—with little evidence—that it destroyed all biological weapons unilaterally in 1991, it is certain that UNSCOM destroyed large biological weapons production facilities in 1996. The large nuclear infrastructure was destroyed and the fissionable material was removed from Iraq by the IAEA.[19]

The record shows that the UN's disarmament efforts in Iraq in the 1990s were substantial, to the point where the Amorim Panel concluded, even after reviewing similar documentation and verification issues with respect to VX, anthrax, and growth agents, that "the bulk of Iraq's proscribed weapons programme has been eliminated"—an assessment that has stood the test of time, including subsequent UN inspections and a post-invasion US search. Indeed, though Blix cited "unresolved disarmament issues" and "key remaining disarmament tasks" in the January 27 report, he also said that such issues "do not contend that weapons of mass destruction remain in Iraq, but nor do they exclude that possibility." They instead "point to lack of evidence and inconsistencies, which raise question marks, which must be straightened out, if weapons dossiers are to be closed and confidence is to arise." These remarks and others indicate that Blix reported no specific evidence of Iraqi WMD possession on January 27, and suggested that the unresolved issues were relevant either to verify Iraq's disarmament in order to close the books on Iraqi WMD, or as possible evidence of Iraqi WMD possession, for which little to no other evidence existed.

Even though Blix never actually said on January 27 that Iraq had any WMD to disarm, the *New York Times* reported in the first paragraph of its front-page story the next day that Blix's report "provid[ed] support to the Bush administration's campaign to disarm Iraq by force if necessary."[20]

The *Times* editorial (January 28) on Blix's report was in some respects fairer than the *Times'* news coverage. It described Blix's report as "mixed," and noted that Blix reported that he "had not yet uncovered hard evidence that conclusively proved that Iraq is developing prohibited weapons." However, a few sentences later, the editorial page went beyond Blix's findings in this regard, and argued that "without Baghdad's full cooperation, inspectors cannot disarm Iraq."[21] If inspectors had found no hard evidence of Iraqi WMD, it was possible there was little or nothing left to disarm.

In addition to ignoring or misrepresenting the reports of the UN inspectors, the *Times* editorial page also ignored a March 3 2003

Newsweek report about a key Iraqi defector, Hussein Kamel, Saddam Hussein's son-in-law, former Iraqi minister of military industry, and "the highest-ranking Iraqi official ever to defect from Saddam Hussein's inner circle," who, for ten years in the 1980s and early 1990s, "had run Iraq's nuclear, chemical, biological and missile programs." Kamel "told CIA and British intelligence officers and UN inspectors in the summer of 1995 that after the 1991 Gulf War, Iraq destroyed all its chemical and biological weapons stocks and the missiles to deliver them."[22]

Newsweek also reported that "Kamel's revelations about the destruction of Iraq's WMD stocks were hushed up by the UN inspectors," and, apparently, also by the CIA, since it too was told about the WMD destruction, and that "the defector's tale raises questions about whether the WMD stockpiles attributed to Iraq still exist."

The implications of this *Newsweek* report were profound. While Kamel's statements without verification did not prove that Iraq had disarmed, the US Central Intelligence Agency nevertheless had information that appears to have been accurate, from Iraq's highest-ranking defector from Saddam Hussein's regime, that Iraq had destroyed its weapons of mass destruction in the early 1990s. The Clinton administration kept this information secret while continuing to support economic sanctions against Iraq for its alleged failure to comply with the disarmament provisions of UN Security Council resolutions. And the Bush administration kept the defector's information secret while justifying an invasion of Iraq on grounds that Iraq had not disarmed. Furthermore, the *Times* editorial page had reported for months with certainty that Iraq in fact possessed WMD; yet it never mentioned the *Newsweek* report or its potential implications.

The editorial page's specific assertions about Iraq's nuclear-weapons program were especially problematic. At one point, the editorial page argued "what really counts in this conflict . . . is the destruction of Iraq's unconventional weapons and the dismantling of its program to develop nuclear arms."[23] Another editorial said Iraq's "failure to provide a full description of its nuclear weapons projects is especially troubling."[24] Other editorials said Iraq had "failed to explain satisfactorily its recent purchase of aluminum tubes that can be used to enrich uranium for [nuclear] bomb-making,"[25] and that Iraq had "failed to mention new efforts to acquire uranium."[26]

Throughout this period, however, there was little evidence of an Iraqi "program to develop nuclear arms," of Iraqi "nuclear weapons pro-

jects," of "aluminum tubes used to enrich uranium," or of any confirmed Iraqi "efforts to acquire uranium." These statements were based
mainly on claims made by the Bush administration, which itself presented little or no supporting evidence. In contrast, there was
considerable evidence, cited above, from the Amorim Panel report and
IAEA inspection reports in the 1990s, that Iraq's nuclear weapons
program had been dismantled by at least 1994.

Furthermore, the idea that Iraq could have reconstituted its nuclear-
weapons program—the most serious WMD issue—was not plausible by
late 2002, when IAEA inspectors had returned to Iraq. In a report to the
Security Council in March 2003, the IAEA's Mohamed ElBaradei spoke
on the issue of Iraq's industrial capacity to support a nuclear-weapons
program:

> At the outset, let me state one general observation: namely, that during the
> past four years, at the majority of Iraqi sites, industrial capacity has dete-
> riorated substantially, due to the departure of the foreign support that was
> often present in the late 1980s, the departure of large numbers of skilled Iraqi
> personnel in the past decade, and the lack of consistent maintenance by Iraq
> of sophisticated equipment. At only a few inspected sites involved in
> industrial research, development and manufacturing have the facilities been
> improved and new personnel taken on. This overall deterioration in
> industrial capacity is naturally of direct relevance for resuming a nuclear
> weapons programme.[27]

Somehow it never occurred to the editorial page at the *Times*—after a
decade in which Iraq's nuclear-weapons program had been dismantled,
and sanctions had degraded industrial capacity while also prohibiting the
sale to Iraq of components related to a nuclear-weapons program—that
Iraq might not have a nuclear program because it had lost the capacity to
have such a program.

The IAEA also investigated the Bush administration's allegations,
supported by the *Times* editorial page, that Iraq had imported aluminum
tubes[28] and uranium[29] to make nuclear weapons. Again, the editorial
page published and credited the administration's claims at face value. In
response to these charges, in his March 2003 report to the Security
Council, ElBaradei reported the IAEA's findings with respect to Iraq's
attempted purchase of aluminum tubes allegedly to enrich uranium:

> With regard to aluminum tubes, the IAEA has conducted a thorough
> investigation of Iraq's attempts to purchase large quantities of high-strength
> aluminum tubes. As previously reported, Iraq has maintained that these

aluminum tubes were sought for rocket production. Extensive field investigation and document analysis have failed to uncover any evidence that Iraq
intended to use these 81mm tubes for any project other than reverse
engineering of rockets.[30]

In the same report, ElBaradei addressed the Bush administration's charge
that Iraq had imported uranium from Africa to build nuclear weapons:

> With regard to uranium acquisition, the IAEA has made progress in its
> investigation into reports that Iraq sought to buy uranium from Niger in
> recent years. The investigation was centered on documents provided by a
> number of States that pointed to an agreement between Niger and Iraq for
> the sale of uranium between 1999 and 2001. . . . Based on thorough analysis,
> the IAEA has concluded, with the concurrence of outside experts, that these
> documents—which formed the basis for the reports of recent uranium
> transactions between Iraq and Niger—are in fact not authentic. We have
> therefore concluded that these specific allegations are unfounded.[31]

Some news-media organizations immediately afterward pursued
ElBaradei's finding that the uranium documents were not authentic:
"ElBaradei: 'Proof' That Iraq Sought Uranium is Fake," *Reuters,* March
7 2003; "Some Evidence on Iraq Called Fake," *Washington Post*, March
8 2003; "CIA Questioned Documents Linking Iraq, Uranium Ore,"
Washington Post, March 22 2003; "UN Official: Fake Iraq Nuke Papers
Were Crude," *Reuters*, March 25 2003.

Unlike these news organizations, which had accurately reported
ElBaradei's March 7 finding that the uranium documents were "not
authentic," that is, were forged, the *Times* editorial page, in a March 8
editorial on ElBaradei's report, neglected to mention that the IAEA had
declared the uranium documents in question to be forgeries. Instead, the
editorial page said only that ElBaradei "found [the uranium charge] to
be unsubstantiated." This misrepresented what ElBaradei said, given that
"unsubstantiated" does not speak to the intentioned deception in this
instance of forged documents.

Given that the *Times* editorial page reported on December 20 2002
that "intelligence on Iraq's recent efforts to acquire uranium" helped
"disprove Iraq's claims to have no unconventional weapons programs,"[32] and that an editorial on January 10 2003 reported that "the
12,000-page declaration Iraq submitted last month . . . failed to mention
new efforts to acquire uranium,"[33] the editorial page should have corrected the record on these charges by accurately reporting what the head

of the IAEA had said about the uranium documents. But it did not do this at the time or soon afterward.

Even though the IAEA director general announced on March 7 that the uranium documents in question had been forged, it took the *Times* editorial page more than two months to acknowledge (on May 26) that the documents were forgeries. In contrast, it took the editorial page one day to support President Bush's claims, issued in his State of the Union address on January 28 2003, that Iraq was seeking uranium and aluminum tubes in order to make nuclear weapons. Here is what the president said on January 28:

> The British government has learned that Saddam Hussein recently sought significant quantities of uranium from Africa. Our intelligence sources tell us that he has attempted to purchase high strength aluminum tubes suitable for nuclear-weapons production. Saddam Hussein has not credibly explained these activities. He clearly has much to hide. The dictator of Iraq is not disarming. To the contrary, he is deceiving.[34]

The next day, the *Times* editorial stated: "Mr. Bush has always done a good job of arguing that Saddam Hussein is dangerous, and he did so again last night."[35] The tendency of the editorial page was to support (sometimes with minor qualifications) whatever the president said about Iraqi WMD and ignore evidence to the contrary with respect to what the inspectors often actually reported, especially ElBaradei.

Six months after President Bush's State of the Union speech, the *Times* editorial page published another editorial devoted to it:

> President Bush cannot be pleased to know that his State of the Union address last January included an ominous report about Iraq that turns out to have been based on forged documents. The incident is an embarrassment for Mr. Bush and for the nation, and he should now be leaning on his aides to explain how they let fabricated information about Iraq's nuclear weapons program slip into his speech. ... In the address, Mr. Bush said the British government had learned that Saddam Hussein had recently tried to get large quantities of uranium from Africa. It is now clear that this accusation was mainly based on counterfeit papers that falsely implied that the West African nation of Niger could be supplying uranium to Iraq. The documents contained obvious factual errors that should have been readily detectable by intelligence analysts.[36]

Obviously aware that it had endorsed the president's speech, including references to the aluminum tubes and uranium, the editorial page was perhaps eager to blame the president's aides (but not the president) for allegations about Iraq that the editorial page itself had endorsed at the time.

But this wasn't the first time the editorial page sought to finesse its record of supporting the president's WMD allegations against Iraq. On May 26, when serious doubts about the truthfulness of the WMD allegations were being widely reported, the editorial page noted "it is disturbing to recall how gravely the administration portrayed the dangers of Iraq's unconventional weapons."[37] Substitute "*New York Times*" for "administration" in this statement, and the resulting statement is equally disturbing.

While the *Times* editorial page reported throughout the pre-invasion period that Iraq had WMD as the Bush administration had claimed, it also reported that Iraq's WMD (which it now appears did not exist at the time) constituted "a serious threat to international order," and it endorsed President Bush's claim that Iraq was "unique in its ability to threaten the world":

> The combination of Saddam Hussein's weapons programs, especially his effort to produce nuclear weapons, and Iraq's brazen defiance of the Security Council represent a serious threat to international order.[38]

> Speaking in Cincinnati, [President Bush] was forceful in outlining the threat presented by Iraq. He laid out the ways in which the Iraqi dictator has brazenly defied United Nations orders to destroy his unconventional weapons, making Iraq, in the president's view, unique in its ability to threaten the world.[39]

These editorial-page endorsements of the Iraqi WMD threat were issued soon after two important speeches by President Bush: the speech before the UN General Assembly on September 12 2002, and a nationally televised speech from Cincinnati, Ohio, on October 7 2002.

In the September 12 UN speech, the president made several references to what he referred to as Iraq's "nuclear program," including its "weapons design, procurement logs, experiment data and accounting of nuclear materials," its "nuclear scientists and technicians," its "physical infrastructure," and "several attempts to buy high-strength aluminum tubes used to enrich uranium for a nuclear weapon."[40] However, none of the nuclear-program components cited by the president in his September 12 speech were ever found, either by UN inspectors before the March 2003 invasion or by US forces during or after the invasion. Yet, despite little or no evidence at the time that such nuclear-program components existed, except for what the president said in his speech, the

Times September 14 editorial on the speech stated that Iraq's "effort to produce nuclear weapons" was "a serious threat to international order."

In his October 7 speech from Cincinnati, President Bush told an American television audience, as the *Times* front page reported the next day, "that Saddam Hussein could attack the United States or its allies 'on any given day' with chemical or biological weapons." The *Times* also reported that "the president likened the threat the country faces today from Iraq to the Cuban missile crisis," that "the president charged for the first time that Iraq's fleet of unmanned aerial vehicles was ultimately intended to deliver chemical and biological weapons to cities in the United States," and that "American intelligence shows that Mr. Hussein is reconstituting his nuclear weapons program with 'a group he calls his nuclear mujahideen, his nuclear holy warriors.' "[41]

But Iraq had no capability to attack the United States with biological or chemical weapons (no such weapons have been found), it had no fleet of unmanned vehicles that were capable of delivering biological or chemical weapons to the United States (no such aerial vehicles have been found), Iraq was not reconstituting its defunct nuclear weapons program (no reconstituted nuclear program or components were found), and Iraq had no nuclear holy warriors (no nuclear holy warriors were found).

Nor were there any grounds to compare the Iraqi threat to the United States to the threat from the Cuban missile crisis. In October 1962, dozens of Soviet ballistic missiles armed with three-megaton nuclear warheads were deployed in Cuba, were operational, and were within striking distance of the United States. Each Soviet warhead was more than 200 times more powerful than the atomic bomb dropped on Hiroshima, and was within fifteen minutes upon launch of most major cities in the United States. Thus, it was obviously a gross exaggeration for President Bush to equate the threat to the United States from Iraq, such as it was, perhaps nothing, with the threat to the United States during the Cuban missile crisis. Yet the *Times* editorial page endorsed the president's October 7 speech in an October 8 editorial, which not only did not challenge the analogy to the Cuban missile crisis, but praised the president for being "forceful in outlining the threat presented by Iraq."[42]

Furthermore, and in keeping with its inconsistent stance as both a hawk and dove with respect to an invasion, the *Times* editorial page inconsistently estimated the extent of the WMD threat from Iraq. After arguing in September that Iraq "represent[ed] a serious threat to international order," and after implicitly endorsing President's Bush's analogy in an October editorial that the threat from Iraq was comparable to the Cuban missile crisis, the *Times* editorial page said in a January 2003 editorial that "even the most alarming estimates of Iraq's unconventional weapons capabilities indicate that there is no imminent danger."[43] Then, less than a month later, the editorial page warned again that "the Europeans and the United Nations must recognize that Saddam Hussein does pose a clear and present danger to the peaceful international order that the United Nations purports to protect." Just three sentences earlier, the same editorial said: "However serious the crimes of Mr. Hussein, we do not find that the administration has made a compelling case that he poses an immediate danger to the vital interests of the United States."[44]

Either the editorial-page vicissitudes of the *New York Times* are the product of incompetence, or they are more calculated, and permit the page to endlessly position itself as an "independent" editorial entity with no consistent allegiance to any party, position, fact, or law.

Upon supporting the Bush administration's assessment of the Iraqi WMD threat, the *Times* editorial page also, for the most part, supported an invasion as an appropriate response to that threat. However, it gave equivocating, even contradictory, advice on this issue as well, which again raises the question whether the *Times* editorial page equivocates in a calculated manner or is simply inept.

Examples of inconsistencies and contradictions are numerous, some of which are presented below, including this excerpt from a November 2002 editorial:

> [W]e hope the Bush administration has not invested the effort in winning unanimous support for [Security Council resolution 1441] only to end up acting unilaterally against Iraq. If Baghdad violates any of these provisions, Washington should insist that the Security Council enforce its decision. Only if the council fails to approve the serious consequences it now invokes—generally understood to be military measures—should Washington consider acting alone.[45]

What is the editorial page's position in this paragraph? The first sentence says the editorial page hopes the administration won't act unilaterally, but the last sentence says the United States "should consider acting alone" against Iraq "if the Security Council fails to approve the serious consequences it now invokes."

Under the UN Charter, if the Security Council does not approve the use of military measures, and unless the United States is under an armed attack or such an attack is imminent, the United States has no option under international law to "act alone" and invade another country. Thus, the editorial page was giving the Bush administration conflicting advice: Don't act unilaterally against Iraq, but consider acting unilaterally (in violation of international law) if the Security Council does not ultimately authorize a military invasion.

Once again, either the argument is confused or its inconsistency is calculated. Given the formulaic repetition of this something-for-everyone kind of reasoning, it looks intentional. For example, conservatives might like the fact that the editorial page would support an eventual unilateral US invasion of Iraq in violation of the UN Charter, a position openly advocated by the Bush administration and its supporters. On the other hand, liberals might see the editorial page's initial statement opposing a unilateral American effort as supporting their case. Thus, the November 9 editorial on Iraq constitutes additional evidence that the *Times* editorial page pursues a self-interested "positioning" strategy that, in the case of its coverage of US policy toward Iraq, is contrary to the UN Charter, undermines the US Constitution (which requires compliance with the Charter), and ignores or misrepresents important facts.

The excerpt below from a January 2 2003 *Times* editorial appears to use a similar positioning approach:

> While Iraq is ostensibly cooperating with U.N. weapons inspectors, Baghdad's overall accounting of its unconventional arms programs has been circumscribed at best and deceptive at worst. The failure to provide a full description of its nuclear weapons projects is especially troubling. Mr. Bush must still exhaust the diplomatic options before ordering American forces into combat.[46]

While the last sentence above favors "exhausting diplomatic options" before "ordering American forces into combat," the second part of this sentence doesn't follow from the first, given that a use of force without Security Council authorization (presumably diplomacy would have been "exhausted" at this point) would violate the UN Charter. Once again, positioning concerns seem to dominate the logic of the editorial—it favors pursuing "diplomatic options," perhaps to make liberals happy, but implicitly endorses a use of force without Security Council approval, to satisfy conservatives.

The positioning occurs not only in the same editorial (or sentence) but between editorials as well. As of January 2 2003, the *Times* editorial page supported the unilateral use of force by the United States against Iraq once diplomatic options were exhausted. In a January 26 2003 editorial, excerpted below, the *Times* modified this position, and tied its support for a US invasion of Iraq to "broad international support":

> We urge the administration to brake the momentum toward war. Saddam Hussein is obviously a brutal dictator who deserves toppling. No one who knows his history can doubt that he is secretly trying to develop weapons of mass destruction. But this war should be waged only with broad international support. To go it alone, or nearly alone, is to court disaster both domestically and internationally.[47]

Less than two weeks later, in yet another instance of either feckless contradiction or political positioning, the editorial page on February 7 reacquired its inclination to support a unilateral American effort, while balancing that position with its standard of "broad international support" for an invasion:

> [T]he pressure is rapidly building on Saddam Hussein to give up his [WMD] evasions or even his office. He may well do neither, inviting an American attack, but we are glad to see the Bush administration turning up the heat before it turns to war. . . . But President Bush confirmed that he was willing to allow the diplomatic dance to swirl a while longer, and would welcome another United Nations Security Council resolution. The decision reflected a wise deference to the widespread sentiment, at home and abroad, that the United States should go to war only if it has broad international support. . . . If Mr. Hussein had hoped for a hung jury after Mr. Powell's [February 5] summation, what he is hearing cannot be of comfort to him. Basically, it is that unless he starts telling the inspectors everything, and starts now, there may soon be no one left trying to hold the Americans back.[48]

What does this editorial say, or appear to say, and what positions does it take? In order of appearance: (a) it assumes Iraqi WMD possession as established fact ("the pressure is building on Saddam Hussein to give up his [WMD] evasions"); (b) it supports the Bush administration's illegal threats to attack Iraq on WMD grounds ("we are glad to see the Bush administration turning up the heat before it turns to war"); (c) it supported the Bush administration's diplomatic efforts at the Security Council (which were narrowly targeted to get an invasion authorization), misrepresented those diplomatic efforts as consistent with anti-war opinion, and aligned itself with the president's narrowly targeted diplomatic efforts at the UN to demonstrate the editorial page's support for going the Security Council route; (d) it supported Secretary of State Colin Powell's February 5 UN report on Iraqi WMD as a credible presentation of evidence of Iraqi WMD possession, and (e) argued that unless the Iraqis reveal their WMD arsenal "now," the US likely will invade with no one left to hold it back. Each of these positions was either misleading, factually wrong, or in conflict with the UN Charter's rules on the use and threat of force.

Also, the difference between the editorial page's advice of January 26 to "brake the momentum toward war" and its February 7 reluctance to hold the president back from invading Iraq reflected the shift from anti-war opinion in the United States that was gaining momentum before President Bush's January 28 State of the Union address and Colin Powell's February 5 UN address, to a pro-war position that picked up after those two speeches.

For example, on January 24, four days before the *Times* editorial page advised the administration for the first time to "brake the momentum toward war," front-page headlines in the *New York Times* read, "Public's Backing of Bush Shows a Steady Decline." The article reported that a *New York Times/CBS News* poll found that "President Bush's public support has eroded steadily over the last 12 months, with a rising number of Americans expressing discontent both with his economic policies and his handling of foreign affairs." Furthermore, front-page headlines in the *New York Times* on January 25 read: "US May Not Press UN For a Decision on Iraq For Weeks." Thus, January 26 may have seemed like a good time for the *Times* editorial page to advise the administration to slow the war momentum, given that the administration had already announced it was delaying an invasion decision, and that public support for an invasion at the time was soft.

On the other hand, by February 7—after American public opinion was swayed by the president's January 28 assertions that Iraq had weapons of mass destruction and ties to Al Qaeda, and by Powell's February 5 claim that Iraq was concealing its prohibited weapons from UN inspectors—the editorial page had reversed its call for restraint. These shifting positions at the *Times* editorial page constitute additional evidence of "positioning" that is less concerned with facts and law and more concerned with where the paper stands politically at a given moment.

There is more evidence of positioning in the February 7 editorial: The editorial page's invocation of "broad international support" as its invasion standard is vague, nor is it the standard for a legal resort to force under the UN Charter. Thus, even when the editorial page appears to take international law into account, as it superficially appears to do here, its careful locution keeps it out of the international law corner.

The positioning approach is evident again in a February 23 *Times* editorial two weeks later:

> Right now, things don't look promising for those of us who believe this is a war worth waging, but only with broad international support. ... It seems clear to us that the United Nations should enforce its own orders and make Iraq disarm, even if that requires force. But in the end, sometime in March, the United States may have to decide whether it should do the job on its own.[49]

While this passage treats Iraqi WMD possession, as always, as an established fact, and cites Iraqi WMD possession as fundamentally justifying an invasion of Iraq, it is also once again internally inconsistent, given that it cites "broad international support" as the editorial page's invasion standard, but also appears to endorse a unilateral US invasion by suggesting that "the United States may have to decide whether it should do the job on its own."

This editorial again reflected either incompetence or calculated positioning, which permitted the editorial page to argue that invading Iraq "is a war worth waging" (good news for right-wingers), "but only with broad international support" (seemingly good news for liberals), and that the United States may have to decide to do the job alone without Security Council approval (more good news for the right).

In March 2003, once a US invasion was nearly imminent, and after driving the war momentum for months with its aggressive promotion of the WMD charge, the *Times* editorial page cited its "broad international support" standard as the basis of its eleventh-hour decision to oppose an Iraq invasion:

> Within days, barring a diplomatic breakthrough, President Bush will decide whether to send American troops into Iraq in the face of United Nations opposition. We believe there is a better option involving long-running, stepped-up weapons inspections. But like everyone else in America, we feel the window closing. If it comes down to a question of yes or no to invasion without broad international support, our answer is no.[50]

After many equivocations and contradictions over several months, this would be the editorial page's final pre-invasion position on an invasion, which President Bush would launch ten days later. Weeks and months later, when no WMD had surfaced and the occupation had bogged down, the editorial page would claim in several editorials that it had opposed the administration's invasion of Iraq—which was true in a narrow technical sense. It was also true, however, that the editorial page supported an invasion of Iraq on principle pending broad international support, that it supported an invasion on principle on WMD grounds, and that it supported an invasion on principle without Security Council approval. Thus, if the invasion and occupation turned out badly for the United States, the editorial page could claim opportunistically (as it did) that it opposed the invasion; if the invasion and occupation turned out well, the editorial page could claim that it supported the invasion on principle.

This "for it and against it" editorial policy is consistent with the fact that the *Times* editorial page rejected the administration's claims about an Iraq–Al Qaeda connection but supported its WMD claims. It was a one-for-one tradeoff that positioned the *Times* comfortably in the center—to the left of the *Wall Street Journal* editorial page, for example, which promoted both the WMD claim and the Iraq–Al Qaeda connection, and to the right, for example, of former UN weapons inspector, Scott Ritter, who rejected both claims and was widely criticized as a result.

Furthermore, opposing an Iraq invasion because it had no "broad international support" was not a legal argument. Rather, it was an argument grounded in feasibility concerns about the effectiveness, difficulty, and expense of an American invasion and reconstruction effort in the absence of UN and allied support. But this kind of advice is analogous to saying you can't rob the bank because it might not go so well without some help.

On the other hand, the March 9 2003 editorial came about as close as the editorial page would to taking an international law position with respect to an invasion of Iraq; that is, while still not mentioning "international law" or "UN Charter." On March 9, the editorial page stated:

> The second argument the Bush administration cites for invading Iraq is its refusal to obey U.N. orders that it disarm. That's a good reason, but not when the U.N. itself believes disarmament is occurring and the weapons inspections can be made to work. If the United States ignores the Security Council and attacks on its own, the first victim in the conflict will be the

United Nations itself. The whole scenario calls to mind that Vietnam-era catch phrase about how we had to destroy a village in order to save it. . . . [The United States] needs to demonstrate by example that there are certain rules that everybody has to follow, one of the most important of which is that you do not invade another country for any but the most compelling of reasons. When the purpose is fuzzy, or based on questionable propositions, it's time to stop and look for other, less extreme means to achieve your goals.[51]

Articulated for the first time ten days before the start of the invasion, the editorial page's brief, indirect reference to international law was too little too late, and, in any event, was contradicted twelve days later in a *Times* editorial supporting the invasion onset: "Nothing could make this invasion look better around the world than evidence that it is welcomed by the Iraqis themselves"; "[J]oyous civilians hailing the invaders as liberators would be very good signs"; "The ultimate prize is Baghdad."[52]

Given the apparent inevitability of the US invasion and the multiple precedents of the editorial page's positioning efforts, it seems that the *Times* editorial page went on record opposing the invasion just before it started, knowing it would support the invasion once it began.

Thus, the *Times* editorial page hit for the cycle, touching nearly every possible political base in its editorials on Iraq. It consistently supported the WMD charge, supported Iraqi WMD possession as a principled justification for invading Iraq, supported at times a unilateral US invasion, opposed at times a unilateral US invasion, ignored "international law" and "UN Charter" but cited "broad international support" as a proxy international law standard, and supported once it began an invasion that it had opposed ten days earlier.

By shifting its positions over several months and scores of editorials, most of the key political stakeholders in the Iraq debate got what they wanted from the *Times*: Its hard-line backing of the WMD claim supported the administration; its last-minute opposition to a unilateral invasion supported the administration's critics. Thus, with respect to Iraq and other US foreign-policy issues, the *Times* editorial page is neither right nor left, neither Republican nor Democrat. In other words, the *Times* differentiates itself by being undifferentiated; or, rather, by being indifferent to its own positions toward important policy issues.

To much of the world, this signifies that the *Times* is unbiased and objective. Scratch the surface, however, and it's clear that the *Times* does not report facts and law objectively; rather, a better description would be that it sits neutrally amidst the rubble it makes of the facts and law. It's basically a Fortune 500 company that positions its product to have broad appeal and credibility (hopefully without too much scrutiny) within the news and information market in the United States.

And until recently it generally has managed to evade public criticism and censure. "The *Times* remains the most important and, on balance, the best newspaper in the world," the *New Yorker*'s liberal political commentator Hendrik Hertzberg wrote.[53] Actually, Hertzberg went even further: "Its authority ... isn't just journalistic; it's down right ontological. It is scarcely an exaggeration to say that the *Times* defines public reality."

A month later, another piece in the *New Yorker* on the *Times* read:

> [I]t is almost impossible to exaggerate the paper's significance. Not only is it bigger and better than its rivals; it enjoys a whole different ontological status. An event it doesn't cover might, in a manner of speaking, just as well not have happened.[54]

While the *Times* has indeed helped define public reality over the past several decades, as it did in its coverage of US policy toward Iraq, that reality with respect to much of US foreign policy is, like the *Times* itself, a facade with respect to representational integrity and credibility. Just as striking is the utterly clear fact that there is no presumption at the *Times*—to accompany the worldwide eminence attributed to it—of international law as the most authoritative criterion for determining whether a contemplated use of force is permissible and wise or not.

2

THE LIBERAL HAWKS ON IRAQ: A PRETENSE OF SOPHISTICATION

Michael Ignatieff is director of Harvard's Carr Center for Human Rights Policy at the Kennedy School of Government. He is also a writer for the *New York Times Magazine*. In January 2003, two months or so before the US invasion of Iraq, the magazine published a cover story by Ignatieff titled "The American Empire: Get Used To It." Lending his influential voice to the call for an Iraq invasion, Ignatieff wrote: "The United Nations lay dozing like a dog before the fire, happy to ignore Saddam, until an American president seized it by the scruff of the neck and made it bark."[1]

Although we know that the UN dog had already disarmed Iraq of its weapons of mass destruction, and that the American president was seizing the UN by the scruff of the neck by threatening to invade Iraq in violation of the UN Charter, deriding the UN and ignoring or mis-representing international law was nearly routine in the *New York Times Magazine*'s coverage of the Bush administration's policy toward Iraq.

At first glance, Ignatieff's stance is not what one might expect from a university-based human-rights intellectual. But Ignatieff was one among other liberal commentators with prestigious academic affiliations who did nothing to challenge the Bush administration's war on Iraq in the pages of the *New York Times*. Among these, perhaps the most notable were Anne-Marie Slaughter, Dean of the Woodrow Wilson School of Public and International Affairs at Princeton University,[2] and Michael Glennon, professor of international law at the Fletcher School of Law and Diplomacy at Tufts University.[3] Other prominent university-based international law scholars who supported an invasion of Iraq in the *New*

York Times included Richard Gardner, professor of international law at Columbia University,[4] and Ruth Wedgwood, professor of international law at Johns Hopkins University.[5]

The *Times* news reports did cite from time to time a number of individuals opposed to an Iraq invasion on international law grounds, but they were usually if not always foreign officials: Russian, French, German, Arab, or Iraqi. Although many university-based US scholars opposed the threat and use of force against Iraq on international law grounds, none, with one exception,[6] were cited or published in the *Times*. Ringing up the usual international law suspects to give unsurprising pro-invasion opinions, and differentiating homegrown US opinion from anti-invasion foreign-based views, contributed to the nationalist momentum in the United States toward war.

In addition to Ignatieff, nearly everyone else who wrote prior to the Iraq invasion for the *New York Times Magazine* supported an invasion. This included James Traub ("Who Needs the UN Security Council," November 17 2002), Barry Bearak ("Scott Ritter's Iraq Complex," November 24 2002), and George Packer ("The Liberal Quandary Over Iraq," December 8 2002). In addition to writing favorable profiles for the *Times* magazine of Paul Wolfowitz ("The Sunshine Warrior," September 22 2002) and President George W Bush ("Reagan's Son," January 26 2003), Bill Keller, at the time a senior writer for the magazine, also supported an Iraq invasion in several *Times* op-ed commentaries ("Masters of the Universe," October 5 2002; "What to Expect When You're Not Inspecting," November 16 2002; "The Selective Conscience," December 14 2002; "Why Bush Won't Wait," January 25 2003; "The I-Can't-Believe-I'm-a-Hawk Club," February 8 2003).

The *Times* also gave a great deal of access to commentators who took a worst-case view of Iraqi WMD and supported an invasion on WMD grounds. Not long after publication in September 2002 of Kenneth Pollack's book, *The Threatening Storm: The Case For Invading Iraq*,[7] the *Times* reviewed it twice within three days. In the first review, Jack Matlock, a former US ambassador to the Soviet Union, wrote: "This book makes the best case possible for an invasion of Iraq."[8] In the second review, Richard Bernstein of the *Times* wrote: "In 'The Threatening Storm,' Kenneth M Pollack makes what is very likely the best and strongest case that can be made for invading Iraq."[9] (Pollack was an analyst at the CIA and for President Clinton's National Security Council on Persian Gulf issues.) Later, Keller wrote on the op-ed page that "Kenneth Pollack, the Clinton National Security Council expert whose argument for invading Iraq is surely the most influential book of this season, has provided intellectual cover for every liberal who finds himself inclining toward war but uneasy about Mr. Bush."[10]

Pollack in fact made no good case for invading Iraq. Essentially, he argued that Iraq had a robust nuclear-weapons program, citing Iraqi exiles and defectors as well as Western intelligence agencies as sources. Pollack's thin case of an imminent or near-term Iraqi nuclear threat led him to conclude that an invasion was "the only sensible course of action left to us."[11] Presumably persuaded by Pollack, Keller echoed: "We reluctant hawks ... are hard pressed to see an alternative [to invasion] that is not built on wishful thinking."[12]

Apparently, little scrutiny was given to the evidentiary foundation of Pollack's claim that Iraq had an active nuclear-weapons program, given that he presented no facts to offset the IAEA's published nuclear-disarmament record with respect to Iraq[13]—a record that Pollack almost entirely ignored in his 500-page book. By ignoring this record, Pollack in effect was asserting outside any evidence-based context that Iraq had a nuclear-weapons program that threatened the United States and justified a US invasion of Iraq. Despite his weak case, Pollack was frequently cited and published in the *Times* as a solid, pro-invasion commentator on US policy toward Iraq.

Even if Pollack had reason to doubt the credibility of the IAEA's reports that it had dismantled Iraq's nuclear weapons program, he should have explained his doubts in the course of addressing the substantive findings of the IAEA's nuclear-inspections record in Iraq. But he never did, except for two dismissive sentences:

> After the Gulf War, the International Atomic Energy Agency (IAEA), which was responsible for eliminating and monitoring Iraq's nuclear program just as UNSCOM was responsible for Iraq's chemical, biological, and missile programs, believed that it had accounted for most of the program. However, there is a consensus that Iraq has resumed work on nuclear weapons.[14]

Although this is the entirety of Pollack's assessment of the IAEA's nuclear-disarmament record in Iraq throughout the 1990s, it is instructive to review even this grudging fragment. For one thing, the IAEA did not merely "account" for Iraq's nuclear-weapons program—it had dismantled what turned out to be the entirety of its program. Also, although Pollack claimed a consensus existed that disputed the IAEA's findings, he doesn't identify anyone belonging to it, except for "defectors" and "intelligence sources." Disturbingly, with respect to Keller—the chief editor at the *Times* today—a discerning reader of Pollack's book would have noticed the absence of credible evidence to support the claim of an Iraqi nuclear program, and the shoddy thesis that the United States needed to invade Iraq due to a lack of alternatives.

Furthermore, the *Times* wasn't only promoting Pollack's dismal book in reviews and commentary; it was also giving Pollack unusually generous access to its op-ed page to make "the case for invading Iraq." While the normal amount of space for an op-ed piece at the *Times* is about 800 words, and while the *Times* op-ed page has long been off limits to progressive opinion, the *Times* published lengthy op-ed pieces by Pollack on September 26 2002 (1,371 words),[15] January 27 2003, with Martin Indyk (1,345 words),[16] and February 21 2003 (1,760 words).[17]

Pollack's op-ed pieces argued (a) that Iraq had a nuclear-weapons program and "there is every reason to believe that the question is not one of war or no war, but rather war now or war later—a war without nuclear weapons or a war with them" (September 26 2002); (b) that "now the United States is firmly stuck in the 'inspections trap,' and our French and German allies appear determined to keep us there ... along with their fellow travelers in Moscow and Beijing, [who] are likely to seize on Mr. Blix's report to insist on delaying any military operation to enforce Iraq's disarmament" (January 27 2003); and (c) that "yes, we must weigh the costs of a war with Iraq today, but on the other side of the balance we must place the cost of a war with a nuclear-armed Iraq tomorrow" (February 21 2003). Despite Pollack's argument that the nuclear-weapons threat from Iraq presented the United States with "a last chance" for "war with Iraq today," none of the editors at the *Times* apparently ever questioned or viewed with skepticism his argument that Iraq was a near-term nuclear threat to the United States.

Undeterred by Pollack's mistaken pre-invasion assertions about Iraq's nuclear-weapons capabilities, which in addition to being speculative and undocumented at the time are now known to have been completely wrong, the *Times* published a 1,900-word op-ed piece by Pollack, titled "Saddam's Bombs: We'll Find Them," on the post-invasion status of Iraqi WMD, where he stated:

> [A]ccusations are mounting that the Bush administration made up the whole Iraqi weapons threat to justify an invasion. That is just not the case—

America and its allies had plenty of evidence before the war, and before President Bush took office, indicating that Iraq was retaining its illegal weapons program. ... The fact that the sites we suspected of containing hidden weapons before the war turned out to have nothing in them is not very significant. ... [T]he failure so far to find weapons of mass destruction in no way invalidates the prewar intelligence data indicating that Iraq had the clandestine capacity to build them.[18]

While appearing to use the article to implicitly deny on his own behalf that he had not "made up the whole Iraqi weapons threat to justify an invasion," Pollack also seemed to distance himself from his own pre-invasion appeals to invade Iraq. This is a tough sell, given that his well-known case for invading Iraq was that its nuclear-weapons program had broken through US containment and deterrence policies, and that invading Iraq sooner would be less costly and more prudent than invading later. Selling-out his own case for invasion, Pollack wrote:

Why was it necessary to put aside all of our other foreign policy priorities to go to war with Iraq in the spring of 2003? It was always the hardest part of the Bush administration's argument to square with the evidence. And, distressingly, there seems to be more than a little truth to claims that some members of the administration skewed, exaggerated and even distorted raw intelligence to coax the American people and reluctant allies into going to war against Iraq this year.[19]

Aside from the impression that this reminds one of *Seinfeld*'s George Costanza extracting himself from a self-inflicted embarrassment, recall that Pollack's February 21 op-ed piece was titled "A Last Chance to Stop Iraq," and that Pollack's last word in support of an invasion in that piece ominously implored us to "weigh the costs of a war with Iraq today" with "the cost of a war with a nuclear-armed Iraq tomorrow."

In short, with Pollack and others, the *New York Times* did little more than present what it packaged as a liberal case for invading Iraq while choreographing a band of liberal and university-based observers to provide "intellectual cover" (Keller's words) for the newspaper's editorial policy of supporting an invasion.

The "I-Can't-Believe-I'm-a-Hawk" account in February 2003 from the *Times*' current executive editor about why he supported an Iraq invasion was a case in point. As with other pro-invasion liberals, Keller's support for war posed as an ironic stance implying a higher level of thoughtfulness in contrast to the right-wing Pentagon civilian intellectuals massing at the gates of Iraq. While the ironic liberalism on Iraq fronted as political and intellectual independence, in reality it insidiously incorporated the right-wing paradigm by assimilating assumptions of the White House strategic-influence campaign (Iraqi WMD), presenting them as ineluctable realities (Iraq's brazen lies denying WMD possession), and ignoring any clash between the advocacy of war and the UN Charter and US Constitution.

This was essentially Michael Ignatieff's pose as well. Because the cover-page title of Ignatieff's January 2003 piece for the *New York Times Magazine*, "American Empire: Get Used To It," appeared to be intentionally exaggerated, an interpretation of first impression was that the title was satirical, given the radical substance and tone of the Bush administration's foreign policy. But the title accurately reflected the content of Ignatieff's article, which displayed no satire or wit, but plodded along in the dull hyperbole of an imperialist realism:

> Being an imperial power, however, is more than being the most powerful nation or just the most hated one. It means enforcing such order as there is in the world and doing so in the American interest. It means laying down the rules America wants (on everything from markets to weapons of mass destruction) while exempting itself from other rules (the Kyoto Protocol on climate change and the International Criminal Court) that go against its interest.[20]

This is the fourth paragraph in Ignatieff's article. The fifth paragraph is the one in which he refers to the UN as a dozing dog picked up by the scruff of the neck by President Bush. In the sixth paragraph, Ignatieff writes:

> The 21st century imperium is a new invention in the annals of political science, an empire lite, a global hegemony whose grace notes are free markets, human rights and democracy, enforced by the most awesome military power the world has ever known. It is the imperialism of a people who remember that their country secured its independence by revolt against an empire, and who like to think of themselves as the friend of freedom everywhere. It is an empire without consciousness of itself as such, constantly shocked that its good intentions arouse resentment abroad.[21]

Here, arguably, the narrative device is descriptive, and Ignatieff conceivably could say that he was merely presenting readers with a hardheaded objective analysis of US policy. But Ignatieff never deconstructs what he might claim to have only described. Instead, he stays the course, and produces an odd read, given what is being presented (an imperial tract), who's saying it (a Harvard human-rights intellectual), and how it's being said (written in a kind of fourth-person narrative that displaces agency and attribution):

> The Americans essentially dictate Europe's place in this new grand design [of the American imperium]. The United States is multilateral when it wants to be, unilateral when it must be; and it enforces a new division of labor in which America does the fighting, the French, British and Germans do the police patrols in the border zones and the Dutch, Swiss and Scandinavians provide the humanitarian aid.
>
> This is a very different picture of the world than the one entertained by liberal international lawyers and human rights activists who had hoped to see American power integrated into a transnational legal and economic order organized around the United Nations, the World Trade Organization, the International Criminal Court and other international human rights and environmental institutions and mechanisms. ... A new international order is emerging, but it is designed to suit American imperial objectives. America's allies want a multilateral order that will essentially constrain American power. But the empire will not be tied down like Gulliver with a thousand legal strings.[22]

This high-end Harvard intellectual sounds a lot like a low-end right-wing satirist when he writes in this manner about the global role of the United States. Three weeks before the September 11 terrorist attacks on New York and Washington, PJ O'Rourke, hitting the same notes as Ignatieff, wrote in the *Wall Street Journal* opinion page:

> [A]merica spends more on defense than the next 12 top defense-spending countries combined. If the US is going to be involved in military multi-lateralism, it should ask its partner nations that ancient question of diplomacy, "You and what army?"...
>
> When America does manage to participate, as an equal, in the community of nations, the results are not pretty. Look at the stupid UN. ...
>
> Is the environment to be cleaned up? What's needed for environmental cleanup is money. America has most of it. A Kyoto treaty that damages the American economy is not going to leave us Americans with extra money to help you foreigners recycle your trash—like all those corrupt, deposed dictators you're always sending here. ...
>
> But the rest of the world should not push America too far with claims upon international relations. The earth is not a family. And only an idiot would try multilateralism in a family, anyway. If you foreigners want America to join in a family marriage of nations, fine. But I warn you, we will be a strict dad. Because it's our planet. And we said so.[23]

In the way that Ignatieff's magazine article appeared to be exaggerated, O'Rourke's piece appeared to be satirical. The extremism of the Bush administration's foreign policy, however, is so severe that even this much exaggeration and satire do not fictionalize the policy. In fact, both Ignatieff and O'Rourke were in keeping with what regularly appeared in the *Wall Street Journal's* editorial page prior to and after September 11, as these excerpts indicate:

> Bush administration initiatives that roil Europeans share the same theme of introducing hard reality into a heady world conversation. They were upset by its rejection of the Kyoto treaty, the international criminal court and the ABM treaty. In each case, Bush diplomacy refused to sacrifice real American interests to what had become international totems. ... Yes, the Americans should engage the Europeans and the rest of their critics. Yes, they should say, we are replacing the old rules with new ones, and the world will be better for it.[24]

> If world opinion wants the US to go along with the likes of the new [International Criminal] court, it's time for world opinion to grow up and get serious.[25]

> It's one thing for a Mexican president to cede his foreign policy to the left for some blather about global poverty. But helping the French block the US in the Security Council, and on a matter of vital national interest [authorizing a use of force against Iraq], is something Americans won't soon forget. ... President Bush repeated yesterday that the US and its real friends will proceed in Iraq with or without the UN's blessing. That little league of nations is going to have to decide whose side it's on.[26]

> If Saddam Hussein figures he can evade the latest UN orders to disarm, we know where he's getting the idea: from the UN's own Kofi Annan. ... Some friend—Richard Holbrooke maybe, or Bill Clinton—ought to do Mr. Annan a favor and tell him to put a sock in it for the sake of his own institution.[27]

These brief excerpts indicate that there wasn't much to differentiate liberal and conservative opinion throughout the pre-invasion period when it came to Iraq and international law, and that the resident (Keller) and guest (Ignatieff) "liberal hawks" at the *Times* endorsed Amercian adventurism at a critical moment rather than stand for a principled advocacy of rule of law in international affairs.

Despite predictably bad results, including thousands of Iraqi and American casualties, Ignatieff persisted in supporting much of the Bush administration's policy toward Iraq well into the post-invasion summer of 2003 in another *New York Times Magazine* cover story.[28] By then it was clear that the administration had exaggerated the Iraqi WMD threat and the Iraq–Al Qaeda terrorist nexus, had violated international law, had not planned adequately for a postwar Iraq, and had generated perhaps unprecedented anti-Americanism abroad. Undisturbed by these developments, Ignatieff wrote, again in an imperialist narrative voice:

> About Iraq, the opinions of mankind told the Bush White House that the use of force was a dangerous and destabilizing adventure, but the intervention went ahead because the president believes that the ultimate authority over American decisions to intervene is not the United Nations or the world's opinion, but his constitutional mandate as commander in chief to "preserve, protect and defend" the United States. This unilateral doctrine alarms America's allies, but there is not a lot they can do about it.[29]

Given the overstated Iraqi WMD and terrorist threats, it's not clear what Ignatieff was referring to when he argued here (in September 2003) that President Bush invaded Iraq to protect the United States. Furthermore, a closer look at Ignatieff's unfortunate attempt to tie the Bush administration's militant unilateralism to the US Constitution shows that the Constitution does not say what Ignatieff said it says. Article II, section 1, paragraph 8 of the US Constitution says, referring to the president's oath of office:

> Before he enter on the Execution of his Office, he shall take the following Oath or Affirmation:—"I do solemnly swear (or affirm) that I will faithfully execute the Office of President of the United States, and will to the best of my Ability, preserve, protect and defend the Constitution of the United States."[30]

Thus, while seeking to give some constitutional legitimacy to the president's unilateral invasion of Iraq, Ignatieff misreported what the Constitution actually says. The president swears an oath to "preserve, protect and defend the Constitution of the United States." Ignatieff's rendition deleted the reference to the Constitution. Furthermore, Article VI, paragraph 2 of the Constitution makes US-ratified treaties, including the UN Charter, "the supreme law of the land." Thus, because the UN Charter prohibits the use of force without Security Council authorization, because the president violated the Charter by invading without such authorization, and because the Constitution (Article VI) makes the Charter "the supreme law of the land," the

THE LIBERAL HAWKS 55

president actually violated the US Constitution, as well as international law, by invading Iraq without Security Council approval. This is the exact opposite of what Ignatieff argued in his September 2003 magazine article for the *Times*.

Furthermore, Ignatieff provided a flimsy constitutional validation of an international crime—the invasion of Iraq—by invoking something that "the president believes." But how would Ignatieff, or anyone else, know what the president believes, especially when what Ignatieff is claiming the president believes in is something that does not exist—that is, a misquoted representation of the Constitution's words. Finally, the president's powers as commander in chief do not reside in Article II, section 1, as Ignatieff indicates, but in Article II, section 2, where the president's powers as commander in chief do not permit him to initiate war unilaterally.

Because the Bush administration hardly bothered to present a formal legal justification for invading Iraq, Ignatieff's attempt to use the Constitution as a legal defense of the president's unilateralism may have reached beyond even what the administration itself had asserted. Perhaps Ignatieff should have referred back to an earlier war that he had opposed to seek legal guidance for the one against Iraq he supported.

In a 1966 memorandum that sought to justify legally the US war in Vietnam, titled "The Legality of United States Participation in the Defense of Vietnam," the US State Department under President Lyndon Johnson asserted, like Ignatieff, that the president's authority as commander in chief "carr[ied] very broad powers, including the power to deploy American forces abroad and commit them to military operations when the President deems such action necessary to maintain the security and defense of the United States."[31]

Supporting this assertion on constitutional grounds, the State Department argued:

> At the federal Constitutional Convention in 1787, it was originally proposed that Congress have power "to make war." There were objections that legislative proceedings were too slow for this power to be vested in Congress; it was suggested that the Senate might be a better repository. [James] Madison and [Elbridge] Gerry then moved to substitute "to declare war" for "to make war," thus "leaving to the Executive the power to repel sudden attacks." It was objected that this might make it too easy for the executive to involve the nation in war, but the motion carried with but one dissenting vote. In 1787, the world was a far larger place, and the framers probably had

in mind attacks upon the United States. In the twentieth century, the world has grown smaller. An attack on a country far from our shores can impinge directly on the nation's security.[32]

Responding to the State Department's reasoning, the Lawyers Committee on Vietnam observed that "the State Department's arguments militate against its own conclusions."[33] In other words, one cannot argue, as the State Department did in this instance, that since the framers confined the unilateral war powers of the president to repelling sudden attacks, the president is somehow therefore justified in sending US troops to Vietnam without UN and congressional authorization. The "smaller world" scenario advanced by the State Department provided little additional constitutional power to the president. The Lawyers Committee elaborated:

> Above all, the Founding Fathers restricted the power of the Executive to "repel sudden attacks." This expresses and foreshadows the philosophy of the United Nations Charter provisions and affirms what is being urged here; namely, that just as the framers of the Constitution accepted the need for carefully restricted powers "to repel sudden attacks," so did the framers of the United Nations Charter acknowledge the need of Member states for special, carefully restricted powers "if an armed attack occurs." Hence, for such emergencies, the United States Constitution permits an exception to the general rule that only Congress can declare war; and the Charter permits an exception from its general rule that only the Security Council can authorize military actions if international peace is threatened. From the standpoint of both instruments, the Constitution and the Charter, exceptional emergency measures are permitted to prevent disaster.[34]

Thus, both the US Constitution and the UN Charter enable the president as commander in chief to unilaterally defend the territorial borders of the United States in order to repel an armed attack, and, thus, permit the president to preserve, protect and defend the United States, as Ignatieff wrote. But neither the Constitution nor the Charter permit the president unilaterally to invade another country, such as Iraq, that had not engaged in an armed attack of the United States, or at the very least posed a credible threat of an imminent attack. In fact, had anyone bothered or dared to point it out, it was Iraq, not the United States, that was being credibly threatened with a massive and imminent armed attack that, if anything, should have prompted the United Nations to support and protect Iraq. Instead, the UN simply witnessed the invasion that took place, and acquiesced in the outcome.

The Lawyers Committee's legal brief was a cogent summary of international law and the use of force. It is relevant today, given that the rules and principles it described were applicable to US policy in the run-up to the Iraq invasion, and were either ignored or denounced by war proponents, who argued that such law was a hindrance in the context of the terrorist threat to the United States. As in the case of Vietnam, however, and Iraq more recently, ignoring international law has proven to be bad policy. And as in Vietnam, the *New York Times* performed little to no journalistic watchdog function with respect to holding the president accountable to the UN Charter and US Constitution. Even worse, much coverage in the *Times* leading up to the Iraq invasion mocked and misrepresented the law that it should have upheld. Furthermore, Ignatieff's post-invasion article in the *New York Times Magazine* proposed liberalizing existing international law standards to permit a broader range of force options for the United States. Before looking at Ignatieff's proposals, however, it might be useful to review briefly what he proposes to change.

UN Charter Article 2(4) as a Prohibition or Limitation on the Use of Force. President Lyndon Johnson's State Department argued in 1966 that UN Charter Article 2, section 4 "imposed an important limitation on the use of force by United Nations Members."[35] Article 2(4) states:

> All Members shall refrain in their international relations from the threat or use of force against the territorial integrity or political independence of any state, or in any other manner inconsistent with the Purposes of the United Nations.

The Lawyers Committee responded that Article 2(4) is not merely a "limitation" on force, but the "keystone to modern international law" that "outlaws" the threat and use of force as an instrument of foreign policy.[36] Most scholars of international law have likewise recognized Article 2(4) not as a "limitation" but as a prohibition on force and a peremptory norm of international law.

In contrast, the State Department's analysis of Article 2(4), which established a precedent for legally justifying a succession of US military interventions since Vietnam, has demonstrated that the "limitation" interpretation in practice permitted the use of force in a wide range of scenarios—an outcome that is hardly consistent with the intent of this cardinal rule with regard to prohibiting (or even limiting) the use of force.

Force as an Instrument of the World Community or the Nation-State. The Lawyers Committee acknowledged that the UN Charter stipulates "for the very purpose of maintaining peace, various measures, and ultimately force may be required" and authorizes the world community, acting through the Security Council, to decide what measures shall be taken with regard to the use of force. According to the Lawyers Committee, "the essential meaning of this rule of international law [UN Charter Article 39] is that no country shall decide for itself whether to use force."[37] Article 39 states:

> The Security Council shall determine the existence of any threat to the peace, breach of the peace, or act of aggression and shall make recommendations, or decide what measures shall be taken in accordance with Articles 41 and 42, to restore international peace and security.

Regarding Article 39, the Lawyers Committee wrote: "Clearly, the United States, as a chief architect and signatory Member of the United Nations is, in principle, bound to admit that the Security Council is the only agent authorized to determine the measures required to maintain or to restore international peace."[38]

Article 51 as the Single, Narrow Exception to Article 2(4), or as Superseding Article 2(4). The State Department argued that UN Charter Article 51 is a "savings clause" designed "to make clear that no other provision in the Charter shall be interpreted to impair the inherent right of self-defense."[39] Article 51 states:

> Nothing in the present Charter shall impair the inherent right of individual or collective self-defense if an armed attack occurs against a Member of the United Nations, until the Security Council has taken the measures necessary to maintain international peace and security. Measures taken by Members in the exercise of this right of self-defense shall be immediately reported to the Security Council and shall not in any way affect the authority and responsibility of the Security Council under the present Charter to take at any time such action as it deems necessary in order to maintain or restore international peace and security.

In response, the Lawyers Committee argued:

> The right of self-defense under the Charter arises only if an armed attack has occurred. The language of Article 51 is unequivocal on this point. The term "armed attack" has an established meaning in international law. It was deliberately employed in the Charter to reduce drastically the discretion of states to determine for themselves the scope of permissible self-defense both with regard to claims of individual and collective self-defense.[40]

Thus, the Lawyers Committee argued that a resort to force in self-defense may be employed only in the event that the victim state experiences an "armed attack," that is, "when military forces cross an international boundary in visible, massive, and sustained form," and when, in the words of Daniel Webster, "the necessity for action [is] instant, overwhelming, and leaving no choice of means, and no moment of deliberation."[41]

In response to what the State Department claimed, then, the Lawyers Committee argued:

> Article 51 purposely restricted the right of self-defense to a situation of armed attack because only these situations require immediate military reaction to avoid disaster. The rationale is persuasive: Other forms of aggression, especially indirect aggression, are so difficult to define and to ascertain, that too many situations might occur in which states, in good faith or bad, would claim the right of self-defense and thereby expand and intensify warfare.[42]

Substitute "terrorism" for "aggression" in this passage and it is clear that international law not only narrows the legal parameters of US counter terrorism policy, but also provides wise counsel, ignored by the Bush administration, given that the Iraq invasion merely "expanded and intensified warfare" with no evident benefit to the national security of the United States, not to mention the expanded and intensified anti-Americanism abroad and an increased threat of terrorism directed at the United States.

Horrific as that day was, the terrorist events of September 11 did not constitute an "armed attack" against the United States within the definition of the term under international law. Nor does Al Qaeda represent a military threat to invade and occupy the United States. Although Al Qaeda today is a threat to US national security, in contrast to Vietnamese nationalism, which posed no such threat, there was no evidence either before or after the Iraq invasion linking Al Qaeda to Iraq. In fact, invading Iraq on post-September 11 grounds not only violated international law, it was a serious strategic and tactical error in US counterterrorism policy, given that it exacerbated anti-Americanism around the world, diverted extensive resources, weakened alliance relations, and increased demand for terrorist retaliation.[43] The invasion of Iraq is the most recent episode in a long series of US violations of international law and the use of force over the past several decades that have arguably undermined rather than enhanced US national security.

The position favored here is that the United States would be best served by adhering to the UN Charter system. If one considers the course of American foreign policy over the last half-century, adherence to the Charter system with respect to the use of force would have avoided disastrous policy failures, especially the wars in Vietnam and Iraq. In fact, US foreign-policy dogma undermines both international law and US interests, and is supported by the reluctance among US journalists and intellectuals to extend the reach of international law and United Nations authority to cover US foreign policy.

It is not the Charter system that is fundamentally in disarray; rather, it is leading states, and above all the United States, that need to be persuaded that their interests are served and their values realized by the pursuit of a law-oriented foreign policy. With respect to the terrorist threat to the United States, the law can be stretched if true necessities arise, but these exceptional situations must, to the extent possible, be in accord with the procedures and norms contained in the Charter system, and with a factually and doctrinally convincing explanation of why particular exceptions are justified.

The international community, with the support of traditional US allies, in fact sanctioned a legally precarious but arguably reasonable stretch of international law by supporting (or not opposing) the US retaliatory invasion of Afghanistan that targeted Al Qaeda and the Taliban in response to September 11. This revealed a broad international consensus that international law should not be used to tie up the United States like Gulliver when legitimate national security issues seemed to be at stake.

The Bush administration overreached, however, when it sought Security Council authorization to invade Iraq in clear violation of international law, given the absence of an Iraqi armed attack on the United States, a credible imminent threat, or an Iraqi link to Al Qaeda and the events of September 11. The preference among a majority of Security Council members and US allies to continue WMD inspections in Iraq, and to commence ongoing monitoring and disarmament verification once inspections were concluded, compares favorably on every front to the reckless and illegal decision by the Bush administration to invade Iraq. Furthermore, note that even this preference was generated to a considerable extent by US arm-twisting of Security Council members. Though it declined to authorize an Iraq invasion, the prewar debate in the Security Council on Iraq was nevertheless tilted in Washington's direction, and the Council ultimately failed to uphold its fundamental mandate to prevent war and protect countries threatened with aggression.

In his September 2003 post-invasion cover story in the *New York Times Magazine*, which on the cover asks, "When should we send in the troops?" Michael Ignatieff proposes easing existing rules of international law and the use of force, paradoxically, as "a way out of this mess of interventionist policy" and "out of American unilateralism."[44]

But no such paradox actually exists for Ignatieff, given that his broad agenda is to grow the interventionist portfolio of the United States by positioning international law to accommodate that expansion. The "mess of interventionism" for Ignatieff, upon examination, lies not in the unilateralism of the Iraq invasion in violation of international law, but in the fact that international law, currently configured, provided no legal support for an invasion of Iraq under the circumstances in which it was proposed and carried out. By expanding interventionist options under international law, however, the international community would be left with fewer legal legs to stand on to oppose US unilateralism.

While Ignatieff writes that his international law reform "entails allowing other countries to have a say on when and how the United States can intervene," this is precisely what Ignatieff rejected by supporting the Iraq invasion in the absence of UN Security Council authorization and support worldwide. And existing rules of international law already permit other countries to have a formal say on US intervention through the procedures of the Security Council.

Ignatieff also writes that his reforms "would mean returning to the United Nations and proposing new rules to guide the use of force," even though one of his proposed new rules already exists in a more precise rendition, another is already in the scholarly and UN pipeline, and the other three would have virtually no chance of becoming law, given the open-ended mandate they would give the United States to resort to force at its own unchecked discretion.

Ignatieff proposes "five clear cases when the United Nations could authorize a state to intervene":

> [W]hen, as in Rwanda or Bosnia, ethnic cleansing and mass killing threaten large numbers of civilians and a state is unwilling or unable to stop it;

when, as in Haiti, democracy is overthrown and people inside a state call for help to restore a freely elected government;

when, as in Iraq, North Korea, and possibly Iran, a state violates the nonproliferation protocols regarding the acquisition of chemical, nuclear or biological weapons;

when, as in Afghanistan, states fail to stop terrorists on their soil from launching attacks on other states; and finally,

when, as in Kuwait, states are victims of aggression and call for help.[45]

Ignatieff's last proposal is already recognized as legal grounds for UN-sanctioned collective self-defense under UN Charter Article 51, except that the intervention standard is a response to "armed attack" and not the more open-ended "aggression" in Ignatieff's proposal. Recall what the Lawyers Committee on Vietnam argued in 1967:

> Article 51 purposely restricted the right of self-defense to a situation of armed attack because only these situations require immediate military reaction to avoid disaster. The rationale is persuasive: Other forms of aggression, especially indirect aggression, are so difficult to define and to ascertain, that too many situations might occur in which states, in good faith or bad, would claim the right of self-defense and thereby expand and intensify warfare.[46]

Diluting the legal standard here from "armed attack" to "aggression," as Ignatieff advocates, would permit the United States to justify legally a much broader range of military intervention under the UN Charter than it is able credibly to do today.

Ignatieff's first proposal, which would permit UN-authorized force to intervene to prevent humanitarian catastrophes, is a subject that is to date under review at the United Nations and among international law scholars. The Kosovo Commission Report in this regard stated:

> The Commission believes that the time is now ripe for the presentation of a principled framework for humanitarian intervention which could be used to guide future responses to imminent humanitarian catastrophes and which could be used to assess claims for humanitarian intervention. It is our hope that the UN General Assembly could adopt such a framework in some modified form as a Declaration and that the UN Charter be adapted to this Declaration either by appropriate amendments or by a case-by-case approach in the UN Security Council.[47]

However, in the course of its proposal to expand the permissible use of military force under international law to prevent humanitarian disasters, the Kosovo Commission carefully considered the circumstances and consequences of such an expansion, and repeatedly cautioned against expansionist pretexts beyond its own proposed narrow expansion—a caution that Ignatieff, a member of the Kosovo Commission, disregarded in his September article in the *Times* magazine.

Ignatieff's additional proposed expansions for the legal resort to force—to "restore a freely elected government," to enforce "nonproliferation protocols," and to "stop terrorists from launching attacks on other states"—are not specifically permitted under existing rules of international law. In each of these cases, remedies short of force are usually available, are preferable, and work better without the costs, risks, and casualties of war. Furthermore, differences of opinion about how to interpret particular situations in each of these instances would complicate rather than clarify international law pertaining to the use of force.

For example, while every other government in the Western Hemisphere opposed it, the Bush administration supported the military overthrow in April 2002 of Hugo Chávez, the freely elected president of Venezuela. Under Ignatieff, several Latin American governments could have petitioned the Security Council to authorize military intervention to restore the ousted left-wing president—an intervention that would undoubtedly have been opposed by the Bush government, especially in light of evidence that the administration provided political and financial support to anti-Chávez forces involved in the coup.[48] A Security Council-authorized use of force against Venezuela, including perhaps with Russian, Chinese, or other foreign troops, would no doubt have been seen by the United States as an inappropriate military intervention in an oil-rich country and a challenge to its proprietary influence in the Western Hemisphere. Likewise, suppose under Ignatieff that the Clinton administration, pursuant to the US Supreme Court decision in *Bush v. Gore* (2000), declared that a freely elected president of the United States, Al Gore, had been deprived of office, and on these grounds requested military intervention from the Security Council to place Gore in the White House.

Or suppose, under Ignatieff, states seeking nuclear disarmament proposed that the Security Council authorize the use of force against the United States to compel US compliance with Article VI of the Nuclear Nonproliferation Treaty, which requires each state party to the treaty "to pursue negotiations in good faith on effective measures relating to ... nuclear disarmament." Actually, no such intervention could be proposed under Ignatieff, since his proposed expansion of the permissible use of force to support nonproliferation protocols was carefully worded to permit force only against states that have not to date acquired chemical, biological, or nuclear weapons. Also, given the fact that Iraq was recently invaded with Ignatieff's support on the false charge that it had not been disarmed of such weapons, while other strategic and business considerations may in fact have motivated the invasion, and given that effective steps short of war were available and had in fact already been taken to disarm Iraq, the problems with Ignatieff's proposal on this count are already evident.

Similarly, Ignatieff's proposal that international law be expanded to permit military intervention against states that "fail to stop terrorists on their soil from launching attacks on other states" is also subject to gray areas, muddled definitions, and above all dangerous geopolitical manipulations. Much of the world views Israeli Prime Minister Ariel Sharon as a terrorist leader who regularly authorizes acts of state terrorism against Palestinians in the West Bank and Gaza. Would Ignatieff's proposal, then, empower the Security Council to authorize an Arab invasion of Israel on antiterrorism grounds? Given that Ignatieff also suggests "the United States should propose enlarging the number of permanent members of the [Security] Council so that it truly represents the world's population," and that it also "ought to propose giving up its own veto so that all other permanent members follow suit," and that the Security Council henceforth would "make decisions to use force with a simple majority vote," opening the floodgates to the permissible use of force at the Security Council suddenly might not look that attractive from the perspective of either Israel or the United States, which like Israel is also viewed as a practitioner and supporter of state terrorism by much of the world.

In most of these instances, enhanced compliance with existing law, especially by the United States, would establish positive policy precedents that would likely produce both short-term and long-term outcomes more favorable to both the United States and the world than simply going to war on the basis of the open-ended criteria proposed by Ignatieff.

The first *New York Times Magazine* article on Iraq in the context of the UN and international law was written by James Traub (a writer for the magazine) and published in November 2002.[49] Though Traub made several references to the Security Council and its deliberations with respect to authorizing force against Iraq, he never cited the basic rules of the UN Charter (summarized above) that give the Security Council, and not the White House, the legal authority to authorize a resort to force against another country that has not attacked the United States.

Ignoring the legal dimension of the relationship between the Bush administration and the Security Council, Traub situated the relationship in a political context and asked an odd question:

> The central question posed by the debate over Iraq remains: Is the blessing of the international community so valuable a good that even this administration, at this moment of American power, is prepared to sacrifice something of its freedom of action in order to secure it? And if it is not, what, exactly, is the Security Council for?

The problem with Traub's approach is that for him the Security Council, not the United States, would be subjected to indictment if the Bush administration invades Iraq without the Council's approval. Suppose the mafia drove around New Jersey and New York running red lights. Most commentators in response would not challenge the law requiring motorists to stop at red lights. Similarly, when the United States does little to align itself with the UN's efforts to help solve the world's very serious problems (with respect to disarmament, human rights, poverty, disease, and the environment), and thus consigns the UN to limited success, for Traub the fault not only lies with the UN itself, but exposes it to ridicule, as he demonstrates:

> This is the domain most of us associate with the UN—high-minded confabulations on intractable global problems, solar-powered cookers, declarations on the rights of historically oppressed communities, etc. This sense of an organization preoccupied with terribly important things it can't actually do very much about has not done much for the UN's reputation, at least in the United States.

Traub also wrote that the UN Charter "makes amazing reading today, when American conservatives talk about signing on to UN treaties as a surrender of national sovereignty." For Traub, a well-rendered paradigm of world legal order and civilized global conduct is "amazing," as in nearly seditious, as he too easily permits the paranoid right-wing assessment of international law to infuse his UN profile.

One week after it published Traub's piece on the UN Security Council, the *New York Times Magazine* published an article on Scott Ritter by Barry Bearak, who like Traub also writes for the magazine.[50]

Ritter's "Iraq complex," as Bearak called it, is catalogued variously in the article as "Ritter-think," Ritter's "messianic side," "the requirements of [Ritter's] self-image," and Ritter's "vainglory." Ritter was seen as nearly psychotic because he opposed the Bush administration's threatened invasion of Iraq, in part by arguing, more accurately than anyone else at the time, that the Iraqis had already been disarmed of "up to 90–95 percent of their most deadly weapons, rendering Saddam fundamentally disarmed."[51]

With respect to what he referred to as "Ritter-think," Bearak wrote:

> On Dec. 16, 1998, the United States, with British support, launched Operation Desert Fox, four days of bombing. With the Clinton administration finally hammering Saddam, one might have expected Ritter to be elated, but in fact, he thought it a travesty. Desert Fox had come without the approval of the Security Council. In Ritter-think, America was bound to the United Nations by treaty, and treaties were backed by the United States Constitution.[52]

In Bearak-speak, then, Ritter-think is defined by what the Constitution actually says and what the UN Charter actually requires. With respect to Ritter's "messianic" complex, Bearak wrote:

> His [Ritter's] messianic side, once solely directed at finding Saddam's lethal weapons, had reversed compass and was targeted now at Washington's failed policies. He spoke often of the thousands of Iraqi children dying because of the sanctions.[53]

If reporting the human cost of the US-supported economic sanctions in Iraq is evidence of a "messianic side" (a subset with "Ritter-think" of Ritter's Iraq "complex"), then perhaps several major medical journals all suffer from the same generalized complex, given that in 1992, for example, the *New England Journal of Medicine* reported "strong evidence that the Gulf war [in 1991] and trade sanctions caused a three-fold increase in mortality among Iraqi children under five years of age," and "estimate[d] that more than 46,900 children died between January and August 1991."[54] In 2000 a study published in the *American Journal of Public Health* "examined the effect of sanctions on mortality among Iraqi children" and found that "the risk of dying increased dramatically."[55] In 2000 the *International Journal of Epidemiology* reported "for 1996, after five years of sanctions and prior to receipt of humanitarian food via the oil for food programme ... mortality among children under five ... reached an estimated 87 per 1000, a rate last experienced [in Iraq] more than 30 years ago."[56] Also in 2000 authors of a study published in *The Lancet* reported that "in the south/center [of Iraq], infant and under-5 mortality increased during the 10 years before the [1999 Iraqi population] survey, which roughly corresponds to the period following the Gulf conflict and the start of the United Nations sanctions," and that "infant mortality [in Iraq] rose from 47 per 1000 live births during 1984–89 to 108 per 1000 in 1994–99, and under-5 mortality rose from 56 to 131 per 1000 live births."[57]

All things considered, these and other facts made Ritter essentially correct about the status of Iraqi disarmament, about the legality of bombing and invading Iraq under the UN Charter and the US Constitution, and about Iraqi children dying due to the sanctions. Rather than give Ritter a fair hearing on any of these issues, Bearak instead dragged Ritter and his arguments through the fact-grinding filter of the *Times* in order to manufacture pathology out of a responsible dissenting position with respect to Iraq.

More of the same was evident from the *New York Times Magazine* two weeks later in another piece on Iraq, this time by George Packer. Packer began his article on American liberals and the pending invasion of Iraq by asking: "If you're a liberal, why haven't you joined the anti-war movement? More to the point, why is there no anti-war movement to join?"[58]

These questions were published about six weeks after tens of thousands of anti-war demonstrators marched in a number of American cities. But Packer disregarded the demonstrators, arguing they were "unnuanced" extremists:

> But this [anti-war] movement has a serious liability, one that will just about guarantee its impotence: it's controlled by the furthest reaches of the American left. Speakers at the demonstrations voice unnuanced slogans like "No Sanctions, No Bombing" and "No Blood for Oil." As for what should be done to keep this mass murderer [Saddam Hussein] and his weapons in check, they have nothing to say at all. This is not a constructive liberal anti-war movement.

Some questions for Packer are indicated: When Packer's article was published, economic sanctions had been in place against Iraq for over a decade with devastating consequences to the Iraqi population, especially young children. Where is the extremism in the "No Sanctions" slogan? It was well established that a US invasion of Iraq would feature an air-war campaign against ground targets in Iraq, which inevitably would cause thousands of Iraqi casualties, which is precisely what happened. Where is the extremism in the "No Bombing" slogan? Given Iraq's oil wealth, and a decades-long US foreign policy toward the Middle East featuring guaranteed US access to oil backed by the threat of a US resort to nuclear war, where is the extremism in the "No Blood [War] for Oil" slogan? Where are Saddam's weapons of mass destruction—the basis of Packer's support for a war against Iraq? Explain how killing thousands of Iraqis by invading Iraq, in addition to the hundreds of thousands already killed by sanctions, permits a pro-invasion American intellectual to make a moral argument for invading Iraq to overthrow the Hussein government, as tyrannical as it was?

Furthermore, Packer was selective in choosing which anti-war arguments to feature. Rather than having "nothing to say," war opponents generally supported a continuation of UN weapons inspections in Iraq, and opposed an invasion on both international law and prudential grounds. Rather than offering "nothing," these reasonable positions ultimately would have verified and monitored Iraq's disarmament, prevented an illegal invasion, prevented the reckless killing of thousands of people, and would have saved the invasion and occupation expenditure of at least $150 billion, all of it borrowed. Many opposed to an Iraq invasion also wisely proposed addressing the Israel–Palestine conflict, consistent with the requirements of international law, as the centerpiece of US policy toward the Middle East—an achievement that would have advanced US counterterrorism policy, rather than set it back, as the Iraq invasion did.

Rather than fairly represent these mainstream views of US anti-war opinion, Packer preferred instead to profile the views of a handful of his "liberal hawks," who are "hardly vast in their numbers" and represent "a [liberal] minority within a [liberal] minority." Packer presents such hawks—Michael Walzer, Christopher Hitchens, David Rieff, Leon Wieseltier, and Paul Berman—as the "ideas" men of the liberal intelligentsia who deserve wider consideration among both the left and right.

In Packer's profiles, Walzer and Rieff were opposed to an invasion of Iraq, but not enough to protest. Wieseltier was "not eager to start" a war with Iraq. Hitchens supported an invasion of Iraq for no specific reasons given in Packer's profile, though Packer writes that "Hitchens has steadily warmed to American power exercised on behalf of democracy." Hitchens himself says, presumably as an argument in support of an invasion of Iraq:

After the dust settles, the only revolution left standing is the American one. Americanization is the most revolutionary force in the world. There's almost no country where adopting the Americans wouldn't be the most radical thing they could do. I've always been a Paine-ite.[59]

Berman "argues for a war in Iraq on three grounds":

To free up the Middle East militarily for further actions against Al Qaeda, to liberate the Iraqi people from their dungeon and to establish "a beachhead of Arab democracy" and shift the region's center of gravity away from autocracy and theocracy and toward liberalization.[60]

Thus, Walzer, Rieff, and Wieseltier were conflicted, and essentially offered no easily identifiable opinion about an invasion—not much in the way of Packer's ideas here. Hitchens on the other hand supported an Iraq invasion presumably to take American-style democracy to Iraq. Berman wanted war to strategically position the United States to fight Al Qaeda and Muslim fundamentalism and to liberate Iraqis from Saddam. With the exception of ousting Saddam, none of these objectives have been achieved to date by invading Iraq.

Assuming that for Hitchens and Berman American-style democracy includes constitutionalism and the rule of law, the invasion they supported, problematically for their position, violated the cardinal rule of international law and was legally precarious under the US Constitution. It also facilitated official systematic lying by the Bush administration, further undermining Hitchens and Berman. The invasion, predictably, has clearly increased anti-Americanism among Muslims worldwide and facilitated Al Qaeda's recruiting. Profound legal and moral issues aside, invading Iraq, which, in any event only two of the five liberal hawks actually clearly supported, was an exceedingly unwise thing for Packer's "Bosnia-generation liberal intellectuals" to support, as post-invasion events have shown.

For Packer, however, another attraction of the liberal hawks was that they could give President Bush an ideas-based promotional campaign to help sell the American people on an Iraq invasion:

Oddly enough, President Bush needs them [the liberal hawks], too. The one level on which he hasn't even tried to make a case is the level of ideas. These liberal hawks could give a voice to his war aims, which he has largely kept to himself. They could make the case for war to suspicious Europeans and to wavering fellow Americans. They might even be able to explain the connection between Iraq and the war on terrorism.[61]

The liberal hawks are apparently so smart they can give voice to the admittedly vague and shifting war aims of the president. These highly differentiated hawks might even explain to the president the connection between invading Iraq and the war on terrorism. This would be a good thing, given that no one, either then or since then, has been able to explain that connection, except to argue with substantial evidence that the Iraq invasion has increased the terrorist threat to the United States.

Three weeks after the United States began its invasion of Iraq, James Traub published another article on the UN Security Council in the *Times* magazine.[62] Traub wrote this article—a sequel to his pre-invasion piece for the magazine on the Council—in the climate of mid-invasion exuberance. Tagging along, Traub was more than willing to support more such successful invasions, backed by the president's global preventive-war strategy, at the expense of the UN and international law. He begins (second paragraph) by informing us that the Security Council will survive the invasion of Iraq the way "that many gravely ill patients do not die." In the same paragraph, he writes:

> While a debate has begun on the role of the UN in postwar Iraq, formulas for replacing or marginalizing the UN are circulating around the conservative policy circles that first drew up the case for war in Iraq in the late '90s. And the Bush administration, should it take its war on terror to other "rogue" or "evil" regimes beyond Iraq, is plainly prepared to dispense with the legitimacy conferred by a Security Council resolution.[63]

As with Iraq, the Bush administration "is plainly prepared" to attack or invade other countries without Security Council authorization. Despite this presumptive intent to violate the most important rules of international law, Traub wrote nothing in response in defense of law. Instead, Traub, like Packer, valued enhancing the administration's arguments for unilateral war while diminishing the role of the UN, international law, and conflict resolution short of invading other countries:

> What drove American officials crazy about [Hans] Blix was his insistence on giving Saddam Hussein points for form—for playing along with the inspections process even while frustrating its object. Blix says that he felt that it was important to preserve his prerogatives: "We being trustees of the Security Council have to at all times be careful about evidence, and not jump to conclusions." But he also seemed to be averting his eyes from the bottom of the barrel. Blix appeared to share the more or less consensual

UN view that continued discussion is almost automatically preferable to fighting—a view in which the belief in peace and the belief in process converge and war is always failure. But talk can also be a form of failure when war is unavoidable.[64]

Even though Iraq had not attacked or threatened to attack the United States, though UN inspections were progressing well with no evidence of Iraqi WMD, and though the Security Council was clearly anxious to mediate the Bush administration's grievances short of authorizing force, the invasion of Iraq for Traub was simply "unavoidable," leaving no time or place for a war-avoidance option of any kind.

What then, is the ultimate position of the United States with respect to the Security Council? Traub writes: "It may very well be true that the United States simply does not need the United Nations anymore," as the neocons quoted in his article argue. "You might say that it almost never has," Traub adds.

But this is not the final word in Traub's article. After knocking down the UN house, Traub picks up a brick and gives it back in the article's last paragraph: "The US does, however, need other countries; and the other countries we need believe in the UN whether we do or not." Thus, Traub is last seen appearing to resuscitate what he has in fact already killed; engaging in what William Safire might call a "counter-consistent conclusion." This is a studied journalistic practice at the *Times* that is mistakenly viewed as fairness and balance.

On Language: "Counter-consistent conclusions" (our words, not Safire's): This is when the *New York Times* covers Ronald Reagan's presidency with kid gloves for eight years (1981–88), then endorses Walter Mondale (1984) and Michael Dukakis (1988) for president. Or when the *Times* hounds President Bill Clinton for eight years over minor issues and allegations (1993-2000), and ridicules Al Gore's presidential candidacy over the last year of those eight years (2000), then endorses Clinton (1996) and Gore (2000). Or when the *Times* gives another hyper right-wing president, George W Bush, what amounts to a free ride, then endorses the Democratic nominee for president in 2004, which it no doubt will. Or when the *Times* in turn will hound and persecute the next Democratic president, and thereby help to disable that presidency as it did Clinton's, then endorse that Democratic president's reelection. Or when the *New York Times* editorial page promotes the Bush administration's campaign to invade Iraq, thereby adding to the war momentum, then opposes the invasion at the eleventh hour when an invasion is nearly imminent.

Similarly, Alan Greenspan, Federal Reserve chair, might look at the same journalistic phenomenon and say that the *Times* eases and tightens editorial policy the way that the Fed eases and tightens monetary policy. Generally, when the economy is overheating (growing too fast), the Fed tightens monetary policy (by acting to increase interest rates); when the economy cools (grows too slowly or retracts), the Fed eases monetary policy (by acting to lower interest rates). By way of analogy, the *Times* eases editorial policy for Republican presidents (that it has not endorsed), and tightens editorial policy for Democratic presidents (that it has endorsed).

Easing editorial policy for right-wing presidents it does not or has not endorsed is a broader example of a "counter-consistent conclusion." This subtle formula for tightening and easing preserves the perception among its readers, advertisers, and stockholders that the *Times* is scrupulously fair and balanced. But what's good for the *Times'* public image and bottom line can be bad for the country, because when the *Times* eases editorial policy for right-wing presidents, it's also easing its oversight responsibilities with respect to the right-wing policies of those presidents. The *Times* in fact is now firmly fixed in the habit of underreporting or ignoring the most significant facts and occurrences that would utterly condemn the policies of George W Bush and his administration if they were reported as often as they happen and as prominently as they deserve to be by the nation's leading newspaper.

Assuming that "counter-consistent conclusions" and "tightening and easing" facilitate the overall editorial mission of the *Times*—which is to position itself in the political center without regard to facts and law—a good hire as executive editor would be someone whose own journalistic ethos reflects this editorial policy.

Bill Keller became executive editor of the *New York Times* on July 30 2003. He was appointed to that position on July 14. Keller was formerly a managing editor and a foreign editor at the *Times*, and as one of its foreign correspondents won a Pulitzer Prize in 1989 for his coverage of the Soviet Union.[65] Just prior to being hired as executive editor, Keller was a senior writer for the *New York Times Magazine* and wrote lengthy twice-monthly commentary for the op-ed page. Like the *Times*, Keller is liberal and urbane, and appears to be infinitely patient with the policies and people of the Bush administration.

In the run-up to war in Iraq, Keller wrote a lengthy profile of Paul Wolfowitz, deputy secretary of defense,[66] and a midterm profile of President George W Bush,[67] both for the *Times* magazine.

As its second-ranking civilian, Wolfowitz was one among other high-ranking hard-liners at the Pentagon who went on record several years ago supporting regime change in Iraq.[68] Keller was apparently attracted to Wolfowitz in part because of "his style, which relies on patient logic and respectful, soft-spoken engagement rather than on fire-breathing conviction." For Keller, Wolfowitz "is [an] interesting and complicated" fox among the prickly hedgehogs in the Bush administration. Keller later positioned himself similarly with respect to Iraq: a complicated pro-invasion liberal hawk among a tedious anti-war liberal cohort. This is also consistent with Packer's portraits of the "liberal hawks," who supported an invasion of Iraq for reasons more complicated than the sloganeering war protestors.

The template for the flattering portraits of the intellectual hawks, however, goes easy on the tough questions. Although Keller apparently had good access to Wolfowitz for a few weeks over the summer of 2003—interviews, discussions, e-mails—Keller apparently posed no probative questions to one of the administration's leading invasion proponents, and elicited from Wolfowitz no sound reasons for invading Iraq. There was no discussion of the legality of an invasion under international law and the Constitution, and Wolfowitz described no imminent or tangible threat from Iraq.

Keller recalls a case for war that Wolfowitz presented to American and British military officers when one of the British officers asked Wolfowitz about Scott Ritter's claim "that Iraq's destructive capability is already neutralized":

> An exasperated look crosses Wolfowitz's wide, boyish face; Ritter's comments are "simply amazing," he says. Then he stops himself. He acknowledges that Ritter knows something about Iraq and concedes that Saddam has probably not been able to rebuild his nuclear program, not yet. But he notes that when inspectors went in after the [1991] gulf war, they found he was far closer than anyone imagined, that in fact he was pursuing four separate avenues for manufacturing a nuclear weapon. And chemical weapons, which he has employed against his own people, or biological weapons are threat enough, and much easier to construct in a secretive, fearsome police state. This is, Wolfowitz tells the [military officers], a man who has been known to have children tortured in front of their parents.[69]

When asked about Iraq's weapons of mass destruction, Wolfowitz did not respond with any precision or confidence that Iraq had such weapons. Iraq no doubt was a "fearsome police state" under Saddam, which tortured people including possibly children. If there is a moral argument for invading Iraq this would be it; that is, if someone could invent a method for invading another country with advanced air power, mechanized armor, and 150,000 heavily armed soldiers that would not also kill and maim children and other innocent people, and would not require a lengthy occupation that would provoke fierce national resistance, resulting in more killing. Furthermore, a global superpower that stood for international law, including in its relations with Israel and other countries in the Middle East, would have much greater political and moral leverage to change the conduct of a dictator like Saddam using methods short of invasion.

In short, with respect to an Iraq invasion, there were many questions to pose to Wolfowitz about the legality of an invasion, a terrorism backlash, post-invasion occupation plans, the cost of an invasion and occupation, in addition to the political and financial divestments from other critical issues. Keller, however, seldom hassled Wolfowitz with such questions. On a substantive note, Wolfowitz did say: "I think the getting in [invasion] is the dangerous part." Then Keller wrote: "He [Wolfowitz] worries considerably less about the day after." The evident absence of rigor displayed here by both Keller and Wolfowitz is indicative of the *Times*' coverage of Iraq policy and post-invasion planning by the Pentagon.

One year later, Wolfowitz declined to speak with David Rieff "about the day after" for an article on post-invasion Iraq, in which Rieff wrote:

> I have made two trips to Iraq since the end of the war and interviewed dozens of sources in Iraq and in the United States who were involved in the planning and execution of the war and its aftermath. It is becoming painfully clear that the American plan (if it can be dignified with the name) for dealing with postwar Iraq was flawed in its conception and ineptly carried out. At the very least, the bulk of the evidence suggests that what was probably bound to be a difficult aftermath to the war was made far more difficult by blinkered vision and overoptimistic assumptions on the part of the war's greatest partisans within the Bush administration.[70]

Rieff then listed Dick Cheney, Donald Rumsfeld, and Paul Wolfowitz as "the core group that would persuade President George W Bush to go to war with Iraq," and who had failed to plan postwar policy adequately.

Rieff also reported that Wolfowitz was unavailable to speak with him for the article.

Keller's midterm profile of President Bush in the *New York Times Magazine* also failed to ask its subject any tough questions. This was a significant feat of journalism considering that by January 2003, the month in which Keller's magazine piece on the president was published, Bush had renounced the Kyoto global-climate treaty, "unsigned" the International Criminal Court treaty, abrogated the antiballistic missile treaty, had repeatedly threatened to violate the UN Charter and US Constitution by saying he would invade Iraq without Security Council approval, had announced a new preventive-war doctrine that had no basis in international law, had placed right-wing Reagan administration officials (including Iran–Contra leftovers John Poindexter, Elliott Abrams, Michael Ledeen, and Otto Reich) in important positions, had withdrawn any minimally meaningful US mediation efforts in the Israeli–Palestinian conflict, had denounced global-warming science, reemphasized coal and oil as America's principal energy sources, announced plans to drill for oil in the Arctic National Wildlife Refuge, declined to increase fuel-economy standards for cars, had proposed relaxing standards for arsenic in drinking water, had proposed tax cuts that would mainly benefit the super-rich while increasing annual budget deficits and the national debt to unprecedented levels, had begun efforts to privatize Social Security and Medicare, and was overseeing the first net loss of American jobs since Herbert Hoover.

On an individual level, President Bush had demonstrated little to no competence to be the country's chief executive, given that he has never written seriously about any of the issues he is charged with deciding, apparently does little to no serious reading, and had never spoken with any evident expertise about the issues he oversees as president. In addition, the president had demonstrated a habit of misrepresenting basic facts of public importance, so much so that David Corn began a popular book on the president as follows:

> George W Bush is a liar. He has lied large and small. He has lied directly and by omission. He has misstated facts, knowingly or not. He has misled. He has broken promises, been unfaithful to political vows. Through his cam-paign for the presidency and his first years in the White House, he has mugged the truth—not merely in honest error, but deliberately, con-sistently, and repeatedly to advance his career and his agenda. Lying greased his path to the White House; it has been one of the essential tools of his

presidency. To call the 43rd president of the United States a prevaricator is not an exercise of opinion, not an inflammatory talk-radio device. This insult is supported by an all too extensive record of self-serving falsifications. So constant is his fibbing that a history of his lies offers a close approximation of the history of his presidential tenure.[71]

Even when the style of the *New York Times*, perhaps understandably, is to forego use of the words "lies" and "liar" when they refer to an American president, an intellectually honest and journalistically appropriate analysis of the first two years of the presidency of George W Bush would seek to hold the president accountable to the facts and the law implicated in his major policies and statements.

But Keller demonstrated no interest, either broadly or with respect to any specific issue, in this approach. Rather, he wrote that his focus "midway into Bush's first term" was to "measur[e] the emerging president against [President] Reagan [as] an instructive way of looking at Bush's qualities and of explaining his popularity."[72]

Keller found that "Bush, like Reagan, is a man of self-discipline, punctual, diet-conscious, religious about his gym time and a good night's sleep," that both are "unashamedly spiritual," that Bush, like Reagan, "tends to measure his counterparts in politics and world affairs by a moral standard," that both are "optimists" and "risk-takers," and quotes Lou Cannon that "both have that presidential temperament." About Bush, Keller wrote: "There is something there, some preexisting quality that avid Bush critics have missed."[73]

While comparing Bush's intellectual prowess with Bill Clinton's, Keller does indulge in one put-down—of Clinton:

> As for the idea that Bush is lazy, incurious or just not very bright, his supporters argue that critics have tended to judge the president by standards that are superficial or misleading. Bush is not, like Bill Clinton, a polymath who can dazzle you with his mastery of detail, who can speak for hours without notes, who can argue an issue from a dozen sides. He is, they say, adept at focusing an issue, asking the pertinent questions, relegating distractions to the sidelines, driving on to a decision and sticking to it. Compare the disciplined Bush of [Bob Woodward's] "Bush at War" with the Bill Clinton of another recent insider book, Kenneth Pollack's "Threatening Storm." That book, a case for going to war against Iraq, portrays the Clinton administration (in which Pollack served) prolonging the discussions while recoiling from the big decisions, equivocating, shifting ground, always looking to keep options open.[74]

Like Keller, Woodward in *Bush at War*[75] was so deferential to President Bush he could have titled his book *Maestro*.[76] But since Woodward had already written a deferential book by that title on Alan Greenspan, he settled for a title depicting the president fighting Al Qaeda and the Taliban in hand-to-hand combat. Also, Pollack's "insider" book, which Keller lauds and cites often, curiously got nearly everything wrong about Iraq in terms of the debate ongoing at the time: Pollack's sources (Iraqi defectors and exiles) were wrong about Iraqi WMD; Pollack's findings (that Iraq had WMD) were the wrong findings; and his policy recommendation (invade Iraq) was the wrong recommendation. While the Clinton administration's policies toward Iraq were among the blackest marks on that administration from a moral and legal standpoint (given its rigid support for economic sanctions), Keller criticizes Clinton via Pollack for failing to muster the intellectual discipline that Bush did in making "the big decision" to invade Iraq.

While embellishing Bush's intellectual gifts, Keller praises the president to the point of contradiction: On one hand, Bush merits points as the hands-on commander in chief; on the other hand, Bush is smartly delegating his presidency to others. In this regard, while paraphrasing Bush's critics, then defending Bush against them, Keller wrote: "In the alchemy of politics, moreover, stupid can be smart. Presidents who don't pretend to be supervising every detail are less likely to be blamed when details go awry." This kind of "stupid can be smart" attribute explains why the president hired Dick Cheney and Karl Rove:

> Much Washington punditry still insinuates that Dick Cheney is the presidential ventriloquist, that Rove is the political mastermind—and that Bush is in over his head. This seems to me wrongheaded. In most of the world an executive who surrounds himself with highly competent advisers is regarded as admirably self-confident.[77]

This is the essence of Keller's midterm profile of the president: He twists nearly every situation, context, and reality while bending over backwards to paint the president as a brighter bulb and better president than he obviously actually is.

And how, finally, did President George W Bush stack up against President Reagan in Keller's article? Keller concluded with these observations (like Ignatieff, with no evidence of any satirical intent):

> What Bush is striving for, on the evidence of the choices he has made so far, is bold in its ambition: markets unleashed, resources exploited. A progressive tax system leveled, a country unashamed of wealth. Government

entitlements gradually replaced by thrift, self-reliance and private good will. The safety net strung closer to the ground. Government infused with, in some cases supplanted by, the efficiency and accountability of a well-run corporation. A court system dedicated to protecting property and private enterprise and enforcing individual responsibility. A global common market that hums to the tune of American productivity. In the world, America rampant—unfettered by international law, unflinching when challenged, unmatchable in its might, more interested in being respected than in being loved.[78]

And the finale in the very next and final paragraph of the article:

> If he fails, my guess is that it will be a failure not of caution but of over-reaching, which means it will be failure on a grand scale. If he succeeds, he will move us toward an America Ronald Reagan would have been happy to call his own.[79]

Perhaps in the way that President Bush is really being smart by not reading, writing, or speaking coherently about any of the issues for which he is responsible, and is being bold and grand by intrepidly setting the country and the world on a course toward multiple disasters, Keller in his own mind is actually practicing good journalism when he writes about the president for the *New York Times* as badly as this. Given that Keller was hired by the publisher a few months later to be the paper's top editor, this article and the ones we review below apparently represent a valued journalistic ideal at the *Times*.

In addition to cutting Wolfowitz and Bush some major slack in the magazine profiles, Keller also supported the administration's invasion of Iraq. Keller justified this support in part by bundling it with the pro-invasion positions of other liberal hawks. Thus, Keller wrote:

> For starters, three men who have little in common with President Bush have articulated the case for war better than the administration itself—at least up until its recent crescendo of case-making. Tony Blair, who so resembles the American predecessor Mr. Bush despises, has been an eloquent and indis-pensable ally in the face of grave political risk. Hans Blix, the Swedish diplomat who embodies the patient, lawyerly internationalism some Bush partisans cannot abide, has managed without endorsing war to demonstrate Iraq's refusal to be contained. Kenneth Pollack, the Clinton National Security expert whose argument for invading Iraq is surely the most influential book of this season, has provided intellectual cover for every liberal who finds himself inclining toward war but uneasy about Mr. Bush.[80]

Tony Blair's case for war, especially as presented in two official dossiers published by the Blair government on Iraqi WMD, both of which were already published at the time of this op-ed piece by Keller,[81] has been so thoroughly discredited that Blair's credibility has been permanently damaged in Britain.[82] With regard to Blix, Keller wrote that he "articulated a case for war . . . without endorsing war." This is hardly a robust endorsement for invading Iraq, given that Blix consistently called for continuing UN inspections in lieu of war. And each pillar of Pollack's case for war was not only surprisingly weak and unconvincing even at the time, especially in light of the reverence with which it was repeatedly saluted by the likes of Keller and others, it fell apart completely in the invasion's wake.

Listing other liberal hawks as fellows in support of an Iraq invasion, Keller wrote:

> The I-Can't-Believe-I'm-a-Hawk Club includes op-ed regulars at this newspaper and The Washington Post, the editors of The New Yorker, The New Republic and Slate, columnists in Time and Newsweek. Many of these wary warmongers are baby-boom liberals whose aversion to the deployment of American power was formed by Vietnam but who had a kind of epiphany along the way—for most of us, in the vicinity of Bosnia.[83]

Keller's brief reference to Bosnia is to the massacres committed by Bosnian Serb and Serbian army regulars in the early 1990s of Bosnian Muslim children, women, and men as part of the campaign at the time by the government of Yugoslavia (Serbia and Montenegro) to engage in ethnic cleansing to create a "Greater Serbia."

Francis Boyle, professor of law at the University of Illinois at Champaign/Urbana, who represented the Bosnian government in that government's case at the International Court of Justice, wrote at the time: "Not since the end of the Second World War and the revelations of the horrors of Nazi Germany's 'Final Solution' has Europe witnessed the utter destruction of a People, for no other reason than they belong to a particular national, ethnical, racial, and religious group as such."[84] Marshall Harris, a former Clinton administration State Department official, wrote that the crisis in Bosnia was, "in reality, a clear case of Serb-sponsored genocide against Bosnian Muslims."[85]

Profoundly exacerbating the tragedy in Bosnia was the refusal, for various reasons, of the UN Security Council to intervene effectively to stop the killing, which included the July 1995 massacre of over 7,000 men and boys in just a few days in the Bosnian town of Srebrenica.

Thus, Keller's reference to Bosnia was designed to be anecdotal of Security Council ineptitude as applied to its reluctance to authorize force against Iraq.

But the two cases were strikingly different. Intervention in Bosnia arguably was legally required "to prevent" genocide under Article 1 of the 1948 Genocide Convention. In contrast, the most pressing humanitarian crisis in Iraq in the years prior to the 2003 invasion was due to US- and British-supported economic sanctions against Iraq. In addition to the studies published in the medical journals cited above, a 1999 report by the UN Children's Fund (UNICEF) found that "there would have been half a million fewer deaths of children under-five in [Iraq] as a whole during the eight-year period 1991 to 1998" in the absence of the US-backed economic sanctions.[86] A year later, *Reuters* reported:

> A senior UN official said Friday about half a million children under the age of 5 have died in Iraq since the imposition of UN sanctions 10 years ago. Anupama Rao Singh, country director for the UN Children's Fund, made the estimate in an interview with Reuters. "In absolute terms we estimate that perhaps about half a million children under 5 years of age have died, who ordinarily would not have died had the decline in mortality that was prevalent over the 70s and 80s continued through the 90s," she said.[87]

If the mortality figures published by UNICEF in 1999 and also in *The Lancet*[88] in 2000 are accurate, then the number of deaths among young children in Iraq in the 1990s exceeded the total number of all Bosnians killed in the 1990s; nevertheless, in his Wolfowitz profile, Keller cynically referred to the sanctions-related deaths in Iraq as "a P.R. nightmare of hungry children" for the Bush administration.[89]

It seems that Keller invoked Bosnia in part "to provide intellectual cover" for himself and his liberal-hawk club to support an Iraq invasion that was not otherwise supportable: "We reluctant hawks may disagree among ourselves about the most compelling logic for war—protecting America, relieving oppressed Iraqis or reforming the Middle East—but we generally agree that the logic for standing pat does not hold."[90] Protecting America from Iraq? Iraq never attacked or threatened to attack the United States, had no military capability to attack the United States, and no evidence linked Iraq to September 11. Relieving oppressed Iraqis? Saddam was a tyrant, but US policy through war and sanctions has greatly exacerbated the killing and suffering of Iraqis, most of which occurred more than ten years earlier when the US government looked the other way because Iraq was our strategic ally at the time.

Reform the Middle East? Such reform more credibly would begin with an Israeli–Palestinian peace agreement consistent with applicable international law, a policy that the Bush administration to date has rejected.

Also, Keller's reasons for invading Iraq satisfy no international law criteria for a resort to force. But the mere existence of the liberal hawk club remedies even this problem. Keller writes: "Thanks to all these grudging allies [that is, the other liberal hawks], Mr. Bush will be able to claim, with justification, that the coming war is a far cry from the rash, unilateral adventure some of his advisers would have settled for."[91]

Is there a Traub-like "counter-consistent conclusion" in Keller's analysis? After indicating that he would support a unilateral invasion of Iraq in violation of the UN Charter, Keller, like Traub, wants to whack the UN back to life. Thus, a month after Ignatieff wrote that President Bush picked up the UN by the scruff of the neck for its own good, Keller wrote, in another instance of tough love favored at the *Times* and by the president:

> Mr. Bush has kicked some new life into the UN, and been well repaid; I'd place a small bet that he will even get a second resolution on Iraq. Now we should stop treating it with such petulance and embrace it as a source of support and legitimacy.[92]

Keller does not go on to say how he reconciles his advocacy for violating the cardinal rule of the UN Charter with wanting to embrace the UN.

Ultimately, like the *Times* itself, Keller is less concerned with facts, law, and consistent arguments than with political positioning. The "liberal hawk" brand of support for President Bush's invasion of Iraq clearly sought to hit the positional sweet spot between hawks who supported an invasion and liberals who opposed it. On this count, Keller writes:

> I think there is a consensus to be built. It is not the ultrahawk view of an America radiating indifference to everyone who gets in its way, keeping aspiring powers in their place, shunning the clumsy implements of international law and leading with its air force. Nor is it the Vietnam-syndrome reticence about American power that still holds portions of both parties in sway.[93]

While seeking political consensus is appropriate for mediating negotiations, it's not a good journalistic model for getting at important facts or exposing lawless policies. This is because a consensus position is easily limited to the positions of the principals involved (the president and the Congress, Republicans and Democrats, ultrahawks and liberal hawks), easily forecloses on facts that exist outside the fact consensus, and easily ignores the US Constitution and the UN Charter when a consensus exists to violate the law, as it did among each of the parties of consensus mentioned here with respect to invading Iraq.

"Yoi Kangae, Yoi Shina!" *Business Week* reports this is Japanese "Toyota-speak" for "Good thinking means good products."[94] Presumably, "Toyota-speak" would apply to news products as well as to cars. But there is no evident good thinking happening at the *Times*. The result is a highly overrated news product, and no discernible editorial policy, except for the paper's ongoing obsession with positioning its editorial products the way a car company might position its cars.

The liberal hawk positioning of the *Times* with respect to Iraq policy was not grounded in any concerns for fairness and accuracy, but in finding a presumptively safe place to position editorial policy between supporters and opponents of an invasion. In other words, the *Times* sought to be exacting with respect to its centrism rather than with the facts and law as they existed. "Liberal hawk" itself indicates taking aspects of two sides, of not being easily pinned down or identified, as does Keller's "I Can't Believe I'm a Hawk." Positioning, as in trawling for an amorphous political center, best describes the editorial policy of the *Times*. This "bad thinking" is what leads the paper to produce its mediocre news and editorial product.

Less than a month before being named executive editor, Keller wrote a review of *Rogue Nation* (2003), a book by Clyde Prestowitz.[95] In his review, Keller wrote:

> If you want to know how the American colossus looks to the rest of the world, "Rogue Nation," by Clyde Prestowitz, is your book—an unsparing but unhysterical catalog of American behavior that has made the world see us as self-centered and hypocritical. The counts in the indictment are familiar: We preach fair trade but underwrite American cotton farmers at such high prices that we keep African farmers in poverty. We guzzle petroleum, and then need a foreign policy that overemphasizes one region of the globe. We preach democracy and dance with tyrants. "Rogue Nation" could serve as an appendix to this month's global poll by the Pew Research Center, which shows a ballooning fear and mistrust of the United States around the world.[96]

Summarizing Prestowitz's proposed remedy to the rogueness, and concluding his review, Keller writes:

> And the solution? Essentially, spontaneous enlightenment. Americans should wise up, throw out unilateralist politicians, treat the world with respect and generally be just a little less ... American. While we're at it, I propose that we eat right, floss daily, tithe generously and stop watching mindless TV shows.[97]

Keeping this review in mind, recall that a hallmark event establishing the reputation of the *New York Times* as a newspaper that reported the news without fear or favor was its publication of the Pentagon Papers in 1971. At that time, the publisher of the *Times*, Arthur Ochs ("Punch") Sulzberger, rejected Attorney General John Mitchell's demand to cease publication of the *Times'* stories on the Pentagon Papers, the leaked secret Pentagon history of US involvement in Vietnam. In the US Supreme Court case that permitted the *Times* to continue its published coverage of the Pentagon Papers, Justice Potter Stewart wrote:

> In the absence of the governmental checks and balances present in other areas of our national life, the only effective restraint upon executive policy and power in the areas of national defense and international affairs may lie in an enlightened citizenry—in an informed and critical public opinion which alone can here protect the values of democratic government.[98]

Now compare the two perspectives presented here on the importance of an enlightened citizenry in the United States: The cynical one expressed by Bill Keller, the current executive editor of the *New York Times*, in his book review above, and the one expressed by Justice Stewart in the Pentagon Papers case, described as that which "alone can here protect the values of democratic government."

Keller in effect rejects, even satirizes, the core constitutional mandate—given to the *New York Times* by the US Supreme Court in the Pentagon Papers case—to "enlighten the citizenry" with respect to national security and international affairs. Keller rejected this mandate in the *Times* while he was widely thought to be the leading candidate to replace Howell Raines as executive editor—a rejection that apparently helped to mark Keller as a good fit to be hired to that position three weeks later.

Ruth Wedgwood is the *New York Times'* leading international law expert, given that she holds the recent record among such experts for most appearances in the *Times*. From January 1 1996 to November 1 2003, Wedgwood was cited as a legal expert in twenty-nine news stories. In the *Times*, Wedgwood has supported the Bush administration's invasion of Iraq,[99] the Clinton administration's threats to bomb Iraq in 1998,[100] and the arrests and imprisonment of American citizens, without being charged of a crime, for suspicion of supporting terrorism.[101]

Wedgwood is currently Edward B. Burling Professor of International Law and Diplomacy at Johns Hopkins University. Her opinions are predictable in that she seldom, if ever, opposes on international law grounds the use of force by the United States. Among international law scholars she is to the right of most in a generally conservative field in the United States.

When political tension in March 2003 between the Bush administration (and its threats to invade Iraq) and the UN Security Council (and its reluctance to authorize an invasion) was at a peak, the *Times* chose to cover this moment by soliciting Wedgwood's right-wing views and those of a like-minded colleague about the US use of force under international law. On March 10, UN Secretary General Kofi Annan said that a US invasion of Iraq without Security Council approval would violate the UN Charter. On March 11, the *New York Times,* after reporting Annan's statement to this effect, quoted Wedgwood in response: "I just disagree with the secretary general's legal view because there are fundamental Security Council resolutions that underlie this."[102] Elsewhere in the article, the *Times* reported:

> Professor Wedgwood said that even if the United States loses the final vote [at the Security Council] and proceeds to war, "the failure of this particular resolution" does "not obviate the prior ones," especially since the prior [Security Council] resolutions gave Washington and its allies authority to disarm Iraq for the sake of the peace and security of the region.[103]

This same article cited Richard N. Gardner, professor of international law at Columbia University, and a consistent supporter over the years of the liberal-hawk position supporting the US use of force in legally dubious circumstances:

> [Gardner] said that since Saddam Hussein has repeatedly violated the conditions of the 1991 [Gulf War] cease-fire, "the United States and other countries revert back to their rights to restore peace and security in the area" under the [Security Council] resolution authorizing that war, passed in 1990. . . . Professor Gardner agreed that the authority [to invade Iraq] existed

in previous resolutions and said he was confident as an international lawyer that Mr. Bush has the authority he needs, "but we are now in a situation where there are certain ambiguities."[104]

Given that Wedgwood and Gardner were arguing on the basis of challengeable assumptions—(a) that Iraq had not disarmed itself or been disarmed of UN-proscribed weapons, (b) that Iraq's presumptive violations of the old resolutions (given its presumptive failure to disarm) permitted an invasion of Iraq even in the context of a contemporaneous refusal by the Security Council to authorize an invasion, and (c) that even assuming an Iraqi failure to disarm and violations of Security Council resolutions, that such grounds satisfied the requirements of the UN Charter for invading Iraq—there were important and time-urgent reasons to respond to these claims.

Though Gardner stated he was "very uneasy about going to war at this stage without authority from the [Security] Council," and cautioned that doing so would "leave us in a world where every country is self-judging what it does, and that leads to world anarchy," the *Times* left unanswered the specious legal arguments of Wedgwood and Gardner that pointed to those results.[105]

"Kosovo" was a common refrain among proponents of an Iraq invasion. In the same article that featured Wedgwood and Gardner, White House spokesman Ari Fleischer said that "from a moral point of view," if the Security Council fails to authorize force against Iraq, it will have "failed to act once again" as it did in Kosovo.[106]

Weeks earlier, the *Times* had reported:

> Not every expert agrees that the United States will even ask for another [Security Council] resolution [to use force against Iraq]. Some say the Bush administration may well use the model of Kosovo in the late 1990's, when President Bill Clinton realized that Russia would veto military action and therefore ignored the Security Council altogether.[107]

In a *Times* op-ed piece, the liberal Michael Glennon quoted without dissent US Secretary of State Colin Powell's statement that "the president has authority [to use force against Iraq], as do other like-minded nations, just as we did in Kosovo." Glennon also argued "it would not be unlawful to attack Iraq, even without Security Council approval."[108]

Similarly, in an op-ed piece published two days before the administration launched the Iraq invasion, Anne-Marie Slaughter argued:

By giving up on the Security Council, the Bush administration has started on a course that could be called "illegal but legitimate," a course that could end, paradoxically, winning United Nations approval for a military campaign in Iraq—though only after an invasion.[109]

Slaughter further wrote:

The relevant history here is from Kosovo. In 1999, the United States, expecting a Russian veto of military intervention to stop Serbian attacks on ethnic Albanians in Kosovo, sidestepped the United Nations completely and sought authorization for the use of force within NATO itself.[110]

The notion of "illegal but legitimate" in Kosovo, Slaughter wrote, came from "the Independent International Commission on Kosovo [which] found that although formally illegal—the United Nations Charter demands that the use of force in any cause other than self-defense be authorized by the Security Council—the [Kosovo] intervention was nonetheless legitimate in the eyes of the international community."[111]

But the rationale for citing the Kosovo intervention as "legitimate" did not apply to Iraq. This was evident in the Kosovo Commission's report:

The Commission concludes that the NATO military intervention was illegal but legitimate. It was illegal because it did not receive prior approval from the United Nations Security Council. However, the Commission considers that the intervention was justified because all diplomatic avenues had been exhausted and because the intervention had the effect of liberating the majority population of Kosovo from a long period of oppression under Serbian rule.[112]

In contrast, "all diplomatic avenues" had not been exhausted prior to the Bush administration's invasion of Iraq. For example, the chief UN weapons inspectors—Hans Blix and Mohamed ElBaradei—had pleaded for continuing inspections in Iraq, which were progressing with good results and without serious obstruction. A majority of Security Council members supported continued inspections in lieu of war, as did a majority of traditional American allies. Iraq certainly posed no immediate military threat to the United States, or any other state, and any future threats were remote and speculative. And there was no humanitarian crisis in Iraq comparable to Kosovo at the time, except for the extensive excessive morbidity and mortality in Iraq due to the effects of the decade-long, US-supported economic sanctions.

Furthermore, the Kosovo Commission Report overall was quite rigorous with respect to limiting and qualifying the Kosovo exception to the prohibition on force. Among numerous other reservations, the Commission wrote that the exception was restricted to "impending and unfolding humanitarian catastrophes," and was undertaken in light of "the inadequacy of the protective response of the UN to the ethnic cleansing in Bosnia a few years earlier," and likewise to "the Rwanda genocide in 1994."[113]

Though Slaughter cited the Kosovo exception to support an Iraq invasion, she made no attempt to apply the details or principles of the exception to the Iraq situation. She did, however, argue that the United Nations "cannot be a straightjacket, preventing nations from defending themselves or pursuing what they perceive to be their vital national security interests." But the Kosovo Commission clearly did not intend its report to be used to justify future military invasions based nakedly on an invading country's "perceptions" of its national security interests.

Perhaps to soothe surprised readers, Slaughter vaguely maintained that "what is most important here is that the contending sides [in the legal debate] continue to regard United Nations approval as a necessary component of the use of force."[114] Rejecting the necessity of UN approval for the use of force at a critical moment, while arguing that UN approval is still necessary, was a fit finale to the *Times'* pre-invasion coverage of Iraq.

3

EDITORIAL POLICY AND IRAQ: A FORTUNE-500 COMPANY POSITIONS ITS PRODUCT

In recently published memoirs about his half-century at the *New York Times*, Arthur Gelb, a founding editor in 1944 of an in-house newsletter called *Timesweek*, tells about taking "*Timesweek* into the field of investigative journalism." Gelb wrote: "My first target was the cafeteria, often maligned by the staff for its practice of serving reheated leftovers—especially knockwurst and sauerkraut—and day-old bread. I thought such an exposé would bring both plaudits for *Timesweek* and culinary improvements; but I miscalculated." As the cafeteria investigation began, Gelb was summoned by the publisher, Arthur Hays Sulzberger, who lectured the twenty-year-old copyboy about editorial policy at the *Times*. "Well, young man," Sulzberger said, "I hear you've assigned a story on complaints about the food served in the cafeteria. . . . *Timesweek*, up to now, seemed to have been guided by the same principles as the *Times*, and you should have learned that we are not a crusading newspaper."[1]

Finding out that the *Times* is not a crusading newspaper is part of the learning curve for reporters at the paper. Gelb recounted how in the 1960s, Clifton Daniel, the *Times* managing editor, "once halfheartedly warned me to keep my crusading spirit under control, but I pretended not to hear him."[2] In 1970 "the most momentous story" of Gelb's tenure as metropolitan editor—a major exposé of the New York City Police Department, which began in part with information provided to the *Times* by Frank Serpico—might not have been investigated and published because one of Gelb's assistant editors told the investigating reporter at the outset (while Gelb was on vacation) "not to bother" since "*The Times* was not interested in 'crusading' stories." The reporter,

David Burnham, continued his investigation anyway and the *Times* eventually published it with Gelb's support.[3]

In his memoirs of the *New York Times*, John Hess, a former *Times* reporter, suggested an investigation of housing corruption in New York City in the 1950s to the *Times* city editor, Frank Adams, who rejected the proposal, telling Hess "the *Times* is not a crusading newspaper."[4]

In addition to its reluctance to pursue worthwhile investigations, from bad cafeteria food on up, the *Times* sees itself as a centrist newspaper that favors no political party or ideology. Gelb tells how his friend, Abe Rosenthal, a top editor in the 1960s, frequently pleaded with the paper's bureaus and desk editors to keep the paper from drifting to the left:

> Over and over, he [Rosenthal] alerted editors to watch the daily copy for editorializing and—most particularly—warned about keeping the paper from moving to the left of center. Center, he insisted, was where the paper must always be.[5]

Hess gives some insight into how Rosenthal's remonstrations were put into practice:

> Back home, the country was shaken by the police riot at the [1968 Democratic] convention in Chicago. Editor Rosenthal changed what [*Times* reporter] Tony Lukas witnessed [at the convention] from [police] "brutality" to "overreaction." When Harrison Salisbury complained on behalf of his staff at the convention that Abe was "taking the guts out of the story," Rosenthal retorted that he was taking out "the goddam editorializing."[6]

The in-house insistence that the *Times* operate as a non-crusading, centrist newspaper originates in the founding principles of its patriarch, Adolph Ochs, who, in 1896—the year Ochs bought the *Times*—declared that its editorial mission was "to give the news impartially, without fear or favor, regardless of any party, sect, or interest involved."[7] Regarding the Ochsian legacy at the *Times*, Gay Talese wrote in his renowned book on the *Times* that "a bronze statue of Ochs stands in the lobby and also up on the fourteenth floor where the stockholders and directors meet, and Ochs' credo—'To Give the News Impartially, Without Fear or Favor'—is on display in various places around the [*Times*] building and in *Times* bureaus around the nation and world."[8]

Talese wrote: "[I]n many ways *The Times* remains Ochs' paper, his shrine, his words of wisdom being reechoed by old sages still under his influence," and that it was Ochs' desire "to have *The Times* run as he wished not only until his death, but long after it." Thus, "[t]his was one reason why, in his final years, Ochs became almost obsessed by his last will and testament, consulting endlessly with his lawyer lest there be confusion about his ultimate dream: *The New York Times* must, upon his death, be controlled only by immediate family, and in turn by their families, and it would be the responsibility of them all to govern during their lifetime with the same dedication that he had during his."[9]

Indeed, the line of Ochs-family publishers since Ochs' death in 1935—Arthur Hays Sulzberger (Ochs' son-in-law), 1935–61; Orvil E. Dryfoos (Sulzberger's son-in-law), 1961–63; Arthur Ochs ("Punch") Sulzberger (Sulzberger's son), 1963–92; and Arthur Ochs Sulzberger Jr. (Punch's son), the current publisher since 1992—have committed themselves to Ochsian "impartiality" as the paper's editorial policy.

Loyalty to the family editorial credo is reflected not only in what the *Times* publishes, but also apparently in whom it promotes. Hess wrote that "[a] Darwinian selection favors the survival of people who see the world as the family does."[10] Talese wrote that "[u]ntil relatively recent years the editors who had risen within the institution had been those most reverential toward Ochs fundamentalism, and the highest-paid reporters were those who were the most objective and accurate, aware of the weight of each word in *The Times*."[11] For Talese, however, the requirement to heed the Ochsian fundamentalism came with tradeoffs for reporters at the *Times*:

> This awareness often stifled their writing style. They might have written with lucidity and freedom on other publications but on *The Times* they felt the weight and became overly cautious, rigid, and dull. Dullness had been no sin during the Ochs era. Better to be a little dull than to dazzle and distort, the thinking went, and as long as they remained faithful to the principles of Ochs, a sense of responsibility and caution, the old morality, they need not worry. They were secure on *The Times*. They were paid well, treated fairly, protected from the sham and uncertainties of the outside world. Economic recessions and depressions did not cut off their income, and threats to world survival seemed not to disturb the inner peace of the *Times* building. *The Times* stood apart, solid and unshakeable. If it sometimes seemed a bit crusty and out of touch with popular trends, this was not so bad. It was, like Ochs, never frivolous. It was almost never caught out on a limb.[12]

One tradeoff is the inherent tension between not wanting to get caught out on a limb and the requirement that the *Times* be seen as the vanguard publisher of national and world news, as Arthur Gelb and others have noted.[13] Gelb's views here are of interest because he clearly struggled with the *Times* policy of non-crusading centrism, but nevertheless in his book remained too loyal and affectionate toward the *Times* to challenge the dogma beyond a few anecdotes. As a young man, however, and prior to his employment at the *Times*, he recognized the journalistic implications of the paper not wanting to get caught out on a limb in its coverage of major political issues. In the first chapter of his book, Gelb wrote about his brief college career, and his take as a young man on the *Times*: "I wasn't as radical as some of my school friends, but I did have a rebellious social conscience, and I often found myself at ideological odds with *The Times*."[14] For example:

> I thought its coverage of the Spanish Civil War had been too pro-Franco. My friends and I—supporters of the Loyalist side and despising Franco as a Nazi ally—had been influenced in our thinking by a letter in *The Times* signed by Archibald MacLeish and Bennett Cerf, among other literary figures, that criticized the paper for allowing its correspondent, William P. Carney, to rely heavily on Franco's propaganda.[15]

And:

> Then there was my sense that *The Times's* coverage of Nazi atrocities—despite the moral loftiness and balance it espoused—was dismayingly thin. While it was true there had been scores of stories about the persecution of European Jews in the paper since 1939, the accounts were brief, rarely appeared on page one and bore no interpretation. Nor did the editorial page express sufficient indignation when our government ignored various proposals by Jewish organizations to rescue those destined for systematic slaughter in what, at the time, were insidiously designated as "reservations."[16]

Gelb also wrote how the *Times,* under its Washington bureau chief in the 1970s, James ("Scotty") Reston, lagged behind the *Washington Post* in its coverage of Watergate, due mostly to "Scotty's warm friendships with Washington's power elite"[17] and Reston's overall disinclination to investigate official Washington: "It seems clear, with hindsight, that it was Scotty's scorn for old-fashioned police reporting that led to our Washington bureau's dismal performance in covering Watergate."[18] Tony Lukas, a former *Times* reporter and for a time one of "Scotty's boys" in the Washington bureau, later wrote that "some of those who have worked for and with Reston over the years may wish that he were a little less cozy with power, a little less reverential toward the System, a little more outspoken about the evils they detect in American society."[19] Reston, though, was a favorite among the *Times* publishers for whom he worked, and Lukas' description of Reston's columns as "lofty, above the fray, moralistic, and often downright banal" could just as easily describe the long-time tone and tenor of the *Times* editorial page.

It could also have described the predictably unoriginal and bland news reporting on the front page today, which is too complacent about taking its news cues from the Bush administration and too eager to follow the administration's agenda. For example, on December 15 2003 the *Times* front page featured a six-column headline announcing that Saddam Hussein had been captured, and included five stories on the capture, a big photograph of Saddam, and a color illustration of his hideout that, taken together, took up the entire front page of the *New York Times* on that day. While Saddam's capture in a different context could have been a welcome event given his long tyrannical rule in Iraq, the triumphalism of the front-page coverage in the *Times* ignored the context in which the capture was accomplished, as if nothing else existed or mattered: No illegal invasion. No humiliating occupation. No casualties. No hundreds of billions of dollars spent. No war profiteering. No lies told (and none investigated by the non-crusading paper).

No doubt the *Times* viewed its coverage of Saddam's capture as an exemplary case-study of how it can mobilize its vast resources to cover an issue overnight more exhaustively than any other US news organization. Predictably, however, the paper's generously proffered coverage ignored the moral and legal tensions involved in the capture of the untidy tyrant by the illicit invader. The next day (December 16), however, when the *Times'* Elvis Mitchell mourned "the price of triumph"—a hint of insight perhaps into the previous day's coverage—he could have been writing about the invasion of Iraq, the capture of Saddam, and the ultimate costs to the United States of "its pounding and operatic martial fury."[20] Mitchell, however, is a film critic for the *Times* and was reviewing "The Lord of the Rings: The Return of the King," not the invasion of Iraq.

Which brings to mind a hypothetical question: What if film critics, who generally write with more imagination, emotion, and intellectual rigor than the *Times* foreign correspondents or editorial-page writers, were assigned to cover US foreign policy as a remedy to Ochsian fundamentalism? How might the film critics review American foreign policy? Perhaps they would argue that "nothing less than the fate of humanity is at stake"[21] in the Bush administration's methodical rout of international law with respect to war prevention, missile treaties, and the environment. Or perhaps they would describe the "sleepless malice"[22] of Cheney and Rumsfeld and the civilian neo-orcs at the Pentagon who wanted an invasion to re-set the stage in the Middle East for geopolitical and oil concerns. Though it might upset Ochsian editorial custom, such coverage would reflect more insight into the current situation than the muffled correspondence from the foreign bureaus of the *Times* and the bland, non-crusading centrism of its editorials.

Another conflict with the Ochsian editorial legacy was perhaps inadvertently highlighted by Arthur Hays Sulzberger in 1935, when, upon assuming the publisher's post after Ochs' death, he wrote:

> Custom among newspapers requires a new publisher to announce his policies and to them pledge adherence. . . . I pledge myself, in the words of [Ochs'] salutatory of August 19, 1896, "to give the news impartially, without fear or favor, regardless of any party, sect, or interest involved," and I join with the many men and women who daily make *The New York Times* in re-dedicating ourselves to the fundamental principles of our democracy and the high dreams of our nation's builders.[23]

The assumption in Sulzberger's statement is that Ochsian editorial policy serves democracy in the United States. The publishing record of the *Times,* however, shows that it cannot easily serve both Ochs and democracy.

For example, what is the value to democracy of Ochsian "impartiality" if the policies of an American president threatened to undermine the US Constitution, and the *Times*, in response, loathe to rock the boat and thus to investigate constitutional subversions, was content to occupy a centrist position that had floated perilously to the right? In fact, the *Times'* rigid adherence to this interpretation of "impartiality" exposes a flank of constitutional vulnerability—providing opportunities for an administration that is both ruthless enough to take the country as far to the right as it pleases, and smart enough to know that the *Times* and the press in general won't do much to report the facts and law as needed to defend the Constitution, as they have declined to do under George W Bush.

Keeping this scenario in mind, the principal threat to the Constitution today comes from the conscious consolidation of executive power via deliberate and flagrant violations of international law, a process that (a) feeds the cycle of state violence and retaliatory terrorism, (b) exacerbates terrorist threats to US national security, and (c) promotes opportunistic alterations to established constitutional principles. Seen in this light, international law is the Minas Tirith of the Constitution and American democracy: If international law falls, restraints on the exercise of US power will fall, world legal order will fall, and the rule of force and terrorism will govern—even more so than it does today. National security and counterterrorism concerns would trump the Constitution, making this once durable framework of our political and legal systems a quaint anachronism.

The cascading harm to world legal order and constitutionalism has already begun. And we have already seen, through its coverage of the Iraq invasion, how the *Times* would likely respond to an escalating world crisis: It refuses even to print the words "UN Charter" or "international law" on its editorial page with respect to US policy; its most favored international law scholar is the right-wing Ruth Wedgwood (who seldom if ever meets a US use of force she doesn't endorse); it defends the Bush administration's WMD claims as "based on the best intelligence available"[24] in order to cover up the substantial complicity of the *Times* itself in the WMD scandal; and its publisher and top editors, Gollum-like, are obsessed with holding the "precious" center to the point of constitutional betrayal. It seems "non-crusading centrism" prevents the *Times* from going out on a limb even to defend the facts and law that have been systematically distorted and violated by the Bush administration.

In 1971, in fact, the US Supreme Court made it the *Times'* business to defend the facts when the US government distorted them, and to uphold the law when the US government violated it. The *Times* inherited this constitutional mandate by way of the Pentagon Papers case, when its publisher, Punch Sulzberger, risked prison to publish excerpts and analyses of the government's secret history of military involvement in Indochina. Publishing this history helped expose the official lies that led to the US war in Vietnam. In his separate opinion in the case, which upheld the right of the *Times* to publish its analysis of the Pentagon Papers despite President Nixon's demands that it not publish them, US Supreme Court Justice Hugo Black helped to define the constitutional role of the press and its leading organ by writing:

> In the First Amendment, the Founding Fathers gave the free press the protection it must have to fulfill its essential role in our democracy. The

press was to serve the governed, not the governors. The government's power to censor the press was abolished so that the press would remain forever free to censure government. The press was protected so that it could bare the secrets of government and inform the people. Only a free and unrestrained press can effectively expose deception in government. And paramount among the responsibilities of a free press is the duty to prevent any part of the government from deceiving the people and sending them off to distant lands to die of foreign fevers and foreign shot and shell.[25]

The last sentence of this passage—read in the context of the *Times'* coverage of Iraq policy—reveals the indifference at the *Times* today to its broad constitutional latitude to expose the deceit and lies of the Bush administration. The *Times* refused, apparently, to consider its constitutional mandate when, in order to fulfill its in-house mandate of non-crusading centrism, it permitted the administration to deceive the American people about the nature of the military threat from Iraq. Rather than perform its "duty to prevent the government from deceiving the people" (Justice Black), the *Times* aided and abetted the administration's deception efforts by reporting without challenge the claims about Iraqi WMD, and by not challenging on international law grounds the illegal unilateralism of the president. Nor has the *Times* to date significantly censured the administration for its WMD deceptions and illegal international conduct. How could it when its own coverage is implicated in the same deceptions that justified the conduct? Despite periodic episodes of commendable coverage, when accidents of events and people have prompted the *Times* to stray from its self-imposed inertia, the paper's record of coverage of the US use of force reflects a protracted failure at the *Times* to assume the burden of oversight on behalf of either the US Constitution or the UN Charter.

Bill Keller's memo to the *New York Times* newsroom on July 30 2003 was issued on his first day of work as the new executive editor of the *Times*. It was also attached to the virtuously titled "Report of the Committee on Safeguarding the Integrity of Our Journalism" ("The Siegal Committee")[26] that was written and published in response to the Jayson Blair scandal.

Blair had worked for the *Times* as an intern and staff reporter from 1998 to 2003, and apparently had engaged in a number of journalistic misrepresentations throughout those years. In April 2003, when a newspaper in Texas notified the *Times* "that portions of Blair's story [in the *Times*] about a missing soldier's mother" were "a near-perfect match to one the Texas paper had published,"[27] the *Times* initiated an investigation of Blair's reporting, and for the first time found extensive journalistic fraud committed by the reporter.

In May 2003 the *Times* published the findings of its investigation of Blair's reporting in a 7000-word front-page story that began:

> A staff reporter for The New York Times committed frequent acts of journalistic fraud while covering significant news events in recent months, an investigation by Times journalists has found. The widespread fabrication and plagiarism represent a profound betrayal of trust and a low point in the 152-year history of the newspaper.
>
> The reporter, Jayson Blair, 27, misled readers and Times colleagues with dispatches that purported to be from Maryland, Texas and other states, when often he was far away, in New York. He fabricated comments. He concocted scenes. He lifted material from other newspapers and wire services. He selected details from photographs to create the impression he had been somewhere or seen someone, when he had not.
>
> And he used these techniques to write falsely about emotionally charged moments in recent history, from the deadly sniper attacks in suburban Washington to the anguish of families grieving for loved ones killed in Iraq.[28]

The *Times* publisher, Arthur Sulzberger Jr., said that the Blair scandal was "a huge black eye" for the *Times* and "an abrogation of the trust between the newspaper and its readers."[29]

The Blair episode was a serious event at the *Times* and a public-relations low point for the paper, especially given the scandal's high-profile coverage in other news organizations. To its credit, the in-house investigation of newsroom and management policies implicated in the scandal was impressive. In the final analysis, however, and apart from the distress Blair may have caused to those personally affected by his reporting, the scandal involved little more than a troubled individual and lax newsroom oversight at the paper; and it hurt the paper a lot more than it hurt the country. Jayson Blair's reporting to our knowledge led to no one's death, and caused no American soldier to leave his or her family to fight in Iraq. Nor did Blair's reporting directly implicate editorial policy at the *New York Times*, which facilitates at an institutional level far more serious episodes of journalistic fraud than those that the *Times* newsroom inadvertently set forth with Blair at the level of an inexperienced individual reporter. Far more experienced reporters and editors routinely misrepresent far more serious issues in ways that the editorial policy supports.

For example, on October 8 2002, the day after a major speech by President Bush on Iraq, the lead paragraph of a front-page story in the *Times* read:

> President Bush declared tonight that Saddam Hussein could attack the United States or its allies "on any given day" with chemical or biological weapons. In a forceful argument for disarming Iraq or going to war with that country, he argued that "we have an urgent duty to prevent the worst from occurring."[30]

Putting aside for a moment questions about international law with respect to invading Iraq, even if WMD had been found, and whether Iraq actually possessed chemical or biological weapons, one might ask in response: Given that Iraq is 10,000 miles from the United States, how might Iraq have delivered a chemical or biological weapon to the United States? Does Iraq have intercontinental ballistic missiles? Strategic bombers? Submarines that can fire ballistic missiles or cruise missiles? These questions are too absurd to even ask, yet President Bush clearly intended to give the impression that Iraq had some such capability to attack the United States. And the fact that Bush, in the same speech, compared the Iraqi military threat to the United States to the 1962 Cuban missile crisis clearly indicated that he was not referring to the threat of terrorist suitcase weapons.

The *New York Times* had at least three chances on October 8 (the day after the president's speech) to correct the impression given by the president concerning Iraq's ability to attack the United States: (a) in a front-page news story by veteran *Times* reporter David Sanger, (b) in a front-page "news analysis" of the president's speech by another veteran *Times* reporter, Todd Purdum, and (c) in the *Times* lead editorial on the speech that was published that day.

In addition to writing in his second sentence that President Bush "presented a forceful argument" for invading Iraq, Sanger wrote: "[t]he president likened the threat the country faces today from Iraq to the Cuban missile crisis," which Sanger presumably viewed as an aspect of the forceful argument. Sanger also wrote "the president charged for the first time that Iraq's fleet of unmanned aerial vehicles was ultimately intended to deliver chemical and biological weapons to cities in the United States." Even if such aerial vehicles existed, how would they deliver any weapons to the United States? No evidence existed that even came close to establishing that Iraq had unmanned aerial vehicles with a range of 10,000 miles, yet Sanger's report implied that Iraq had a fleet of such vehicles that were capable of attacking the United States.

Purdum's "news analysis" was equally inept. Thus, in response to the speech in which President Bush had compared the threat from Iraq to the Cuban missile crisis, Purdum wrote that the president "us[ed] simple metaphors and concrete examples in a fatherly reminder of a president's ability to rise above elite diplomatic debates."[31] Apparently, writing "news analysis" for the *Times* in this case also meant analyzing the president's speech as "plain-spoken" and "stern," but did not entail presenting simple evidence that the president was seriously and dangerously misleading the public.

Also with regard to the speech, the editorial page said: "Speaking in Cincinnati, [President Bush] was forceful in outlining the threat presented by Iraq."[32] Like Sanger's news report and Purdum's news analysis, the editorial opted to flatter the president rather than flag the president's analogy to the Cuban missile crisis. Thus, even though the *Times* covered the president's Cincinnati speech with two veteran reporters (Sanger and Purdum) and a lead editorial, the paper nevertheless permitted the president to compare without challenge or serious reflection the threat from Iraq to the Cuban missile crisis. This was an inexcusable though not unsurprising performance by veteran reporters and the editorial page of the *Times*, yet it was apparently not recognized by the paper's editors or publisher as signaling a serious problem with the *Times*' coverage of what the president was saying about Iraq.

Given the extent to which institutional custom at the *Times* permits the paper to publish presidential misrepresentations as news on a regular basis, a "Siegal Committee Report" on editorial policy at the *Times* would almost certainly reveal more serious problems at the paper than the Blair investigation did. However, the Siegal report in fact took a moment to stipulate that its inquiry into the Blair scandal "was not an examination of the editorial policies of the newspaper, its story choices or its news values."[33] To our knowledge, no such recent or modern published inquiry of editorial policy at the *Times* exists. Nor is there much evidence that the *Times* has ever systematically explored exactly what "non-crusading" (Sulzberger), "centrist" (Rosenthal), or "impartiality" (Ochs) mean as the foundational principles of editorial policy at the paper, or how and why editorial policy at the *Times* has permitted a succession of American presidents over several decades to fabricate reasons to go to war without appropriate journalistic oversight from the *Times*.

While Adolph Ochs invoked "impartiality" as the editorial policy of the *Times* over a hundred years ago, today it fronts for a staff (with some exceptions*) of apparently uninspired and unprincipled functionaries who toe the line for a "non-crusading" newspaper that seems indifferent to the welfare of the United States, the preservation of the Constitution, and a world order ruled by law rather than power. While Ochsian "impartiality" as a foundational principle of editorial policy is abstract at best, and would seem to require some clarification as a workable editorial policy, it would also appear to require occasional updating and adjustments as required to meet the critical political challenges of the day. To our knowledge, no such formal or public sharpening of editorial policy at the *Times* has occurred since Ochs or within the fifty-year framework of our analysis.

Thus, what is often a muddle of non-crusading, centrist, impartiality has functioned as editorial policy at the *Times* both before and after, for example, the advent of nuclear weapons, the onset of global warming, and a clear history of American presidents using force in violation of international law while lying about underlying facts and political intent. In other words there is no differentiated application of editorial policy at the *Times* that would allow it to cover events and conditions that can end human life on earth any differently than it would cover less consequential issues. Certainly, the truth or falsity of official claims to justify invading Iraq demanded an application of the most discerning editorial policy and the strictest possible journalistic scrutiny. If anything, the record indicates that the *Times* lowered its standards of editorial policy to accommodate the invasion agenda.

An overhaul of editorial policy at the *Times* is long overdue. For one thing, like a story that mutates from its starting point after passing through several storytellers, Sulzberger's "non-crusading" and Rosenthal's "centrism" represent subtle evolutions of Ochs' "impartiality" that do not appear to have been consciously thought through. Depending upon how it's interpreted, Ochs' "impartiality" may have some merit. A courtroom (ideally) is impartial though rigorous in its assessment of the facts and law, and ultimately it must take sides. Centrism, however, means not taking sides and mandates no journalistic rigor. And non-

---

* Exceptions in our view include a number of reporters that do not cover foreign policy for the *Times*, including, for example, Linda Greenhouse, Gretchen Morgenson, and Robert Pear.

crusading has led in practice to complacency and an absence of due diligence. The *Times'* coverage of the run-up to the Iraq invasion was a model of "non-crusading centrism" that at best sought to split the difference between the pro-war and anti-war camps while demonstrating little journalistic truth-seeking.

Thus, whereas Ochsian impartiality might be obliged ultimately to expose and take sides against an administration that lies and violates the law, non-crusading centrism would feel no such obligation. Also, complications arise when centrism must also bear the burden of credible—even exemplary—journalism. This is a tough assignment when centrism as the official political position of the newspaper sits highest in the hierarchy of editorial policy, while the facts and law are slighted and viewed as junior partners in the venture.

Furthermore, even if there were some virtue in non-crusading journalism, it exists at the *Times* only to the extent that it can maintain the paper's centrism. Thus, leveraging as it does the myth of the left-leaning *Times,* the paper has significant leeway to lean to the right in its coverage of major issues in order to fix its "centrist" position in the public's consciousness. This permits the *Times* to cover stories with more or less zeal, depending upon its ultimate effect on the perception of the *Times'* centrism. The *Times* hounded the Clintons for years over Whitewater and other assorted trivial matters, while it ignores the serial lying and ideological extremism of the Bush administration. This selective application of crusading versus non-crusading coverage permits the *Times* to maintain the perception of a centrist non-partisan paper.

Furthermore, the categories "crusading" and "non-crusading" can be applied simultaneously to the same set of circumstances. Thus, the *Times* took a non-crusading approach to the WMD issue by ignoring pre-invasion evidence of WMD disarmament in Iraq. On the other hand, it took a crusading approach—in its editorial-page and in Judith Miller's coverage—by promoting the administration's WMD claims.

Ultimately, the decision to resort to crusading or non-crusading is determined not by impartiality, but by how one or the other approach positions the paper politically at a given time. "Positioning," then, as in Rosenthal's "center," appears to be the functional editorial policy of the *Times*. While Ochs' "impartiality" in principle has potential merit for a national newspaper of distinction, the centrist/positioning adaptation of Ochs' legacy has been de facto policy at the *Times* for several decades.

Having a reputable name, either as an organization or an individual, was apparently a liability in terms of being a source for the *Times* on Iraqi WMD. Certainly the *Times* ignored identifiable sources that might have cast doubt on the administration's Iraqi WMD claims, while featuring unidentified sources that supported the claims.

For example, the *Times* ignored the IAEA's reports from 1991 to 2002, which were issued pursuant to UN Security Council resolutions 687 (1991) and 1051 (1996), and which document the agency's record of dismantling Iraq's nascent nuclear-weapons program.[34] Despite this easily available published record, the news and editorial pages of the *Times* barely cited it as part of its WMD coverage, nor is there much evidence that its reporters and editorial-page writers even read the IAEA's reports on Iraq.

Nor did the *Times* make use of the nearly 100 "Baghdad Press Briefings" by Hiro Ueki, the Baghdad UNMOVIC and IAEA spokesman, who reported almost on a daily basis from November 27 2002 to March 17 2003 on the inspections of suspected WMD sites in Iraq. By December 19 Ueki had reported that UNMOVIC and the IAEA had inspected at least eight of the nine suspected WMD sites listed in the Blair government's September 2002 WMD dossier. The nine sites listed in the British dossier were the following: (a) a chlorine and phenol plant at Fallujah 2 near Habaniyah; (b) The Ibn Sina Company at Tarmiyah, a chemical research center; (c) The al Qa Qaa chemical complex, including a phosgene production plant; (d) Project Baiji at al Sharqat in northwest Iraq, a large chemical complex; (e) the castor oil production plant at the Fallujah III facility; (f) the al-Darwah Foot and Mouth Disease Vaccine Institute, which was involved in biological agent production and research before the 1991 Gulf War; (g) the Amariyah Sera and Vaccine Plant at Abu Ghraib; (h) the al-Rafah/ Shahiyat Liquid Propellant Engine Static Test Stand; and (i) the al-Mamoun Plant for rocket-propellant mixing and casting.[35]

In the context of having inspected these sites, UNMOVIC chief Hans Blix reported to the UN Security Council on December 19: "With respect to the results of our inspections, I should note that several sites, which have been the subject of public discussion, have been inspected and questions as to their use may have been answered."[36]

The inspections record published by Ueki, in addition to Blix's public statement, appeared to indicate that the Blair dossier's suspected WMD sites had been inspected with no preliminary findings of WMD evidence. This deserved news coverage at the time, but received none from the *Times*, which almost certainly didn't bother to check off the list of UNMOVIC- and IAEA-inspected sites from the Blair dossier to ascertain whether the sites were WMD facilities as the Blair government had charged.

The *Times* also ignored an important conclusion of the March 1999 Amorim Panel report to the UN Security Council that "although important elements still have to be resolved, the bulk of Iraq's pro-scribed weapons programmes has been eliminated." That report also described the substantial disarmament record of UN inspectors in Iraq up until late 1998.[37]

Nor did the *Times* report the October 2003 statement by Greg Thielmann, described by *CBS News* as formerly "the person responsible for analyzing the Iraqi weapons threat for Colin Powell." Thielmann told CBS "that at the time of Powell's [February 5 UN] speech, Iraq didn't pose an imminent threat to anyone—not even its own neigh-bors," and: "I think my conclusion now is that it's probably one of the low points in [Powell's] long distinguished service to the nation."[38]

Though the *Times* editorial page described Powell's February 5 UN speech as "the most powerful case to date that Saddam Hussein stands in defiance of Security Council resolutions and has no intention of revealing or surrendering whatever unconventional weapons he may have,"[39] neither the *Times* editorial page nor its news or op-ed pages showed any interest in Thielmann's statement. When he worked for Powell, Thielmann was director of the Strategic, Proliferation and Military Affairs Office of the State Department's Intelligence Bureau, which allowed him to speak authoritatively about the discernible status of Iraqi WMD at the time of Powell's February 5 presentation. Despite these qualifications and his insider status, the *Times* ignored Thielmann and what he had to say about Iraqi WMD.

The *Times* also failed to fairly consider the important assessment by Scott Ritter, a former UN inspector in Iraq, that the Iraqis had already been disarmed of "up to 90–95 percent of their most deadly weapons, rendering Saddam fundamentally disarmed."[40] And the *Times* apparently disregarded Ritter's more comprehensive analysis of Iraq's disarmament, published in June 2000:

> What is often overlooked in the debate over how to proceed with Iraq's disarmament is the fact that from 1994 to 1998 Iraq was subjected to a strenuous program of ongoing monitoring of industrial and research facilities that could be used to reconstitute proscribed activities. This monitoring

provided weapons inspectors with detailed insight into the capabilities, both present and future, of Iraq's industrial infrastructure. It allowed UNSCOM to ascertain, with a high level of confidence, that Iraq was not rebuilding its prohibited weapons programs and that it lacked the means to do so without an infusion of advanced technology and a significant investment of time and money.

Given the comprehensive nature of the monitoring regime put in place by UNSCOM, which included a strict export-import control regime, it was possible as early as 1997 to determine that, from a qualitative standpoint, Iraq had been disarmed. Iraq no longer possessed any meaningful quantities of chemical or biological agent, if it possessed any at all, and the industrial means to produce these agents had either been eliminated or were subject to stringent monitoring. The same was true of Iraq's nuclear and ballistic missile capabilities. As long as monitoring inspections remained in place, Iraq presented a WMD-based threat to no one.[41]

That Iraq had been disarmed by the United Nations also appears to have been the position of Secretary of State Colin Powell prior to September 11 2001. In a statement issued in Egypt in the company of the Egyptian foreign minister, Powell said with respect to Iraqi WMD and the sanctions against Iraq:

We had a good discussion, the Foreign Minister and I and the [Egyptian] President and I, had a good discussion about the nature of the sanctions—the fact that the sanctions exist—not for the purpose of hurting the Iraqi people, but for the purpose of keeping in check Saddam Hussein's ambitions toward developing weapons of mass destruction. We should constantly be reviewing our policies, constantly be looking at those sanctions to make sure that they are directed toward that purpose. That purpose is every bit as important now as it was ten years ago when we began it. And frankly they have worked. He [Saddam Hussein] has not developed any significant capability with respect to weapons of mass destruction. He is [also] unable to project conventional power against his neighbors.[42]

This statement was posted on the US State Department website throughout the pre- invasion period. It was still posted as of June 2004 (our manuscript deadline). Given that it contradicts Powell's post-September 11 claims with respect to Iraqi WMD, and especially Powell's February 5 2003 speech to the UN Security Council that the *Times* editorial page endorsed, the *Times* should have reported this statement in its coverage of Iraqi WMD. But the non–crusading paper ignored it.

In contrast to the "non-crusading" *New York Times,* which ignored credible, identifiable sources that undermined the administration's claims about Iraq, the "crusading" *Times* repeatedly used anonymous Bush administration sources and Iraqi defectors to support the administration's WMD claims against Iraq. This is essentially how Judith Miller covered the WMD story for the paper.

In an important September 8 2002 front-page article, published only days after the Bush administration had initiated a public-relations campaign to convince the American public of the need to invade Iraq,[43] the *Times'* Michael Gordon and Judith Miller cited anonymous Bush administration sources and anonymous Iraqi defectors to report the administration's claims that Iraq had WMD and posed a threat to the United States. To underscore the extent of their use of anonymous sources, excerpts from the September 8 piece by Gordon and Miller are presented below, with anonymous sources highlighted in italics. None of the sources in italics below were ever identified in the article, and nothing of what these anonymous sources stated below turned out to be true or accurate.

> More than a decade after Saddam Hussein agreed to give up weapons of mass destruction, Iraq has stepped up its quest for nuclear weapons and has embarked on a worldwide hunt for materials to make an atomic bomb, *Bush administration officials said today.* . . .

> The diameter, thickness and other technical specifications of the aluminum tubes had persuaded *American intelligence experts* that they were meant for Iraq's nuclear program, *officials said,* and that the latest attempt to ship the material had taken place in recent months. . . .

> *Iraqi defectors* who once worked for the nuclear weapons establishment have told *American officials* that acquiring nuclear arms is again a top Iraqi priority. . . .

> *An Iraqi defector* said Mr. Hussein had also heightened his efforts to develop new types of chemical weapons. *An Iraqi opposition leader* also gave American officials a paper from Iranian intelligence indicating that Mr. Hussein has authorized regional commanders to use chemical and biological weapons to put down any Shiite Muslim resistance that might occur if the United States attacks. . . .

> "The jewel in the crown is nuclear," *a senior administration official* said. "The closer he [Saddam] gets to a nuclear capability, the more credible is his threat to use chemical or biological weapons. Nuclear weapons are his hole card." . . .

Still, Mr. Hussein's dogged insistence on pursuing his nuclear ambitions, *along with what defectors described* in interviews as Iraq's push to improve and expand Baghdad's chemical and biological arsenals, have brought Iraq and the United States to the brink of war. ...

Bush administration officials say the quest for thousands of high-strength aluminum tubes is one of several signs that Mr. Hussein is seeking to revamp and accelerate Iraq's nuclear weapons program. ...

Officials say the aluminum tubes were intended as casing for rotors in centrifuges, which are one means of producing highly enriched uranium. ...

In addition to the special aluminum tubes, *a senior administration official* said Iraq had made efforts to purchase other equipment, epoxy and resins that could be used for centrifuges. A key issue is whether the items Iraq tried to buy are uniquely designed for centrifuge use or could have other applications. ...

Senior administration officials insist that the dimensions, specifications and numbers of the tubes Iraq sought to buy show that they were intended for the nuclear program. ...

In interviews in a European capital late last month, *an Iraqi who said he was involved in the chemical weapons program before he defected two years ago* said that Mr. Hussein had never stopped producing VX and other chemical agents, even when international inspectors were in Iraq. ...

Speaking on the condition that neither he nor the country in which he was interviewed be identified, Ahmed al-Shemri, his pseudonym, said Iraq had continued developing, producing and storing chemical agents at many mobile and fixed secret sites throughout the country, many of them underground. ...

Mr. Shemri [the pseudonym] said Iraq had produced 5 tons of stable VX in liquid form between 1994 and 1998, before inspectors were forced to leave Iraq. Some of this agent, *he said*, was made in secret labs in the northern city of Mosul and in the southern city of Basra, which Unscom inspectors confirmed they had rarely visited because of their long distance from Baghdad. *He said* Iraq had the ability to make at least 50 tons of liquid nerve agent, which *he said* was to be loaded into two kinds of bombs and dropped from planes. ...

Of even greater concern is *Mr. Shemri's allegation* that Iraq had invented, as early as 1994, and is now producing a new, solid VX agent that clings to a soldier's protective clothing and makes decontamination difficult. ...

Mr. Shemri said Iraq had received assistance in its chemical, germ and nuclear programs from Russian scientists who are still working in Iraq. At least two

Iraqi scientists traveled to North Korea in early 2002 to study missile technology, *he said.* . . .

Mr. *Shemri* said he had been told that Iraq was still storing some 12,500 gallons of anthrax, 2,500 gallons of gas gangrene, 1,250 gallons of aflotoxin and 2,000 gallons of botulinum throughout the country. . . .

American officials have also expressed intense concern about [Iraqi possession of] smallpox, one of history's greatest scourges, which was declared eradicated from human populations in 1980. . . .

Although *administration officials* say they have no proof that Baghdad possesses the smallpox virus, *intelligence sources* say they cannot rule that out. "There's a number of sensitive things," said *a senior government official* who has studied the evidence for more than a decade. *He added* that "on a scale of one to 10, I'd say it's probably a six" that Iraq has the virus.[44]

Despite the number of Bush administration officials with whom Gordon and Miller apparently spoke, and despite the length of the article (3600 words), the *Times'* Gordon and Miller never cited a single Bush administration official by name in the article, with the exception of non-substantive references to President Bush. Gordon, Miller, and the editors at the *Times* apparently gave a blank check to nameless high-ranking officials to make empty but provocative statements in this front-page story about Iraqi WMD. With journalism like this, why not eliminate the press as the middleman, and permit the executive branch as a practical matter to print its own daily newspapers and lie directly to the public? Given that the *Times* itself reported on September 7 that "White House officials said today [September 6] that the administration was following a meticulously planned strategy to persuade the public, the Congress and the allies of the need to confront the threat from Saddam Hussein,"[45] the *Times* article by Gordon and Miller of September 8 looks like an intentional contribution to that effort.

In another front-page article two months later using anonymous sources, Miller reported "Iraq has ordered large quantities of a drug that can be used to counter the effects of nerve gas."[46] Even though "hospitals and clinics around the world commonly stocked atropine [the drug in question] to resuscitate patients who have had heart attacks," Miller wrote that the drug is also "highly effective at blocking such nerve agents as sarin and VX." The purchase of atropine was a signal, according to an anonymous administration official, that "if the Iraqis were going to use nerve agents, they would want to take steps to protect their own soldiers, if not their population." Miller cited anonymous

Bush administration officials thirteen times in the article to support the claim, published by the *Times* on its front page, that the purchase of atropine by Iraq indicated that Iraq had chemical weapons.

Three weeks later, Miller cited anonymous "senior American officials" to report that "the C.I.A. is investigating an informant's accusation that Iraq obtained a particularly virulent strain of smallpox from a Russian scientist who worked in a smallpox lab in Moscow during Soviet times."[47] The essence of this story was that an anonymous informant told anonymous Bush administration officials who told Miller that a deceased Soviet scientist might have traveled to Iraq in 1990 to give the Iraqi government a virulent strain of smallpox. No smallpox in Iraq has been found or is known to be there.

In January 2003, using anonymous "senior administration officials," Miller wrote that "former Iraqi scientists, military officers and contractors have provided American intelligence agencies with a portrait of Saddam Hussein's secret programs to develop and conceal chemical, biological and nuclear weapons that is starkly at odds with the findings so far of the United Nations weapons inspectors."[48] No such chemical, biological or nuclear weapons were found in Iraq.

On March 19, a day before the US invasion of Iraq began, and again citing anonymous Bush administration officials, Miller reported that the administration "[is] determined to find illegal weapons before Mr. Hussein can send them out of the country and perhaps sell them to other rogue nations or terrorist groups."[49] There is no evidence that the Iraqi government sent or sold outlawed weapons to any country or terrorist group.[50]

In the run up to the March 2003 Iraq invasion, Miller repeatedly cited unidentified Bush administration sources to report that Iraq had weapons of mass destruction that later it was found not to have. Though this was the focus of her pre-invasion reporting on Iraq, she made an occasional attempt to balance that reporting. For example, in January 2003 Miller reported "[d]ays after delivering a broadly negative report on Iraq's cooperation with international inspectors, Hans Blix on Wednesday challenged several of the Bush administration's assertions about Iraqi cheating and the notion that time was running out for disarming Iraq through peaceful means." Miller reported that Blix's UNMOVIC inspectors had rejected the administration's claim that an Iraqi location photographed by US satellites was a chemical weapons site, and that "inspectors concluded that the site was an old ammunition storage area often frequented by Iraqi trucks, and that there was no reason to believe it was involved in weapons activities."[51]

Even here, however, as on other occasions, anonymous administration officials beckoned, and Miller gave them the last word:

> But an [anonymous] administration official said there was "good reason" to believe the site was suspect, and that Unmovic had waited a week before visiting it.
>
> "Whether something was removed, or whether it was ever there remains an open question," he complained. He noted that although the C.I.A. was still providing inspectors with sensitive information, concerns remained about Unmovic's ability to safeguard it.
>
> "Iraqis may have bugged offices or hotel rooms of some Unmovic people," he said, noting there were "several examples" in which Iraqis seemed to have either "advance knowledge, or very good luck in going to places before inspectors."

The ethics, journalistically, of Miller's reporting these and the other anonymous speculations about Iraqi WMD in so many of her articles is obviously questionable. Though there were apparently few formal restrictions on the use of anonymous sources at the *Times*, the Siegal Committee Report weightily intoned with respect to the Blair case that "[u]nidentified sources cannot be allowed to speculate in our pages."[52] Miller's excessive use of anonymous administration sources to speculate (falsely) about Iraqi WMD predated the onset of the Jayson Blair scandal and the Siegal Committee Report. Through that report the *Times* has expressed its justifiable annoyance with Blair; however, the *Times* has remained silent to date about Miller.

Given that the *Times* apparently had few clear standards in place to prevent the abuse of anonymous sources,[53] there were few institutional incentives for Miller to discontinue her pre-invasion abuses of such sources in her post-invasion coverage of Iraqi WMD. One month after the onset of the invasion, and thus one month after Iraqi WMD had not surfaced, Miller cited an unidentified Iraqi scientist as her main source for a front-page WMD report:

> A scientist who claims to have worked in Iraq's chemical weapons program for more than a decade has told an American military team that Iraq destroyed chemical weapons and biological warfare equipment only days before the war began, members of the team said.
>
> They said the scientist led Americans to a supply of material that proved

to be the building blocks of illegal weapons, which he claimed to have buried as evidence of Iraq's illicit weapons programs.

The scientist also told American weapons experts that Iraq had secretly sent unconventional weapons and technology to Syria, starting in the mid-1990's, and that more recently Iraq was cooperating with Al Qaeda, the military officials said.[54]

Miller wrote that US military officials "declined to identify [the scientist], saying they feared he might be subject to reprisals" and "this reporter [Miller] was not permitted to interview the scientist or visit his home." However, for the benefit perhaps of *Times* readers who still have faith in the rigorous journalistic standards of the paper, Miller also reported:

> While this reporter [Miller] could not interview the scientist, she was permitted to see him from a distance at the sites where he said that material from the arms program was buried. Clad in nondescript clothes and a baseball cap, he pointed to several spots in the sand where he said chemical precursors and other weapons material were buried.[55]

Apparently in order to corroborate the claims of the anonymous Iraqi scientist, Miller wrote:

> The officials' account of the scientist's assertions and the discovery of the buried material, which they described as the most important discovery to date in the hunt for illegal weapons, supports the Bush administration's charges that Iraq continued to develop those weapons and lied to the United Nations about it. Finding and destroying illegal weapons was a major justification for the war.[56]

Miller then wrote: "The officials' account also provided an explanation for why United States forces had not yet turned up banned weapons in Iraq."[57]

In a follow-up story two days later, Miller wrote that the anonymous Iraqi scientist had helped everyone come to a new view of the WMD search in Iraq. Rather than look for actual weapons, "the paradigm has shifted," Miller wrote, and US forces would henceforth look for Iraqi WMD scientists, like the anonymous scientist who had pointed to the sand as proof of Iraqi WMD, and that the discovery of such scientists would show, in the absence of actual WMD, that Iraq had WMD as the administration had claimed.[58]

In this regard, Miller reported:

Based on what the Iraqi scientist had said about weapons being destroyed or stocks being hidden, military experts said they now believed they might not find large caches of illicit chemicals or biological agents, at least not in Iraq. They said this would increase their reliance on documents and testimony from individual Iraqis to help them piece together the scope, organization, and goals of the programs that the United States has said Saddam Hussein created and concealed from the world.

Thus, for Miller, the story one month after the invasion was not that no Iraqi WMD or any related programs had been found; the story was that Iraq concealed its WMD, and that the absence of WMD was potential evidence to support the administration's claims that Iraq had WMD.

In May 2003 Miller published three articles on the Bush administration's claim that it had found mobile biological-weapons labs in Iraq.[59] Miller began the first of the three articles by following her usual routine of citing administration officials issuing a WMD charge: "Senior Bush administration officials in Washington said today that a joint British–American team of experts had concluded that a tractor-trailer truck found in northern Iraq several weeks ago could be a mobile biological weapons lab."[60]

This charge not only proved to be false, there was little evidence at the time that the trailer was a weapon. Miller even cited the conclusion of the US WMD search team in Iraq that the trailer might not be a mobile weapons lab: "Two days ago at the headquarters of the Exploitation Task Force, or XTF, which is responsible for the hunt for unconventional weapons, officials said the unit's experts had not concluded that the equipment constituted a mobile biological weapons lab."[61]

If the US XTF team in Iraq had not concluded that the trailer was a mobile weapons lab, on what basis did the Bush administration and Miller report that the trailer was a weapons lab? The answer is grounded in assertions made by an Iraqi defector that were given undue prominence in the article. While the XTF team's assessment of the trailer was printed in the nineteenth paragraph of Miller's story, the opinion of the unidentified Iraqi defector was featured in the second, third, and eighth paragraphs:

> The trailer's design closely fits that of a mobile biological weapons laboratory described by a defector, but the officials could not say whether it had ever produced biological agents for weapons.

"While some of the equipment on the trailer could have been used for purposes other than biological weapons agent production, U.S. and U.K. technical experts have concluded that the unit does not appear to perform any function beyond what the defector said it was for, which was the production of biological agents," said Stephen A. Cambone, the undersecretary of defense for intelligence. ...

The defector said [Iraqi] mobile laboratories had been used to produce anthrax, botulism, and staphylococcus.[62]

Three days later, while the XTF team presumably still did not view the trailer as a mobile weapons lab, Miller cited the findings of a second team of US technical experts who examined the trailer:

A team of experts searching for evidence of biological and chemical weapons in Iraq has concluded that a trailer found near Mosul in northern Iraq in April is a mobile biological weapons laboratory, the three-team members said today.[63]

This three-man team of technical experts, including one from "Special Operations forces" and "a former marine," also proved to be wrong about the trailer, although, as technical experts, they volunteered a number of fishy political observations, including the team's opinion that the trailer was a "smoking gun" that "substantiate[d] the Bush administration's allegations that Iraq was making biological and chemical weapons." While Miller noted that "the team did not find any protective clothing or biocontainment system to safeguard the scientists or technicians who worked inside the trailer from exposure to deadly germs"—indications that the trailer might not be a weapons lab—Miller quoted the team leader, who rendered the expert technical explanation that "we've already seen what a low regard for human life this regime had."[64]

When, for the sake of balance, Miller reported that "some scientists say the trailers could have been used for peaceful purposes," she qualified this in the same sentence with "none of them have seen the labs or talked to the experts who reject such contentions." In the next sentence, she reported that all three team members "said they were certain that future tests would confirm that the trailer was evidence of a weapons program." However, future tests showed that the trailers were not weapons labs, "but were for the production of hydrogen to fill artillery balloons, as the Iraqis have continued to insist."[65] Furthermore, in January 2004, the New York Times reported that David Kay, the Bush-appointed head of the Iraq Survey Group, "added that there was now a consensus within the United States intelligence community that mobile trailers found in Iraq and initially thought to be laboratories for biological weapons were actually designed to produce hydrogen for weather balloons, or perhaps rocket fuel."[66]

Upon reporting with certitude the "technical" findings and clumsy opinions of the three-person team, which spoke to Miller "on the condition of anonymity," Miller slips into a speculative frenzy as she invokes other anonymous sources and mobile weapons labs multiply like rabbits:

> Other [unidentified] American experts say they believe that teams hunting for biological and chemical weapons may now have located parts of three mobile labs, military and civilian officials said today.
>
> Those experts said that in addition to the Mosul trailer and another one found in northern Iraq, a smaller trailer was discovered last week by American forces near Baghdad. They said the smaller trailer, like the one near Mosul, had been taken to Baghdad International Airport for further examination.
>
> The experts also said they believed that based on intelligence information, there might be as many as eight mobile labs in Iraq, adding that the locations of the other five have not yet been determined.[67]

Not only were there not eight mobile weapons labs in Iraq, or five, or two, as Miller reported, no such labs at all have been found in Iraq.

Miller's third and last article on the mobile weapons labs was published on May 21 2003. This marked two months since the onset of the invasion. It also marks Miller's failure after two months of unsubstantiated reporting from Iraq to find WMD.

Also by May 21, the absence of evidence that the "mobile weapons labs" had made any weapons (none had been found) or had even made any biological agents (none were detected on the trailers) was beginning to undermine Miller's story that the Iraqi trailers were mobile germ labs. In the absence of evidence to support what she had already concluded about the trailers, Miller ramped up her compromised reporting by steeling herself against emerging indications that the trailers were not weapons, and calling upon her anonymous administration sources once again to say that the trailers were weapons. Thus, Miller begins her third article on the trailers by reasserting the administration's view that the trailers are weapons, despite growing doubts:

> United States intelligence agencies have concluded that two mysterious trailers found in Iraq were mobile units to produce germs for weapons, but

they have found neither biological agents nor evidence that the equipment was used to make such arms, according to senior administration officials.[68]

Despite doubts, this story like the others is overtaken by the determination of both Miller and the Bush administration to have the trailers seen as weapons. In this piece, Miller invoked anonymous administration sources at least seventeen times to assert that the trailers were weapons. Thus, Miller's last piece on Iraqi WMD in late May 2003 resembled the September 2002 piece, bookends of compromised journalism from a veteran *New York Times* reporter who ignored key facts about the WMD story—including that there weren't any—and mostly reported what anonymous administration sources told her about Iraqi WMD, as she did in her May 21 piece: "[Anonymous] officials said that they expect that the intelligence community's conclusion about the mobile units to become a centerpiece of their argument that Iraq had a well-concealed germ weapons program."[69]

Miller's WMD crusade apparently went beyond her inappropriate and excessive use of anonymous Bush administration sources. A few days after her third report (May 21) on the Iraqi trailers, the *Washington Post* reported:

> A dustup between two New York Times reporters over a story on an Iraqi exile leader raises some intriguing questions about the paper's coverage of the search for dangerous weapons thought to be hidden by Saddam Hussein.
> An internal e-mail by Judith Miller, the paper's top reporter on bioterrorism, acknowledges that her main source for such articles has been Ahmad Chalabi, a controversial exile leader who is close to top Pentagon officials. Could Chalabi have been using the Times to build a drumbeat that Iraq was hiding weapons of mass destruction?[70]

Although the dustup had to do with Miller filing a May 1 story on Chalabi without the prior knowledge of John F. Burns, her bureau chief in Baghdad, the *Post* somehow acquired Miller's e-mailed responses to Burns, and published some excerpts, including this one:

> I've been covering Chalabi for about 10 years, and have done most of the stories about him for our paper, including the long takeout we recently did on him. He has provided most of the front-page exclusives on WMD to our paper.[71]

The circumstances behind three front-page articles in the *Times* by Judith Miller—August 15 1998, December 20 2001, and September 8 2002—suggest Chalabi's well-timed involvement in each of them.

On January 26 1998, a group of neoconservative policy intellectuals wrote a letter to President Bill Clinton because they were "convinced that current American policy toward Iraq is not succeeding, and that we may face a threat in the Middle East more serious than any we have known since the end of the Cold War." The letter was signed by several who were to become high-ranking officials in the Bush administration—Donald Rumsfeld, Paul Wolfowitz, Richard Perle, John Bolton, and others. The authors of the letter sought "the removal of Saddam Hussein's regime from power," and argued "we believe the U.S. has the authority under existing U.N. resolutions to take the necessary steps, including military steps, to protect our vital interests in the Gulf," and "[i]n any case, American policy cannot continue to be crippled by a misguided insistence on unanimity in the U.N. Security Council."[72]

On May 29 1998 the same letter writers wrote to Speaker of the House Newt Gingrich and Senate Majority Leader Trent Lott to express their concern "that the U.S. policy of 'containment' of Saddam Hussein was failing" and recommended "the removal of Saddam and his regime from power."[73]

Shortly afterward, the Congress began to consider legislation that would implement the principal recommendation of Rumsfeld, Wolfowitz, Perle and the others with regard to regime change in Iraq. This legislation would soon be passed by the US House of Representatives on October 5 1998 and the US Senate on October 7, and would be signed into law on October 31 by President Clinton, as the Iraq Liberation Act of 1998.[74] The act stated that "[i]t should be the policy of the United States to support efforts to remove the regime headed by Saddam Hussein from power in Iraq." Perhaps most importantly for Ahmed Chalabi, it also allocated $97 million "to the Iraqi Democratic opposition," which Chalabi and his organization, the Iraqi National Congress, led. In a *New York Times* article published a few weeks after President Clinton signed the Iraq Liberation Act, the *Times'* James Risen and Barbara Crossette reported: "Mr. Chalabi lobbied Congress to pass the $97 million funding plan, and now hopes to push the Administration to designate his group as a prime beneficiary."[75]

Three months after the letter to Lott and Gingrich, and two months before the Iraq Liberation Act became law—a law in which Chalabi, who was acquainted with the letter's authors, had a huge personal stake—the *New York Times* published a front-page article by Judith Miller using an Iraqi defector apparently introduced to her by Chalabi. This defector claimed to have knowledge that Iraq was poised to resume its nuclear-weapons program. Miller began her story as follows:

> An Iraqi scientist who defected to the United States has publicly described for the first time the inner workings of Iraq's three-decade effort to build a nuclear bomb.
>
> The scientist, Khidhir Abdul Abas Hamza, said that before he fled Iraq in 1994, he helped train a cadre of young scientists who with other scientists still working together on other projects would be capable of quickly resuming Iraq's atomic weapons program if the United Nations cut back on its inspections and, ultimately, lifted economic sanctions.

Miller reported that Hamza's information "come[s] as a new confrontation is building over whether Baghdad has dismantled its chemical, nuclear and biological programs," and that Hamza "insisted that Mr. Hussein remains determined to reconstitute the chemical, biological and nuclear programs in which he invested so much."[76]

This article was almost certainly one of Chalabi's "front-page exclusives on WMD" to the *Times*. In a *PBS Frontline* program broadcast in October 2003, Miller reported that Chalabi had originally provided her with access to Hamza. Miller said "Chalabi had proven absolutely credible with respect to Khidir Hamza" and "at that point, I began to take Chalabi very seriously about people that he was bringing out, because the CIA had doubted Hamza was for real."[77]

Chalabi clearly had a huge financial and political interest in introducing Hamza to Miller for a story on Iraqi WMD in the *Times* while the Iraq Liberation Act—which Chalabi reportedly helped write—was under consideration in 1998. According to an article by Jane Mayer in the *New Yorker*, and referring to the 1998 act, "Chalabi, [Francis] Brooke [Chalabi's aide], and their allies in Congress crafted the legislation together" and "Chalabi had lobbied tirelessly for the legislation" in Washington.[78] Thus, according to these reports, Chalabi helped write legislation that would benefit him and his organization, then lobbied the Congress, and in effect the American people through the *New York Times*, to pass it. In addition to the funds appropriated to Chalabi's organization as a result of the 1998 Iraq Liberation Act, Mayer also reported that "the current Bush administration gave Chalabi's group at least thirty-nine million dollars."[79]

The coincidence of Miller writing and publishing a front-page article in the *Times*, based on sources introduced to Miller by Chalabi, at an opportune moment for Chalabi and those who would become his close contacts at the Pentagon, would occur again in two other front-page stories in the *Times* by Miller.

Miller's next front-page WMD article using Chalabi as a source was published on December 20 2001—two months after September 11 and one month before President Bush's "Axis of Evil" speech in January 2002. According to Bob Woodward, prior to September 11, "the Pentagon had been working for months on developing a military option for Iraq" and "Rumsfeld was raising the possibility that they could take advantage of the opportunity offered by the terrorist attacks to go after Saddam immediately."[80] And according to *CBS News*, "barely five hours after American Airlines Flight 77 plowed into the Pentagon, Defense Secretary Donald H. Rumsfeld was telling his aides to come up with plans for striking Iraq."[81]

Rumsfeld's chief deputy, Paul Wolfowitz, also wanted to invade Iraq in response to September 11, according to published reports, including Woodward's:

> Rumsfeld raised the question of Iraq. Why shouldn't we go against Iraq, not just al Qaeda? He asked. Rumsfeld was speaking not only for himself when he raised the question. His deputy, Paul D. Wolfowitz, was committed to a policy that would make Iraq a principal target of the first round in the war on terrorism.[82]

Chalabi wanted the United States to invade Iraq as well. And he was close to Wolfowitz, Perle, and Rumsfeld. In a *New Yorker* article published in May 2003, Seymour Hersh wrote:

> There was a close personal bond, too, between Chalabi and Wolfowitz and Perle, dating back many years. Their relationship deepened after the Bush Administration took office, and Chalabi's ties extended to others in the Administration, including Rumsfeld; Douglas Feith, the Under-Secretary of Defense for Policy; and I. Lewis Libby, Vice-President Dick Cheney's chief of staff.[83]

The focus of Hersh's *New Yorker* article was the creation of the Office of Special Plans (OSP) by Wolfowitz and Rumsfeld. The OSP was a

Pentagon intelligence cabal that sought to make a stronger case than the CIA, the DIA, and the State Department had made that Iraq had weapons of mass destruction and links to Al Qaeda. A principal OSP intelligence source was Ahmed Chalabi, as Hersh describes:

> If Special Plans was going to search for new intelligence on Iraq, the most obvious source was defectors with firsthand knowledge. The office [OSP] inevitably turned to Ahmad Chalabi's Iraqi National Congress. The I.N.C., an umbrella organization for diverse groups opposed to Saddam, is constantly seeking out Iraqi defectors. The Special Plans Office developed a close working relationship with the I.N.C., and this strengthened its position in disputes with the C.I.A. and gave the Pentagon's pro-war leadership added leverage in its constant disputes with the State Department.[84]

Hersh also reported that the OSP, with Chalabi as one of its principal intelligence sources, "began their work in the days after September 11, 2001."

Shortly after OSP "began their work" using Chalabi, the *New York Times* published a front-page article by Judith Miller on Iraqi WMD. In the article, Miller used as her principal source an Iraqi defector introduced to Miller by Chalabi. The first few paragraphs of Miller's article, published on December 20 2001, read as follows:

> An Iraqi defector who described himself as a civil engineer said he personally worked on renovations of secret facilities for biological, chemical and nuclear weapons in underground wells, private villas and under the Saddam Hussein Hospital in Baghdad as recently as a year ago.
>
> The defector, Adnan Ihsan Saeed al-Haideri, gave details of the projects he said he worked on for President Saddam Hussein's government in an extensive interview last week in Bangkok.
>
> Government experts said yesterday that he had also been interviewed twice by American intelligence officials, who were trying to verify his claims. One of the officials said he thought Mr. Saeed had been taken to a secure location. The experts said his information seemed reliable and significant.
>
> The interview with Mr. Saeed was arranged by the Iraqi National Congress, the main Iraqi opposition group, which seeks the overthrow of Mr. Hussein. If verified, Mr. Saeed's allegations would provide ammunition to officials within the Bush administration who have been arguing that Mr. Hussein should be driven from power partly because of his unwillingness to stop making weapons of mass destruction, despite his pledges to do so.[85]

The weapons facilities described in this article by the INC's defector were never found and the "government experts" who worked with

Miller and the INC on this story were never identified. And the timing of this front-page story using a defector brought to Miller by Chalabi, like Miller's front-page story in August 1998, was impeccable. Rumsfeld and Wolfowitz were hoping to invade Iraq in response to September 11 and President Bush would deliver his "Axis of Evil" speech in January, which included an implied threat to invade Iraq. In between, Judith Miller's front-page article was published using Chalabi's Iraqi defector as her source on Iraqi WMD, which thereafter would become the main rationale for an Iraq invasion.

In addition to the circumstantial evidence, at a minimum, of an alignment of interests among Chalabi, the Pentagon's civilian leaders, and Miller, who henceforth would repeatedly seek to "provide ammunition to officials within the Bush administration" with respect to WMD, Seymour Hersh reported in the *New Yorker* in May 2003 that "[w]ith the Pentagon's support, Chalabi's group [the INC] worked to put defectors with compelling stories in touch with reporters in the United States and Europe" and "the resulting articles had dramatic accounts of advances in weapons of mass destruction or told of ties to terrorist groups."[86] A few months later, the British newspaper, the *Independent*, reported:

> Information from Iraqi defectors made available by Ahmed Chalabi and the Iraqi National Congress before the US invasion was of little or no use, a Pentagon intelligence review shows.
> The Defense Intelligence Agency (DIA) said defectors introduced to US intelligence agents by the organization invented or exaggerated their claims to have personal knowledge of the regime and its alleged weapons of mass destruction. The US paid more than $1 million for such information. ...
> Information provided by Mr. Chalabi was used extensively by the administration and US journalists. Sources said *The New York Times* reporter Judith Miller relied on the INC for many of her stories about Iraq's alleged weapons of mass destruction.[87]

Also, if Hersh's report was correct—that "with the Pentagon's support, Chalabi's group worked to put defectors with compelling stories in touch with reporters in the United States and Europe"—it seems that officials in the Pentagon, if such "support" included payments to Chalabi, may have paid Chalabi to provide Miller and the *Times* with compromised information about Iraqi WMD.

The *New York Times* itself confirmed part of what the Pentagon's DIA had reported about Chalabi and the *Times*. In a front-page article published on September 29 2003, the *Times* reported:

> An internal assessment by the Defense Intelligence Agency has concluded that most of the information provided by Iraqi defectors who were made available by the Iraqi National Congress was of little or no value, according to federal officials briefed on the arrangement.
>
> In addition, several Iraqi defectors introduced to American intelligence agents by the exile organization and its leader, Ahmad Chalabi, invented or exaggerated their credentials as people with direct knowledge of the Iraqi government and its suspected unconventional weapons program, the officials said.
>
> The arrangement, paid for with taxpayer funds supplied to the exile group under the Iraq Liberation Act of 1998, involved extensive debriefing of at least half a dozen defectors by defense intelligence agents in European capitals and at a base in the northern Iraqi city of Erbil in late 2002 and early 2003, the officials said.

In the same article, the *Times* also reported, without mentioning Miller, "the Iraqi National Congress had made some of these defectors available to several news organizations, including The New York Times, which reported their allegations about prisoners and the country's weapons programs."[88] Thus, if Chalabi and his Iraqi National Congress were paid by the US government to make Iraqi defectors available to US intelligence agents, and if the INC also made these defectors available to Judith Miller and the *New York Times*, which reported the defectors' allegations about Iraqi WMD, it seems that Chalabi may have been paid by the US government to give what was known to be false or suspect information to the *Times* about Iraqi WMD at critical moments that supported the work of the Pentagon's Office of Special Plans.

The front-page article by Judith Miller published in the *Times* on September 8 2002—which reported numerous false claims by anonymous Bush administration officials about Iraqi WMD, and which also featured Iraqi defectors making false WMD allegations, and which was published in the midst of the Bush administration's marketing campaign to generate public support for an invasion of Iraq—also contributes to the impression that the Bush administration, Chalabi, and Miller coordinated their efforts to promote the WMD claim and regime change in Iraq.

Given these circumstances, the US Congress should initiate an investigation into whether US tax dollars were used by the Pentagon and Ahmed Chalabi to plant stories in the *New York Times* about Iraqi WMD. Furthermore, given the Jayson Blair precedent, the *New York Times* should have already conducted an in-house investigation to determine whether Ahmed Chalabi was paid by the US government to plant stories in the *Times* using Judith Miller as his principal contact, and should publish the findings. The Miller–Chalabi affair potentially is a far more serious matter than the Jayson Blair episode, and the country should know whether the Bush administration planted what amounted to propaganda in the *Times* about an issue of major national and global importance.

4

A CRIME AGAINST PEACE: IRAQ AND THE NUREMBERG PRECEDENT

One of the first public accounts about what was happening near the town of Hilla in central Iraq in early spring 2003 was by *Agence France Press*:

> Reports of coalition forces killing dozens of Iraqi civilians stoked growing international unease at the US-led war, already high after seven women and children were shot dead at a US checkpoint in Central Iraq. Thirty-three people, including women and children, died and 310 were wounded in a coalition bombing on the outskirts of the farming town of Hilla, 80 kilometers south of [Baghdad] on Tuesday [April 1], local hospital director Murtada Abbas said.[1]

One day earlier, according to the report, "fifteen members of one family were killed nearby late Monday [March 31] when their pickup truck was blown up by a rocket from a US Apache helicopter in the region." Sitting "among 15 coffins in the local hospital," a man reported that "his wife, six children, his father, his mother, his three brothers and their wives" had been killed by the attack.[2]

On April 2, the British newspaper, the *Independent,* reported "at least 11 civilians, nine of them children, were killed in Hilla in central Iraq yesterday, according to reporters in the town who said they appeared to be the victims of bombing." In the same article, the *Independent*'s reporter, Robert Fisk, wrote:

> Terrifying film of women and children later emerged after Reuters and the Associated Press were permitted by the Iraqi authorities to take their cameras into the town. Their pictures—the first by Western news agencies from the Iraqi side of the battlefront—showed babies cut in half and children

with amputation wounds, apparently caused by American shellfire and cluster bombs.

Much of the videotape was too terrible to show on television and the agencies' Baghdad editors felt able to send only a few minutes of a 21-minute tape that included a father holding out pieces of his baby and screaming "cowards, cowards" into the camera. Two lorryloads of bodies, including women in flowered dresses, could be seen outside the Hilla hospital.[3]

Fisk reported more of what he saw: an Iraqi doctor said "almost all the patients were victims of cluster bombs dropped in Hilla and in the neighboring village of Mazarak"; one woman reported that "she lost six of her children and her husband in the attacks"; another man "is seen with an arm missing, and a second man, whose wife and two of his children were killed, can be seen sitting next to his third and surviving child, whose foot is missing"; and "the mortuary of the hospital, a butcher's shop of chopped up corpses, is seen briefly on the tape." Fisk reported: "Iraqi officials have been insisting for 48 hours that the Americans have used cluster bombs on civilians in the region but this is the first time that evidence supporting these claims has come from Western news agencies."[4]

Near midnight on April 2, Amnesty International issued a press release on the cluster-bombing of Hilla:

> Amnesty International is deeply concerned about the high toll of civilian casualties and the use of cluster bombs in US military attacks in heavily populated areas. On April 1, at least 33 civilians including many children were reportedly killed and around 300 injured in US attacks on the town of al-Hilla. Amnesty International is particularly disturbed by reports that cluster bombs were used in the attacks and may have been responsible for some of the civilian deaths. The use of cluster bombs in an attack on a civilian area of al-Hilla constitutes an indiscriminate attack and a grave violation of international humanitarian law.[5]

On April 3, the *Asian Times* (Hong Kong) reported that a spokesman for the International Committee of the Red Cross in Iraq described what happened in Hilla as "a horror of severed bodies and scattered limbs."[6] Also on April 3, the *Independent*'s Fisk reported "the wards of the Hillah teaching hospital are proof that something illegal—something quite outside the Geneva Conventions—occurred in the villages around the city once know as Babylon." Fisk reported: "the wailing children, the young women with breast and leg wounds, the 10 patients upon whom doctors had to perform brain surgery to remove metal from their heads, talk of the days and nights when the explosives fell 'like grapes' from the sky. Cluster bombs, the doctors say—and the detritus of the air raids around the hamlets of Nadr and Djifil and Akramin and Mahawil and Mohandesin and Hail Askeri shows that they are right."[7]

On April 4, the *Canadian Press* reported that a Red Cross worker "said doctors were horrified by the casualties they found in the hospital in Hilla," that "we saw that a truck was delivering [to the hospital] dozens of totally dismembered dead bodies of women and children," and that "it was an awful sight" and "really very difficult to believe this was happening." The Red Cross worker said "in the case of Hilla, everybody had very serious wounds and many, many of them small kids and women. We had small toddlers of two or three years of age who had lost their legs, their arms. We have called this a horror."[8]

Also on April 4 the *Financial Times* of London reported "confirmation by the US and Britain of widespread use of cluster munitions in Iraq" and, "although many are unleashed as so-called cluster bombs, both the US and British armies have also fired large numbers from the ground in artillery barrages." The *Financial Times* reported that the British Minister of Defence, Geoffrey Hoon, "confirmed in Parliament that British forces were in fact using cluster munitions." Hoon said the cluster munitions were "absolutely justified ... because it is making the battlefield safer for our armed forces." The *Financial Times* also reported that "the US was put on the defensive yesterday after the International Red Cross backed Iraqi claims that BLU-97 cluster bombs had been used in the town of Hilla."[9]

On April 8, Amnesty International reported again that it was "deeply concerned about the mounting toll of civilian casualties in Iraq and the reported use of cluster bombs by US forces in heavily populated areas," and:

> The devastating consequences of using cluster bombs in civilian areas are utterly predictable. If, as accounts suggest, US forces dropped cluster bombs in residential areas of al-Hilla, even if they were directed at military targets, such an action could constitute a disproportionate attack. This would be a grave breach of international humanitarian law. An independent and thorough investigation must be held and those found responsible for any violations of the laws of war should be brought to justice.[10]

This is a brief summary of a week's worth of foreign press coverage of the US bombing of Hilla. The *New York Times* covered the cluster-bombing of Hilla differently.

On April 2 the Iraqi government invited Western journalists to travel by bus from Baghdad to Hilla to witness the death and damage done by at least two days of US bombing. The *New York Times* Baghdad bureau chief, John F. Burns, made the fifty-mile bus trip down to Hilla with other reporters.

In his report in the *Times* published the next day (April 3), Burns wrote that "[Iraqi] officials marshaling the buses from the Palestine Hotel in the capital made it plain that, for them, the case was open and shut, an example of American weapons being used indiscriminately to kill civilians." Burns wrote that Hilla was "a showcase of what Mr. Hussein's government wants the world to believe about the American way of war." Burns also wrote about "confusing accounts" of Iraqi eyewitnesses, that "it was difficult to mesh accounts from the hospital with the scenes where the attacks were said to have occurred," that "whatever had occurred at Nadir [near Hilla], the incident was part of a wider pattern of increasing tension among Iraqi officials and American troops," and "reporters were led on a tour of sinuous alleyways to see the damage from what was described as the cluster bombing of an entire neighborhood." Burns grudgingly reported that eyewitness claims about cluster bombs "seemed probable to the eye," that "houses appeared to have been hit ... by thousands of shards of shrapnel," and that "small, grayish-black pieces of unexploded ordnance, possibly a form of cluster bomb, lay scattered in profusion."[11]

While Amnesty International and Robert Fisk reported that the cluster-bombing of Hilla was almost certainly a war crime, Burns himself made no such observation. Rather, he channeled this responsibility to a 38-year-old Iraqi man who lost his mother and his right arm in the bombing. After telling Burns that "people's heads were snapped off their bodies," the man says: "I have just one thing to say to George Bush. He is a criminal and a liar to talk of bringing us freedom. He attacks civilians for no reason. This is a crime, a crime, a crime."[12] Although Burns did not intend to imply that the man was correct in his assessment of criminal responsibility, the Iraqi man nevertheless was correct: the US invasion of Iraq, because it violated the UN Charter, was a "war of aggression" and a "crime against peace" under international law, and the cluster-bombing of Hilla and surrounding areas was almost certainly a "war crime" under the Geneva Conventions of

August 12 1949 Relating to the Protection of Victims of International Armed Conflicts. These were issues that the *Times* was eager to ignore except for its cynical use of the justifiably hysterical charges of Iraqi civilians.

While much of what Burns reported came from his visit to the general hospital in Hilla, he apparently made no effort to visit the hospital mortuary ("a butcher's shop of chopped up corpses") or to see the trucks that had arrived at the hospital (with "dozens of totally dismembered dead bodies of women and children"), given that he never mentioned the mortuary in the hospital basement or the trucks around back.

Overall, Burns reported the US cluster-bombing of Hilla with a minimum of facts and insight, but perhaps with just enough detail to carry out his journalistic duty the way some people go to church on Sunday to fulfill a nagging obligation. Upon returning to Baghdad the next day, however, Burns appeared to be uplifted by the intense US bombardment of the capital that was under way, and wrote "American air power, as the 21st century begins, is a terrible swift sword that strikes with a suddenness, a devastation and a precision, in most cases, that moves even agnostics to reach for words associated with the power of gods."[13]

In the same day's *New York Times* (April 4), Susan Sachs, a Cairo-based correspondent, complained scornfully that Arab-based news media were unfairly covering the story of civilian casualties in Iraq: "Horrific vignettes of the helpless—armless children, crushed babies, stunned mothers—cascade into Arab living rooms from the front pages of newspapers and television screens." She argues that "the rage against the United States is fed" not by the bombing itself, but "by this steady diet of close-up photography and television footage of dead and wounded Iraqis, described as victims of American bombs." Fortunately, from her perspective:

> Sensationalism has not gripped all media. Some mainline government-owned newspapers like the staid Al Ahram in Egypt and two of the privately owned international Arabic papers in London, Al Hayat and Asharq Al Awsat, have reported the war in neutral language. They show bandaged victims in Iraq hospitals but not the gory pictures of ripped bodies that fill the pages of their competitors.[14]

Like Burns, Sachs trades her humanity for her service to the *Times*, and dutifully sees Arab rage about Arab children bombed by the United

States as "sensationalism," while her own rage against Arab anger presumably reflects the higher journalistic standards at the *Times*.

The US bombing of Hilla in central Iraq on March 31 to April 2 occurred shortly after the decision was made at US Central Command to continue the US ground march to Baghdad despite unexpected resistance from armed Iraqis. Before the start of the invasion on March 20, Bush administration officials had predicted a less contentious conquest. By March 26, however, headlines in the *New York Times* read: "Unexpected Resistance and a Change in Plans";[15] "Decade of Plans to Topple Hussein Yields Mixed Results";[16] "Top General Concedes Air Attacks Did Not Deliver Knockout Blow";[17] "Republicans Depict War as Harder Than Hoped";[18] "Opinions Begin to Shift as Public Weighs Costs of War";[19] "Constant Iraqi Attacks Are Holding Up the Allied Forces Trying to Reach Baghdad";[20] "A Tough Fight, a Retreat and a Look Ahead";[21] "New Reality, Hard Choices";[22] and "A Pause in the Advance, and Some Time to Reflect."[23] The headlines were similar in other newspapers and on network and cable news television programs.

Right-wing commentators in the United States, including Rush Limbaugh, with a weekly radio audience of twenty million, and William Kristol, editor of the *Weekly Standard*, viewed such "negative" news coverage as "undermin[ing] the war effort" (Limbaugh) and "com[ing] close to being disgraceful" (Kristol).[24] In this case, however, as in many others that rouse the right-wing news media critics, the press was simply reporting what was evident, as noted even by US military commanders in Iraq. For example, on March 28 the *New York Times* reported that Colonel Ben Saylor, chief of staff of the US First Marine Division in Iraq, said: "We've been contested every inch, every mile on the way up" to Baghdad. In short, due to Iraqi resistance and US supply-line problems one week into the invasion, the expected fast march from Kuwait to Baghdad had been momentarily stymied. US military planners suddenly found themselves having to make a choice between continuing the march to Baghdad with possibly an insufficient number of troops, poorly supplied, or to wait, perhaps for weeks, for troop and supply-line reinforcements.[25]

A front-page article in the *Times* by Michael Gordon on March 28 summarized the dilemma: "The United States military now faces a series of difficult calculations in its efforts to overthrow Saddam Hussein and his government. One way to accomplish that goal is to try to advance quickly to the outskirts of Baghdad, destroy the Republican Guard troops defending the approaches to the capital and then win the fight inside the city." The other "possible approach" was "to defer the rush to Baghdad."[26] The following day (March 29), the *Times* reported that "the timing of any thrust to Baghdad was under intense review," and that the outcome of that decision "would determine the immediate future of the war."[27]

Within a day of that report the decision was made, at least as much for political reasons as military ones, to continue the march to Baghdad. This is because the operational pause, US casualties, and high-profile TV commentators talking about bad military planning and a potential quagmire in Iraq had begun to undermine US domestic political support for the invasion.

The decision, then, to continue the march to Baghdad without troop and supply-line reinforcements was both politically and militarily risky. To reduce such risks, the Bush administration made the additional decision to proceed to Baghdad using maximum force, which turned the eighty-mile corridor from Najaf to Baghdad literally into a US warpath.

On April 1 the *New York Times* reported that the US vice-chairman of the Joint Chiefs of Staff, upon resumption of the US march to Baghdad, had indicated that US forces would proceed to the capital despite the likelihood of high casualties:

> [T]he United States was prepared to pay a "very high price" in casualties to capture Baghdad and topple President Hussein. "We're prepared to pay a very high price because we are not going to do anything other than ensure that this regime goes away," the officer told reporters. "If that means there will be a lot of casualties, then there will be a lot of casualties."[28]

Unfortunately for the town of Hilla, it happened to be located between US forces in central Iraq—the Third Infantry Division, the US First Marine Division, and the US 101st Airborne Division—and Saddam Hussein in Baghdad. In an article written on March 31 and published on April 1, *Times* correspondent Jim Dwyer, reporting "With the 101st Airborne Division, near Hilla, in central Iraq," wrote:

> It was possible today to drive 30 miles north from Najaf toward Baghdad and not see a single living person other than American soldiers. The roads were littered with the hulks of pickup trucks and taxi cabs that had been fired on by American soldiers. As for the occupants of several of those cars—singled out as members of paramilitary forces loyal to President Saddam Hussein—their bodies were sprawled on the ground nearby.

> So it was that a swath of the Iraqi countryside along the Euphrates, about 60 miles from Baghdad, was all but devoid of ordinary life on this beautiful spring day, as American troops from the 101st Airborne Division hunted down Iraqi soldiers and guerrillas in a relentless show of force.[29]

Even assuming that the Americans were somehow able to determine with any accuracy which of the Iraqi pickup trucks and taxi cabs were carrying Iraqi paramilitary forces, this report indicates that such forces occupied only "several" and not all of the trucks and cabs. Thus, with no signs of life for thirty miles among destroyed heaps of cars and trucks, a sky's-the-limit proclamation on casualties declared by the US vice-chairman of the Joint Chiefs of Staff, and the powerful political motivation to get to Baghdad as quickly as possible, an obvious question here is whether US forces indiscriminately killed civilians during the course of its "relentless show of force" on that beautiful spring day on March 31. Dwyer never asked the question.

The relentless use of force apparently continued once US forces reached Hilla. Reporting from Hilla, Dwyer wrote in the same article, and on the same day that Iraqi eyewitnesses reported that the cluster-bombing of Hilla had begun: "Today, the Americans launched a blizzard of shells, bombs and bullets, flushing out soldiers of an Iraqi artillery unit near Hilla, north of Najaf on the road to Baghdad."[30] Also reporting from Hilla on March 31, the *Times'* Dexter Filkins wrote: "Night fell to sounds of American artillery bombarding the remnants of an Iraqi force that soldiers here said had been weakened severely by an American advance team early this morning."[31] Filkins continued, describing the bombardment of Hilla and nearby localities with the intellectual and emotional detachment prized by the *Times*:

> At last, Baghdad was getting closer again, and everyone seemed to feel it. Marine officers strutted about their headquarters compound, set up hours before in an abandoned building at the highway's edge. American jets streaked freely about the skies.
>
> The horizon, too, offered its own display of American power. To the left, an Iraqi city glimmered in the distance. Then, with an airstrike, its lights faded black. To the right, a huge orange glow rose in the darkness, illuminating the night sky, until it, too, shrank to nothing. Seconds later, a pair of American jets skylarked to the south.[32]

Aside from the eerie cheerfulness of these reports, how might the *Times* reporters claim to know that the US was "bombarding the remnants of an Iraqi force" and "flushing out soldiers" near Hilla, rather than simply bombing a town? In the block quote above, Filkins doesn't even pretend that the Americans were bombing anything but a town. Indeed, a month later, the *Associated Press* reported:

> A month after U.S. cluster munitions fell in a deadly shower on Hillah's teeming slums as U.S. forces drove toward victory in Baghdad, 55 miles to the north, the most telling evidence may lie in the crowded, fly-infested wards of the city hospital, where the toll of dead and wounded still mounts.
>
> At least 250 Iraqis were killed and more than 500 wounded during 17 days of fighting in the area, most of them civilians and many the victims of cluster munitions, according to hospital medical staff.[33]

The *AP* reported that "gaps and uncertainties remain" with respect to the details of what happened in Hilla, "including the question of whether Iraqi troops were still in Nadr, Amira and other Hillah-area districts when they were attacked." Upon closer inspection, the gaps and uncertainties cited in the *AP* report had to do mostly with the fact that the Bush administration would not confirm using cluster bombs in Hilla. Meanwhile, visual evidence and eyewitness reports from numerous Iraqis quoted in the article clearly indicated that cluster bombs were used.[34]

On March 28, a little more than a week into the invasion, a missile hit a crowded market in Baghdad. John F Burns reported in the *New York Times* (March 29) that the explosion from the missile killed "as many as 35 people, possibly as many as 55, many of them women and small children."[35] Though Burns reported that witnesses near the market had "seen the vapor trail of a high-flying aircraft" and "heard the roar of an engine they likened to cruise missiles," indicating that the missile had come from a US or British bomber or fighter plane, Burns had other ideas about who might have been behind the Baghdad-market bombing.

In another case study of self-imposed denial among the *Times* foreign correspondents, Burns reported "it was impossible to determine the cause" of the bombing. Given statements from Iraqi eyewitnesses that a missile from an airplane had hit the market, and the fact that US air power in Iraq was so dominant that no Iraqi fighters were known at the time to have taken off from an Iraqi air base anywhere in Iraq (none had been reported shot down by US forces), the circumstantial evidence available to Burns logically indicated that a US or British missile hit the market. However, with little evidence—that is, a relatively small crater for a US cruise missile or gravity bomb—Burns saw Saddam's finger-prints on the bombing. He thus spun the carnage he witnessed into a censure of the Iraqi regime, and, like Judith Miller, cited anonymous Iraqi opposition sources to "corroborate" unsubstantiated speculation about the incident:

> With an [US] invading force already hung up in southern Iraq by unexpectedly fierce resistance, Mr. Hussein and his associates in the Baghdad leadership are certain to use any incident involving large numbers of civilian deaths to mobilize opinion against the war at home and abroad.
>
> Ultimately, the Iraqi ruler appears to hope that growing opposition to the war abroad, especially in the United States and Britain, will force a turn-around in allied war aims, saving him from being ousted the same way he was spared by the American decision to seek a cease-fire after Iraqi forces were pushed out of Kuwait in 1991.
>
> This alone, Iraqi opposition leaders say, would give Mr. Hussein an incentive to organize incidents like the two bombing attacks [including the Baghdad-market bombing] this week.[36]

Having blamed Saddam for the bombing, Burns freed himself to fulfill the technical requirement of having to report civilian casualties. Thus, Burns wrote:

> At the market, fragments from the blast killed people up to 80 yards away, including three brothers from a single family in a home beside the market and two traders putting up their shutters for the night at shops just down the road. ...
>
> One victim was a 6-year-old girl, Iman Fadil, who died along with her mother and small brother, neighbors said.[37]

Burns reported other statements of Iraqis who witnessed the bomb-ing. By highlighting the absence of ambiguity in the statement below from an Iraqi doctor, Burns signaled that the doctor's statement might not meet the reporting standards of the *Times*:

> After the marketplace explosion Friday night, there was no ambiguity in the response of Iraqis struggling to deal with the carnage. Dr. Hassan Razouki, 50, director of Al Noor Hospital half a mile from the explosion, broke away from directing surgery to talk to reporters.
>
> "At 5:30 p.m. this evening, an enemy plane deliberately hit the local market," he said. "It was crowded with lots of people, including many children and many elderly, who went there to buy food. The number of martyrs from this criminal act is 35, most of them under 15 years of age, elderly or female, and we have treated 47 others who were injured."

He added: "The bodies were shattered by the missile, which was intended to kill as many people as possible. It was daylight. It was clear to anybody that the market was crowded, and there are no military or strategic facilities in this area."[38]

While concluding, Burns reintroduced the hand of Saddam in the bombing, as well as the ghost of Iraq's ancient history, to situate the market-bombing killing of women and children not in the context of the US invasion, but in the inexorable reality of Iraqi suffering:

> In the prayer on that muddy ground, in the mosque, at the marketplace amid the pools of blood, at the hospital, nobody, at least nobody directly affected by the bombing, made any mention of Saddam Hussein. In the darkness, it seemed suddenly, to an outsider, that these were people who had made their own quittance with the Iraqi leader, at least in their souls, and that what mattered to them now were ancient truths, and ancient sufferings, that would far outlast the Iraqi ruler, whatever the outcome of the war.[39]

This was how the *Times* and its Baghdad bureau chief reported and left the story of the March 28 marketplace bombing. A day after the *Times* published the March 29 report by John F Burns, the *Independent*'s Robert Fisk published a story on the same incident.[40]

Fisk reported that a piece of metal bearing a series of numbers "was retrieved only minutes after the missile exploded ... by an old man whose home is only 100 yards from the 6-foot crater." The metal bore two sets of coded numbers—30003-704ASB 7492 and MFR 96214 09—that Fisk surmised might be the serial and lot numbers of the missile that hit the market, and that might identify the type of missile, its manufacturer, its nation of origin, and ultimately the identity of who fired the missile into the market.

In a follow-up report three days later, the *Independent* reported:

> An American missile, identified from the remains of its serial number, was pinpointed yesterday as the cause of the explosion at a Baghdad market on Friday night that killed at least 62 Iraqis.
>
> The codes on the foot-long shrapnel, seen by the Independent correspondent Robert Fisk at the scene of the bombing in the Shuale district, came from a weapon manufactured in Texas by Raytheon, the world's biggest producer of "smart" munitions.
>
> The identification of the missile as American is an embarrassing blow to Washington and London as they try to match their promises of minimal civilian casualties with the reality of precision bombing.[41]

The *Independent* reported that the Pentagon and Raytheon declined to comment on the serial number evidence. It also reported that "the American military has confirmed that a navy EA-6B 'Prowler' jet, based on the USS *Kittyhawk*, was in action over the Iraqi capital on Friday [March 28] and fired at least one Harm missile to protect two American fighters from a surface-to-air missile battery."

The *Independent* also reported that the serial and lot numbers of the metal fragment showed that what hit the market was either a Harm (High-Speed Anti-Radiation Missile) missile or a Paveway laser-guided bomb sold by Raytheon to the US Navy. The *Independent* reported that "defence experts said the damage caused at Shuale was consistent with that of Paveway or, more probably, a Harm weapon, which carries a warhead designed to explode into thousands of aluminium fragments." This is consistent with what John F Burns reported on March 29 that "fragments from the blast killed people up to 80 yards away."[42] It is also consistent with the relatively small crater left by the impact and immediate dispersal of Harm missile fragments. In his report, published on March 30, Fisk was more descriptive: "The missile sprayed hunks of metal through the crowds—mainly women and children—and through the cheap brick walls of local homes, amputating limbs and heads."[43]

In short, John F Burns misreported the market-bombing story for the *Times* by supporting the Bush administration's spin that an Iraqi anti-aircraft missile had fallen on the market, and by volunteering the part about Saddam having motives for bombing the market himself.

The cluster-bombing of Hilla that began on March 31 spread to Baghdad as the US march to the capital advanced. The reports that follow of civilian casualties during the siege of Baghdad represent a sample of such reports from a number of news organizations.

On April 3, Suzanne Goldberg reported for the *Observer* from Sueb. This is an Iraqi town located between Hilla and Baghdad that, according to Goldberg, had the bad fortune to "lie directly on the Americans' path":

> Yesterday's strike [April 2] took out two homes of an extended family of about a dozen. Tuesday's raid [April 1] destroyed the local school, and on Monday a poor baklava seller, pitied by the entire neighborhood, lost his wife, mother, sister, nephew, and two sons to American missiles.[44]

Referring to the US decision to resume the march to Baghdad after the operational pause a week earlier, Goldberg wrote: "After the US troops suffered setbacks in the south of Iraq in the early days of the war, the people on the next frontline are ruing their fate." She described how "the last five days" in Sueb "have seen intense, round-the-clock bombardments," and quotes an Iraqi man who told her "there are bombings—missiles and airplanes—all day long, and all night long."[45]

Also on April 3 Samia Nakhoul of *Reuters* reported that "U.S. missiles hit a Red Crescent maternity hospital in Baghdad and other civilian buildings on Wednesday [April 2], killing several people and wounding at least 25, hospital sources and witnesses said," and that "this correspondent saw at least five burned-out and twisted cars" where "witnesses said the drivers burned to death inside."[46]

On April 5 Robert Fisk of the *Independent* reported:

> There was new evidence yesterday of the use of cluster bombs, on Baghdad itself this time, not just in the villages outside. From Furad, in the Doura district and Hay al-Ama and other areas west of Baghdad, civilians were arriving in emergency wards with the usual terrible wounds—multiple and severely deep gashes made by shrapnel released by bombs that explode in the air.
>
> The death toll at Furad alone was said to be more than 80. One central hospital received 39 wounded, four of whom died in surgery. One young man had run for his life when he saw white canisters dropping from the sky but he was hit as he tried to run through his own front door.[47]

On April 6, Mary Riddell reporting for the *Observer* wrote:

> Be mindful, as the endgame plays out, of the Home Secretary's guidelines on war coverage. Some British journalists, he complains, are reporting the conflict in a manner that lends "moral equivalence" to the Iraqi regime and encourages a "progressive and liberal public" to believe this distorted version. Mr. Blunkett, who yesterday embellished his assertions, is doubly wrong. There is no bias, nor the slightest hint that Bush, Blair and Saddam register equally on the weighbridge of tyranny.
>
> On the separate question of whether Iraqi acts of war are on a par with those of the coalition, the answer is simple. Ours are sometimes worse. The spectre of chemical attack remains, but, amid Iraqi Scuds unfired and bio-weapons undiscovered, reality trumps fear. The cluster-bombing of civilians by an invading force proclaiming its superior power is an outrage against humanity and the Geneva Convention.[48]

Also on April 6, the *Associated Press* reported:

> The number of casualties in Baghdad is so high that hospitals have stopped counting the number of people treated, the International Committee of the

Red Cross said Sunday [April 6]. "No one is able to keep accurate statistics of the admitted and transferred war wounded any longer as one emergency arrival follows the other in the hospitals of Baghdad," the ICRC said in a statement.

The *AP* also published a photograph of a man and two children in a hospital, with the caption: "Dahoud Salim holds his nieces Dalhia Nasser, 10, left, and Mihad Ali, 3, at al-Kindi hospital Sunday, April 6, 2003, in Baghdad. Both children were injured when their house collapsed, killing their father, during bombing raids on the outskirts of Baghdad Saturday."[49]

On April 7 Robert Fisk asked questions that no *Times* reporter had asked or would ask:

Why do we aid and abet the lies and propaganda of this filthy war? How come, for example, it's now BBC "style" to describe the Anglo-American invaders as the "coalition." This is a lie. The "coalition" that we're obviously supposed to remember is the one forged to drive Iraqi occupation troops from Kuwait in 1991, an alliance involving dozens of countries—almost all of whom now condemn President Bush Junior's adventure in Iraq. There are a few Australian special forces swanning about in the desert, courtesy of the country's eccentric Prime Minister, John Howard, but that's about it.

Then there's the famous "war in Iraq" slogan which the British and American media like to promote. But this is an invasion, not a mere war.

And isn't it turning into an occupation rather than a "liberation"? Shouldn't we be remembering in our reports that this whole invasion lacks legitimacy? Sure, the Americans claim they needed no more than the original UN resolution 1441 to go to war. But if that's the case, why did Britain and the US vainly seek a second resolution? I can't help thinking readers and viewers realize the mendacity of all this sleight of hand, and that we journalists go on insulting these same readers and viewers by thinking we can con them.

Thus, we go on talking about an "air campaign" as if the Luftwaffe was taking off from Cap Gris Nez to bomb London, when not a single Iraqi aircraft has left the ground. So, it's "coalition forces," a war not an invasion, liberation rather than occupation, and the taking of cities that are "secured" rather than "captured," and when captured, are insecure.[50]

On April 8, Fisk reported in the *Independent*, again in stark contrast with the hollowed-out reports filed by the *Times* Baghdad correspondents:

It's becoming harder to visit these places of pain, grief and anger. The International Committee of the Red Cross yesterday reported civilian victims of America's three-day offensive against Baghdad arriving at the hospitals now by the hundreds. Yesterday, the Kindi [hospital] alone had taken 50 civilian wounded and three dead in the previous 24 hours. Most of the dead—the little boy's family, the family of six torn to pieces by an aerial bomb in front of Ali Abdulrazek, the car salesman, the next-door neighbors of Safa Karim—were simply buried within hours of being torn to bits.

On television, it looks so clean. On Sunday evening [April 6], the BBC showed burning civilian cars, its reporter—"embedded" with US forces—saying that he saw some of their passengers lying dead beside them.

That was all. No pictures of the charred corpses, no close-ups of the shrivelled children. So perhaps I should warn those of what the BBC once called a nervous disposition to go no further. But if they want to know what America and Britain are doing to the innocent of Baghdad, they should read on.[51]

On April 10, Fisk reported:

The Iraqi civilians and soldiers brought to the Adnan Khairallah Martyr Hospital in the last hours of Saddam Hussein's regime yesterday—sometimes still clinging to severed limbs—are the dark side of victory and defeat; final proof, like the dead who are buried within hours, that war is about the total failure of the human spirit. As I wandered amid the beds and the groaning men and women lying on them—Dante's visit to the circles of hell should have included these visions—the same old questions recurred. Was this for 11 September? For human rights? For weapons of mass destruction? ...

Florence Nightingale never reached this part of the old Ottoman Empire. But her equivalent is Dr Khaldoun al-Baeri, the director and chief surgeon, a gently-spoken man who has slept an hour a day for six days and who is trying to save the lives of more than a hundred souls a day with one generator and half his operating theatres out of use—you cannot carry patients in your arms to the 16th floor when they are coughing blood.

Dr Baeri speaks like a sleepwalker, trying to describe how difficult it is to stop a wounded man or woman from suffocating when they have been wounded in the thorax, explaining that after four operations to extract metal from the brains of his patients, he is almost too tired to think, let alone in English. As I leave him, he tells me that he does not know where his family is.

"Our house was hit and my neighbors sent a message to tell me they sent them away somewhere. I do not know where. I have two little girls, they are twins, and I told them they must be brave because their father had to work night and day at the hospital and they mustn't cry because I have to work for humanity. And now I have no idea where they are." Then Dr Baeri choked on his words and began to cry and could not say goodbye.[52]

On April 12 Kim Sengupta reported in the *Independent*:

> "Why do you all want to talk to Ali? There are hundreds of children suffering like him, and we are getting more every day," said Moufak Gabriel, the hospital director, as we arrived to see Ali Ismail Abbas, the injured 12-year-old boy who has become the centre of a British media frenzy. . . .
>
> The facts of what happened to Ali are as follows: An American missile smashed into his home in the village of Zafaraniya, 30 miles from Baghdad, as his family slept, just after midnight. He was severely burnt and both his arms had to be amputated.
>
> His father, Ismail, and mother, Azhar, who was pregnant, were killed.
>
> Ali has black curly hair and hazel eyes. His aunt Jamila and a nurse brushed away the flies. "If I had hands, I would shake your hand," he said. "They cut them off after the bomb. I want my hands."
>
> We stood there awkwardly. Rahim al-Kinani, the doctor treating him, said he had been told that newspapers in Britain had launched an appeal on his behalf and that he would have artificial arms soon. . . .
>
> Two floors away, in another ward of Saddam general, lay 11-year-old Fouad Abu Haidar. He has lost his left arm, half his face is hidden by bandages, and he may lose one of his eyes. He suffered his injuries during another air attack, 10 days ago, near Iskandiriyak, in the southern suburbs of Baghdad. A 14-year-old cousin, Karim, died when the missile struck their house just after nine o'clock in the evening.
>
> Fouad has not had anyone visit him from the Western media, and no promises that he will also benefit from the generosity of the British people. His father, Haidar Hussein, said he was glad to know about the concern of the British people but felt nothing but anger about what had happened. "No one has told me anything about money from Britain. But this is a war by Bush and Blair. They did this to my son and other children, women, men. Why didn't the British and American people stop their leaders from doing this? What is the justification in bombing ordinary people?"[53]

Not only have Americans to date not stopped their leaders from killing ordinary people in Iraq, some Americans in effect have urged their leaders to do more of it. Well into the occupation of Iraq, after Iraqi insurgents blew up the UN and Red Cross headquarters in Iraq, killing dozens of civilians, *New York Times* columnist David Brooks argued that the American forces in Iraq might well have to resort to more brutal measures:

> It's not that we can't accept casualties. History shows that Americans are willing to make sacrifices. The real doubts come when we see ourselves inflicting them. What will happen to the national mood when the news

programs start broadcasting images of the brutal measures our own troops will have to adopt? Inevitably, there will be atrocities that will cause many good-hearted people to defect from the cause. They will have us be tempted to retreat into the paradise of our innocence.[54]

This illustrates the downward spiral of advocacy among American intellectuals who supported the invasion: First, support for the invasion, then support for the "inevitable" American atrocities, as in the case of Brooks; or, support for the invasion, then for the kind of counter-insurgency and pacification programs that killed hundreds of thousands of people in Vietnam, as in the case of Max Boot (see below); or, support for the invasion, then for "coercive interrogations," as in the case of Michael Ignatieff (see chapters 2 and 5). And all of this is stipulated by high-profile commentators in the New York Times.

For example, Max Boot, a war historian who wrote in the New York Times op-ed page in August 2003 that "there was nothing wrong with President Bush's decision to invade Iraq without United Nations blessing" and that "the issue of whether to involve the United Nations in a particular problem should be based" not on considerations of international law but on "pragmatic considerations,"[55] wrote a short time later that the United States should resort to Vietnam-style counterinsurgency warfare in part because "our [conventional] military" forces in Iraq "may simply be too Boy Scoutish for the rougher side of a dirty war."[56] For these and other such views, Boot was given generous access to the Times op-ed and book-review pages, where he wrote 10,000 words of commentary on Iraq and related military issues from October 2002 to February 2004.[57] And the right-wing Brooks was hired by the publisher in 2003 to offset Paul Krugman's commentary on the op-ed page.[58]

Other prominent regulars at the Times have made a point either of ignoring altogether the issue of Iraqi civilian casualties or of casually recommending the use of cluster bombs. In an article on March 27 2003 titled "Delicate Calculus of Casualties and Public Opinion," veteran Times reporter Todd Purdum asked: "What level of casualties does the White House think the American public will tolerate?" Purdum was not referring to US and Iraqi casualties, just US casualties. In a 1300-word article, he never referred to or otherwise mentioned in any way the issue of Iraqi casualties.[59] Similarly, during the US operational pause in central Iraq, the Times veteran military reporter, Michael Gordon, appeared to suggest, without mentioning potential civilian casualties, the use of cluster bombs during the US march to Baghdad: "During the stretch of bad weather, the Army hopes to keep the pressure on by firing Atacms surface-to-surface missiles. The weather will make it difficult for allied pilots to hit mobile targets, but the air war commanders could try to keep the heat on by dropping gravity bombs or cluster bombs."[60]

Once the cluster-bombing began, it was almost completely ignored by the *Times*. Among the few articles that even mentioned cluster bombs, one by *Times* reporter Douglas Jehl casually confirmed their use in Iraq and coldly described their capabilities:

> Among other advances or new weapons singled out by American commanders is the so-called sensor-fused weapon, a cluster bomb that General Moseley said on Saturday [April 5] had been used in combat against Iraqi forces for the first time.
>
> Each bomb releases 10 warheads that in turn each send out 4 armor-piercing weapons that scan the battlefield with infrared sensors for armored vehicles or troops to attack. The weapons are designed to inflict heavy damage on targets over a 30-acre area.[61]

Four other articles mentioned the use of cluster bombs. One of the four, published on April 17, briefly mentioned a cluster bomb but didn't say who used it or where it came from:

> On the other side sat Abdul Wali, 15, whose intestines and stomach were shredded by a cluster bomb. Doctors said he would recover: rebuilding an abdominal wall is something the personnel at Wasiti know how to do well.[62]

Two of the remaining three articles, published on April 3 and April 8, reported possible cluster-bomb casualties under cover of supposed US investigations into the incidents:

> Hospitals in Iraq reported dozens of civilians killed and many more injured as United States Army and Marine forces stormed Baghdad and engaged in firefights with Iraqi defenders. In Hilla, south of Baghdad, the International Committee of the Red Cross visited the local hospital following attacks by American forces and reported 300 civilian casualties. American officials said they are investigating reports that cluster bombs were used against villages.[63]

> A team from the International Committee of the Red Cross said one of its doctors had seen 280 wounded civilians at the Hilla surgical hospital from tank fire and cluster bombs. Local officials said the victims included many women and children. American military officials said the incidents were under investigation.[64]

The findings of these investigations were presumably indicated a month later when the US Chairman of the Joint Chiefs of Staff, General

Richard Myers, reported that only one Iraqi civilian was killed by cluster bombs throughout the course of the invasion.[65]

This leaves only one other mention in the *Times* during the period of major US combat on the use of cluster bombs in Iraq. This mention was the most descriptive one published by the *Times*, though still only a few paragraphs in an article not focused on cluster bombs:

> On Friday, three Iraqi men captured during fighting on Thursday described how their unit, part of the Medina Division of the Republican Guard, had been ravaged by American air strikes.
>
> The three men said they had been stationed with other members of the Medina Division at Dorra, a town near Baghdad. They said their brigade had moved its tanks there in recent weeks to take advantage of the cover provided by the trees the town is known for. On Thursday morning, the men said, they came under heavy bombardment for two hours by American planes using cluster bombs.
>
> "It was a surprise; we didn't realize we could be hit there," said Alahwi Muhammad, one of the soldiers, as he sat cross-legged in a Marine compound near Aziziya. "When the bombs hit the tanks, many people got in their cars. Then the bombs hit the cars. It was terrible."
>
> They said that many civilians had been killed in the town during the American bombardment and that 25 of their brigade's tanks had been destroyed.[66]

Though scant, the *Times*' coverage of US cluster-bombing in Iraq helps confirm that cluster bombs were used and that many Iraqi civilians were killed by such bombs. These brief references to the US cluster-bombing of Iraqi civilians also in effect confirmed the extent to which the *Times* under-reported the story, which, once again, appeared limited to fulfilling a minimal technical requirement of having to report the fact of the cluster-bombing in some manner in the paper.

Beyond these limited reports, the *Times* did its best to ignore the issue, including reports from Amnesty International and Human Rights Watch. On April 16, for example, Human Rights Watch issued a press release about the use of cluster bombs in Iraq:

> The U.S. Central Command should respond publicly to evidence that U.S. forces used cluster munitions in a populated area of Baghdad. According to a report in yesterday's Newsday, a Central Command spokeswoman has anonymously confirmed that U.S. forces have hit urban areas of Baghdad with cluster munitions, stating that they were aimed at Iraqi artillery and missile systems located inside the city.
>
> "U.S. commanders should never use cluster munitions in populated

areas," said Kenneth Roth, executive director of Human Rights Watch. "These are wholly inappropriate weapons when civilians are around. The reported use of cluster munitions in Baghdad is a serious charge and the Pentagon must respond publicly to it."[67]

Before the *Times* ignored this report, it ignored the report a day earlier (April 15) by *New York Newsday,* which reported that a US Central Command spokeswoman, in response to questions from *Newsday*, said "we had to use them [cluster bombs] in an urban environment because that was where Saddam Hussein put those weapons."[68] *Newsday* also reported how some children in Baghdad were still dying at the time from unexploded cluster bombs:

> The little boy wailed and moaned and squirmed on the hospital bed stained with his own blood. A doctor struggled to hold a gauze bandage over the boy's eyes, which no longer existed. Ali Mustapha had found a small cylindrical object on the street near his Baghdad home Monday morning. He picked it up. He played with it. He had it in his hands and the object—a live explosive—literally blew up in his face. At Kadhymia Hospital, Dr. Ausama Saadi's diagnosis was blunt: "He will be blind for the rest of his life."[69]

Also:

> Hussain Hamed said one cluster bomb was fired into his Baghdad neighborhood. Four days ago, a group of children, including Hamed's son, Ali, 10, started playing with what Hamed said turned out to be a small explosive, about the size of a medicine bottle with a hollowed-out bottom. Two children were killed when it exploded, Hamed said. His son's stomach was cut open, spilling out his intestines.[70]

The *Associated Press* had also reported three days earlier how children were dying from unexploded cluster bombs in Baghdad:

> In the deserted emergency room, Mohammed Suleiman hysterically looked for his 8-month-old daughter, Rowand, brought in after a bomb her brother unwittingly brought home exploded. "Please look at her face and see how beautiful she is," he screamed when he found the baby's lifeless body, covered with a blanket, her eyes half open, her nose and mouth bloodied.[71]

In short, the *New York Times* ignored the reports of human rights organizations and other news organizations that US forces were killing Iraqi civilians with cluster bombs. And it apparently spent none of its substantial journalistic resources to investigate the factual and legal status of the US use of cluster bombs in Iraq. Instead, the *Times* spent its resources elevating the US military victory in Iraq and lionizing its principal architects in the Bush administration.

While noting on the front-page for April 9 that "American troops had thrown a noose around Baghdad"—one of several evasive euphemisms used in the *Times* to describe what was happening throughout Iraq during the course of the invasion—the eminent *Times* reporter, RW Apple, in an article titled "Bush's War Message: Strong and Clear," wrote: "At least for the moment, the political planets seem to be sliding into alignment for President Bush."[72] The next day, in an article titled, "A High Point in 2 Decades of Military Might," Apple wrote on the front page, first paragraph: "The collapse of government authority in Baghdad, dramatized by a toppling of a colossal statue of President Saddam Hussein, constitutes the high-water mark for a new American determination to use the nation's military might to project its power around the world."[73] Though Apple notes the actual and potential downsides of the invasion—"a hardening of Islamic and Arab resentment into hatred," for one—he, the *Times,* and the administration are one in celebration: "Not since Alfred Eisenstadt documented the end of World War II with his iconic shot of a sailor locking a nurse in extravagant embrace in Times Square has the United States enjoyed a similar catharsis."

Apple is also with the administration and its counterterrorism rationale for the war:

> Secretary of Defense Donald H. Rumsfeld suggested today that victory in Iraq had the potential to reshape "the future of the region," bringing democracy to countries that have never known it. That would no doubt diminish the prospects of another terrorist attack like those of Sept. 11, 2001, which has always been an underlying if seldom spoken motive for this war.

And Apple is with the White House (the words in parentheses are Apple's):

> Some of the Iraqis in the streets today were jubilant. Some dragged the head of the shattered statue through the streets, which provided pictures that must have gratified the White House. (Photographs of Mr. Hussein himself, strung up by the heels like the Italian dictator Benito Mussolini in the final months of World War II, would have been even more welcome.)[74]

Taking his cues from the president and the defense secretary, Apple exalts "the supreme international crime" under international law (an invasion of another country without UN Security Council approval) and the cluster-bombing of children as a moment of resurgent national glory. This was how it went throughout the siege of Baghdad, as the newsreel-like headlines in the *Times* read: "U.S. Commander, Evoking MacArthur, Hops Past Cities to Baghdad" (by RW Apple);[75] "Marines Move Into 'Bad Guy' Land";[76] "Onward Toward the Tigris; With Iraq's Capital in Mind";[77] "U.S. Columns Roll Forward Near Baghdad";[78] "Cheers and Smiles for U.S. General in Captured City";[79] "U.S. Ground Forces Sweep Toward Baghdad";[80] "U.S. Tightens Grip; Rockets Rain on Baghdad";[81] "U.S. Forces Take Control in Baghdad; Bush Elated; Some Resistance Remains";[82] "Americans See Clear Victory in Iraq, Poll Finds."[83]

Though the *Times* published some of the agony of the invasion to balance the glory—"Abuse, Distrust and Fear Leave Scars on Children in Battered Iraqi Town";[84] "G.I. Who Pulled the Trigger Shares Anguish of 2 Deaths";[85] "In a Functioning Hospital, Scenes of Chaos and Horror";[86] "Discovering Doubt and Death on Drive Toward Baghdad";[87] and "A Grenade on the Road, The Death of the Enemy: The Human Side of War"[88]—most of this was narrowly descriptive, an unfortunate slice of life in the victorious invasion of Iraq. Meanwhile the battlefield victory brought its own set of celebrated headlines on behalf of the invasion's architects: "After the War, New Stature for Rumsfeld";[89] "Mideast Next for Bush: After Iraq a Strong Hand";[90] "Bush Declares 'One Victory in a War on Terror.'"[91]

Even a rare skeptical headline—"News Analysis: Cold Truths Behind the Pomp"—published on the front page after the president's flight-suit appearance on a US aircraft carrier, produced no actual skepticism. *Times* correspondent Elisabeth Bumiller wrote (first sentence, first paragraph): "President Bush's made-for-television address tonight on the carrier Abraham Lincoln was a powerful, Reaganesque finale to a six-week war." There were three "cold truths" behind the pomp —none of which were identified as the illegality of the invasion, the WMD strategic disinformation campaign, and the civilian casualties.[92] Rather, the "cold truths" simply reflected the president's post-invasion political agenda, and were suggested by the administration itself:

The president declared an end to major combat operations, White House, Pentagon and State Department officials said, for three crucial reasons: to signify the shift of American soldiers from the role of conquerors to police, to open the way for aid from countries that refused to help militarily and—above all—to signal to voters that Mr. Bush is shifting his focus from Baghdad to concerns at home.

Though these "cold truths" merely described the president's political agenda, Bumiller did volunteer one of her own observations: "Mr. Bush was careful, though, not to close the door completely on his greatest political strength, his role as the warrior president who struck back after Sept. 11."[93]

Though it provides no comfort, there was a brief, candid report of Iraqi casualties published by the *Times* on April 14. The report by Ian Fisher, one of the paper's Baghdad correspondents, began:

> "I don't know how I'll tell him," Sindous Abbas, 30, said today. At her back was a window, which looked out to the sidewalk where her husband, Saad, 34, sat in pain and ignorance. He had been out of the hospital for just two days. She spoke inside so he would not hear.
>
> "It wasn't just ordinary love," Ms. Abbas said. "He was crazy about them. It wasn't like other fathers."
>
> What all his neighbors and relatives and his own wife have not yet been able to say to him is that three of his daughters—Marwa, 11, Tabarek, 8, and Safia, 5—did not survive the missile that punched down into their apartment on the third night of American airstrikes. No one has any reason to believe it was anything other than an American missile.[94]

Fisher visited the family's apartment and reported "the walls of the home were still spattered with blackened pieces of flesh. One of the girls legs had blown off and was suspended that night from the top of the ceiling fan." Fisher wrote: "there are still no definitive estimates, but it is clear that several hundred died and many more were wounded both from bombs and from soldiers firing on suspected combatants." Fisher also wrote:

> "So many people were killed," said Ali Samurai, who said he had gone to the hospital straight from the funerals of nine people killed by what he said were American bombs. "There was no need for this. The Americans are greedy and just want our resources. We never attacked the United States."[95]

A cousin of the family that lost three of its daughters told Fisher: "There is no reason for this. It's a criminal act."

The cousin, like so many other Iraqis who repeated the same charge, was right. The invasion of Iraq and the killing of these three girls and more than 15,000 Iraqi civilians, in addition to injuring and maiming over 20,000 civilians,[96] were crimes under international law. And ultimate responsibility for such crimes would lie with the high American officials who planned and ordered the invasion in violation of international law.

When the United States invaded Iraq in March 2003 without UN Security Council approval, it violated UN Charter Article 2(4), which prohibits states to use or threaten force without the Council's approval except in response to an actual or clearly imminent armed attack. President Bush's decision to invade Iraq, then, violated the most important rule of the UN Charter—the world's most important treaty.

Because it violated the Charter, the US invasion of Iraq constituted "a war of aggression" under international law, the definition of which under a definitive UN General Assembly resolution is the following:

> Article 1
> Aggression is the use of armed force by a State against the sovereignty, territorial integrity or political independence of another State, or in any other manner inconsistent with the Charter of the United Nations, as set out in this Definition.
>
> Article 2
> The First use of armed force by a State in contravention of the Charter shall constitute prima facie evidence of aggression . . .
>
> Article 3
> Any of the following acts, regardless of a declaration of war, shall . . . qualify as an act of aggression:
>
> (a) The invasion or attack by the armed forces of a State of the territory of another State, or any military occupation, however temporary, resulting from such invasion or attack.
>   . . .
> (b) Bombardment by the armed forces of a State against the territory of another State or the use of any weapons by a State against the territory of another State;
>   . . .
>
> Article 5
> 1. No consideration of whatever nature, whether political, economic, military or otherwise, may serve as a justification for aggression.
> 2. A war of aggression is a crime against international peace.[97]

Because the US invasion of Iraq (a) was initiated in a manner inconsistent with the Charter of the United Nations, (b) was a first use of armed force, (c) included the bombardment of Iraq, (d) was undertaken in defiance of the Security Council's refusal to authorize force despite unprecedented US pressure, and (e) resulted in the US military occupation of Iraq, however temporary, the invasion was "a war of aggression" under international law.

Furthermore, "no consideration of whatever nature," including speculative considerations about Iraqi WMD, or considerations on humanitarian grounds or of bringing democracy to Iraq or to the Middle East, permitted the United States under international law to invade Iraq in violation of the UN Charter.

In addition, under international law, "a war of aggression" constitutes a "crime against peace," the legal lineage of which should be of interest to every American citizen. The Nuremberg Principles of 1950 define "crimes against peace" as follows:

Crimes against peace:
(i)   Planning, preparation, initiation or waging of a war of aggression or a war in violation of international treaties, agreements or assurances;
(ii) Participation in a common plan or conspiracy for the accomplishment of any of the acts mentioned under (i).[98]

Upon reviewing these definitions, it is a simple matter to recall that President Bush and the highest officials of his administration planned, prepared, initiated, and waged the invasion of Iraq—"a war of aggression" and thus a "crime against peace." By committing this international crime, the Bush administration rejected not only the most basic norms of civilized global conduct, but in effect renounced one of the most celebrated aspects of modern history—the defeat of Nazism and the successful prosecution of major German war criminals after World War II.

In August 1945 the allied powers—the United States, the Soviet Union, the United Kingdom, and France—agreed to prosecute and punish "the major war criminals of the European Axis" and to establish "an International Military Tribunal for the trial of war criminals."[99] The London Agreement of 1945 was signed on behalf of the United States by US Supreme Court Justice Robert H Jackson.

Shortly afterward, the allied nations issued the Charter of the International Military Tribunal, which defined "crimes against peace":

Article 6
The following acts, or any of them, are crimes coming within the jurisdiction of the Tribunal for which there shall be individual responsibility:

(a) Crimes Against Peace: namely, planning, preparation, initiation or waging of a war of aggression, or a war in violation of international treaties, agreements or assurances, or participation in a common plan or conspiracy for the accomplishment of any of the foregoing.[100]

The Tribunal's Charter directed the Tribunal to indict suspected German war criminals. The indictment was issued in October 1945, and it reported the list of defendants as follows:

Defendants.

I. [P]ursuant to the Agreement of London dated 8 August 1945, and the Charter of this Tribunal annexed thereto, [the allied powers] hereby accuse as guilty, in the respects hereinafter set forth, of Crimes against Peace, War Crimes, and Crimes against Humanity, and of a Common Plan or Conspiracy to commit those Crimes, all as defined in the Charter of the Tribunal, and accordingly name as defendants in this cause and as indicted on the counts hereinafter set out: HERMANN WILHELM GOERING, RUDOLPH HESS, JOACHIM VON RIBBENTROP, ROBERT LEY, WILHELM KEITEL, ERNST KALTENBRUNNER, ALFRED ROSENBERG, HANS FRANK, JULIUS STREICHER, WALTER FUNK, HJALMAR SCHACHT, GUSTAV KRUPP VON BOHLEN UND HALBACH, KARL DOENITZ, ERICH RAEDER, BALDUR VON SCHIRACH, FRITZ SAUCKEL, ALFRED JODL, MARTIN BORMANN, FRANZ VON PAPEN, ARTHUR SEYSS-INQUART, ALBERT SPEER, CONSTANTIN VON NEURATH AND HANS FRITZSCHE, individually and as members of any of the groups or organizations next hereinafter named.[101]

The defendants were charged with being "leaders, organizers, instigators, or accomplices in the formulation of a common plan or conspiracy to commit . . . Crimes Against Peace," in addition to "crimes in the conduct of warfare" (war crimes) and "crimes against humanity." With regard to crimes against peace, the Tribunal stated: "The common plan or conspiracy embraced the commission of Crimes Against Peace, in that the defendants planned, prepared, initiated, and waged wars of aggression, which were also wars in violation of international treaties, agreements or assurances."[102]

A year later, in September 1946, the Tribunal issued its judgment. With respect to crimes against peace, the Tribunal stated:

The Tribunal now turns to the consideration of the Crimes Against Peace charged in the Indictment. . . . The charges in the Indictment that the defendants planned and waged aggressive wars are charges of the utmost gravity. War is essentially an evil thing. Its consequences are not confined to the belligerent states alone, but affect the whole world.

To initiate a war of aggression, therefore, is not only an international crime; it is the supreme international crime differing only from other war crimes in that it contains within itself the accumulated evil of the whole.[103]

The Tribunal found many of the accused guilty of crimes against peace, and sentenced many of those to death by hanging.

A year after the Nuremberg Tribunal issued its judgment, the UN General Assembly directed the UN's International Law Commission (ILC) to "formulate the principles of international law recognized in the Charter of the Nurnberg Tribunal and in the judgment of the Tribunal."[104] Three years later, in 1950, the ILC issued the seven "Principles of the Nuremberg Tribunal," some of which are listed below:

Principle I

Any person who commits an act which constitutes a crime under international law is responsible therefore and liable to punishment. . . .

Principle III

The fact that a person who committed an act which constitutes a crime under international law acted as Head of State or responsible Government official does not relieve him from responsibility under international law. . . .

Principle VI

The crimes hereinafter set out are punishable as crimes under; international law:

    a.   Crimes against Peace:

        i.   Planning, preparation, initiation or waging of a war of aggression or a war in violation of international treaties, agreements or assurances;

       ii.   Participation in a common plan or conspiracy for the accomplishment of any of the acts mentioned under (i).

Principle VII

The crimes hereinafter set out are punishable as crimes under; international law.[105]

By invading Iraq in violation of the UN Charter, the Bush administration committed "the supreme international crime" under the international law principles embodied in the Nuremberg precedent. Though the United States in large part established this precedent as an expression of global condemnation of Nazi aggression, the Bush administration not only violated Nuremberg-related law by invading Iraq, it did so without even a mention from the *New York Times* that such laws were violated or even exist.

The *New York Times* did the people of the United States no favor by ignoring international law in its coverage of the US invasion of Iraq. From a national- interest perspective, ignoring international law in the conduct of US foreign policy in our view undermines the national security of the United States. If the American people are not outraged on moral grounds with respect to the atrocities in Iraq committed in their name and with their tax dollars, perhaps we might be persuaded by the fact that our own security is threatened when our highest government officials plan and initiate "a war of aggression" and commit "a crime against peace" heedless of the expressed will and wishes of most of the rest of the world, or when US military officials authorize the use of cluster bombs against civilians and thus almost certainly committed "crimes in the conduct of warfare" under international law.

By ignoring international law, the *Times* contributed to the downward spiral of news coverage of Iraq that amounted to disarming the American citizenry of the information we need to make our government accountable to the UN Charter and the US Constitution. In contrast, integrating international law and the Constitution into the paper's coverage of US foreign policy would not only demonstrate "a decent respect to the opinion of mankind," it would promote respect for the law among the citizenry as a rational policy framework that is uniquely consistent with the most fundamental principles of US constitutional democracy.

Taking up international law, and its constitutional relevance, would also improve the news and editorial products at the *Times*. The evidence to support this statement is abundant. In short, by ignoring international law, the *Times* could not report (a) that the Iraq invasion violated the UN Charter; (b) that the invasion therefore was "a war of aggression"; (c) that a war of aggression is a "crime against peace" under the Nuremberg Principles; (d) that a crime against peace is "the supreme international crime" under international law that "contains within itself the accumulated evil of the whole," including in this case the killing and injuring of more than 35,000 Iraqis; (e) that heads of state and high government officials who plan and initiate a crime against peace bear criminal responsibility for the commission of such crimes; and (f) that officials who are responsible for such crimes are punishable under international law.

Because people outside the United States recognize the historical and legal genealogy of these crimes, they have compared the highest elected officials of the United States government to Hitler and the Nazis. We do not agree with this comparison. The Bush administration has not committed the crime of genocide and has no plans to commit genocide or acts of genocide against a national, ethnical, racial or religious group. It has not engaged in the kind or scale of state propaganda engaged in by the Nazi regime. And it has not engaged in the wholesale deprivation of civil rights and liberties of its own citizens. Passing the Hitler test, however, is the lowest possible standard to measure the conduct of the highest elected and appointed leaders of the United States. And while one might not agree with the comparison, one must nevertheless face certain facts—again unreportable without international law.

The facts are that the major German war criminals were charged with the commission of four crimes under international law: (a) conspiracy to commit aggression, (b) the commission of aggression, (c) crimes in the conduct of warfare (war crimes), and (d) crimes against humanity. By planning to invade Iraq in violation of international law, the Bush administration engaged in a conspiracy to commit aggression. By invading Iraq in violation of international law, the Bush administration committed the crime of aggression. By apparently indiscriminately attacking civilians with cluster munitions, the administration may have committed crimes in the conduct of warfare. By reportedly arresting and holding captive more than 10,000 Iraqi men and boys for several months, most of whom are "probably not dangerous,"[106] and by providing little to no public information on their whereabouts and status, the administration may have committed "crimes against humanity."[107]

While friends of the United States might make comparisons to Hitler on these grounds in the hope that such policies will end, enemies of the United States might make such comparisons to justify terrorist attacks on the United States and its citizens. International law does not recognize, nor do we, any legal or moral right to engage in any terrorist attack against the United States or its citizens in response to the US invasion of Iraq. However, victims of US crimes—parents whose children have been blown apart by US missiles and cluster bombs in violation of international law, and without legal accountability or criminal prose-cution of the principal architects of such crimes—might not likewise recognize any legal or moral proscriptions on retaliatory terrorism against the United States. Nor might their relatives or countrymen.

Thus, sound US counterterrorism policy would in our view mandate integrating fundamental principles of international law into US foreign policy. The current model of foreign policy considers international law only in ways that reject it, as in the Bush administration's "preventive-war" doctrine, which by definition represents a conspiracy to wage wars of aggression, the first example of which was the Iraq invasion.

Likewise, editorial policy at the *New York Times* is also quite far not only from incorporating international law into editorial policy, but apparently from having any grasp of international law at all. Thus, the *New York Times* staff of editors and reporters unfortunately titled its book on the Iraq invasion—"A Time of Our Choosing: America's War in Iraq"—with words that describe under the circumstances not only a conspiracy but the commission of a war of aggression under international law.[108]

5

THE TORTURE OVERTURE: HUMAN RIGHTS, HARVARD, AND IRAQ

Michael Ignatieff's third cover story for the *New York Times Magazine,* written on the wrong side of the Abu Ghraib torture photographs, was an instructive case of bad timing. On May 2 2004 the magazine published Ignatieff's proposal to give US presidents discretionary authority to preventively detain US citizens in response to another major terrorist attack in the United States, and to engage in "coercive interrogations" of detainees in US custody. With respect to interrogations, and in a section titled "Torture," Ignatieff wrote (the words in parentheses are Ignatieff's): "Permissible duress might include forms of sleep deprivation that do not result in lasting harm to mental health or physical health, together with disinformation and disorientation (like keeping prisoners in hoods) that would produce stress."[1] Ignatieff's article was written, printed, and put into the distribution pipeline for delivery to retail outlets and homes across the country too late for the *Times* to recall it following the *CBS News* broadcast on April 28, which showed for the first time photographs of tortured Iraqi detainees, including a hooded Iraqi standing on a box at Abu Ghraib prison.[2]

Though it could not withdraw Ignatieff's piece, the *Times* did issue a correction of sorts by publishing three weeks later a hastily arranged cover story by Susan Sontag, who eloquently denounced the torture of Iraqi detainees.[3] The magazine also published a June 27 story by Ignatieff, wherein he criticized the torture at Abu Ghraib and the legal memoranda by lawyers in the Bush administration that appeared to justify it.[4]

We were disturbed but not surprised by the publication of Ignatieff's May 2 cover story in the *Times* magazine. We were disturbed because

Ignatieff, director of the Carr Human Rights Center at Harvard, proposed institutionalizing governmental conduct that would certainly
violate international humanitarian law and constitutional rights and
liberties as they are generally understood. We were not surprised,
however, because both Ignatieff and the *Times,* up to May 2 2004, had
already signaled their willingness to disregard huge swaths of law with
respect to US foreign policy, and the Ignatieff piece on May 2 simply
exhibited the predictable infiltration of that outlook into the US constitutional order.

   We also were not surprised by Ignatieff's article, given his prior
failures to heed applicable systems of legal reasoning and logic. First
among these is the judgment of the Nuremberg Tribunal in 1946 that
concluded—with historical and predictive accuracy—that a war of
aggression contains within itself "the accumulated evil of the whole."[5]
Illegally invading Iraq, in fact, initiated the context wherein complementary illegalities and atrocities were committed, including those
that we have witnessed to date: a brutal and insensitive US military
occupation; the killing and injuring of thousands of Iraqi civilians,
including many hundreds of children; the cluster-bombings of towns
and cities; the beheadings committed by Iraqi fanatics; prolonged illegal
detentions of thousands of Iraqis; the car bombings of public and private
facilities by Iraqi anti-occupation insurgents that have killed and maimed
additional hundreds of people, and the torture and otherwise cruel
treatment of Iraqi detainees. Anyone who advocated on behalf of the
illegal invasion of Iraq—a "crime against peace" and "the supreme
international crime" under international law—as Ignatieff did, in effect
advocated on behalf of this cascade of violence and terror. Like the logic
of senseless violence that leads predictably to more violence, Ignatieff's
exquisitely witless logic in support of an Iraq invasion (see chapter 2)
appeared to initiate his slide down a slippery slope to his flirtation with
torture.

   The slide for Ignatieff began when he favored an invasion of Iraq
while disavowing the laws that disallowed it. Recall that he supported
an invasion in his first cover story, in part to strengthen an American
empire that would "enforc[e] such order as there is in the world" while
"laying down the rules America wants," including "exempting itself
from other rules" like those embodied in the procedures of the International Criminal Court,[6] which has jurisdiction over crimes against
humanity and war crimes, including torture.[7] Ignatieff's American
empire "is multilateral when it wants to be, unilateral when it must be"

and presents "a very different picture of the world than the one entertained by liberal international lawyers and human rights activists." It "is designed to suit American imperial objectives" and "will not be tied down like Gulliver with a thousand legal strings."[8]

In his second cover story, Ignatieff misquoted the Constitution when he invoked what he mistakenly asserted were powers of the president to disregard law in the war against terrorism. Ignatieff argued with evident admiration that President Bush, despite "the opinions of mankind," invaded Iraq anyway, "because the president believes that the ultimate authority over American decisions to intervene is not the United Nations" but "his constitutional mandate as commander in chief." "This unilateral doctrine alarms America's allies," Ignatieff wrote, "but there is not a lot they can do about it."[9]

In his third cover story, Ignatieff espoused "trafficking in evils" as part of US counterterrorism policy. While writing that "defeating terror requires violence," Ignatieff argued "it may also require coercion, secrecy, deception, even violation of rights." These methods, according to Ignatieff, are the "lesser evils" in the war against terrorism, about which Ignatieff wrote:

> [T]hinking about lesser evils is unavoidable. Sticking too firmly to the rule of law simply allows terrorists too much leeway to exploit our freedoms. Abandoning the rule of law altogether betrays our most valued institutions. To defeat evil, we may have to traffic in evils: indefinite detention of suspects, coercive interrogations, targeted assassinations, even pre-emptive war. These are evils because each strays from national and international law and because they kill people or deprive them of freedom without due process. They can be justified only because they prevent the greater evil. The question is not whether we should be trafficking in lesser evils but whether we can keep lesser evils under the control of free institutions. If we can't, any victories we gain in the war on terror will be Pyrrhic ones.

Ignatieff argues that the authority to initiate and regulate these "lesser evils" should be given to our "free institutions," which he characteristically does little to define or explain.

Undaunted and unembarrassed by his broad rejection of the rule of law as we know it in the United States, Ignatieff proposes one outrage after another, each accompanied by vague notions of legislative or judicial oversight of what amounts to an authoritarian executive power. For example:

> On all fronts, keeping a war on terror under democratic scrutiny is critical to its operational success. A lesser-evil approach permits preventive detention, where subject to judicial review; coercive interrogation, where subject to executive control; pre-emptive strikes and assassination, where these serve publicly defensible strategic goals. But everything has to be subject to critical review by a free people; free debate, public discussion, Congressional review, in camera if need be, judicial review as a last resort.

Even with robust congressional and judicial review, these proposals are problematic to say the least. For one thing, very little of the constitutional system of checks and balances is functional today when it comes to foreign policy and national security issues. There is no reason to believe it would work any better within the framework of Ignatieff's brave new world and within the context of a gravely harmed US Constitution. For example, Ignatieff's proposals would increase the power of the executive well beyond what the Constitution intended. Furthermore, how would "free people" engage in "free debate" in dissent from the president's policies if the president had the power to preventively detain US citizens at will, subject to a congressional or judicial review a month or two down the road, which may or not correct presidential excess? And which member of Congress, judge, or justice would actually compel the president to release the "terrorists" that he had already detained in the wake of another September 11?

Despite such problems, Ignatieff continues, apparently finding kinship in a proposal by Bruce Ackerman,

> a liberal law professor at Yale, [who] has recently proposed a wholesale revision of the president's current power to declare a national emergency, suggesting that if terrorists strike again, the president should be given the authority to act unilaterally for a week and to arrest anyone he sees fit. After a week, Congress would have to vote to renew his powers for a period of 60 days. Thereafter, an overwhelming majority would be required to extend the term further. Better to formalize and control emergency power, Ackerman argues, than to allow the president to slowly accumulate the power of tyranny.

Thus, a liberal Yale Law School professor and a prominent Harvard human rights intellectual propose to give the president the power to arrest and imprison any US citizen, or any number of US citizens, indefinitely, subject to review by what is now a predominantly right-wing and excessively deferential Congress. Ignatieff and apparently Ackerman weakly argue that this proposal is designed to co-opt unregulated executive tyranny. But if the executive is powerful enough now to elicit such proposals today, what proposals would a greatly strengthened executive, in the wake of this proposal and others, elicit at some point in the future?

Ignatieff's banana republic of the United States would also apparently reserve the right to abuse detainees in US custody. (Ignatieff neglected to clarify whether he would subject US as well as foreign detainees to such treatment.) His brief discourse on torture begins by appearing to reject torture. Thus, he wrote:

> An outright ban on torture, rather than an attempt to regulate it, seems the only way a democracy can keep true to its ideal of respecting the dignity even of its enemies. For that is what the rule of law commits us to: to show respect even to those who show no respect for us.

However, the very next passages in Ignatieff's article read as follows:

> To keep faith with this commitment, we need a presidential order or Congressional legislation that defines exactly what constitutes acceptable degrees of interrogation. Here we are deep into lesser-evil territory. Permissible duress might include forms of sleep deprivation that do not result in lasting harm to mental or physical health, together with disinformation and disorientation (like keeping prisoners in hoods) that would produce stress. What crosses the line into the impermissible would be any physical coercion or abuse, any involuntary use of drugs or serum, any withholding of necessary medicines or basic food, water and essential rest.
> Fine idea, you say, but who is to enforce these safeguards? It ought to be the rule that no detainee of the United States should be permanently deprived of access to counsel and judicial process, whether it be civilian federal court or military tribunal. Torture will thrive wherever detainees are held in secret. Conduct disgracing the United States is virtually inevitable, and quite predictable, if suspects are detained beyond the reach of the law.

This concluded Ignatieff's section on torture. The best that one can say about these passages, in defense of Ignatieff, is that any inference that he supports some permissible level of torture or cruel, inhuman, and degrading treatment, as he indicates that he does on "lesser-evil" grounds, would be inconsistent with his premise that there should be an outright ban on torture. Another defense of Ignatieff might be that, despite being director of the human rights center at Harvard, he writes without any apparent knowledge of the laws that already unconditionally ban torture and cruel and inhuman treatment of detainees in US custody. While this is implausible, Ignatieff in fact barely references any law while arguing that we should not be inhibited by it while making room for the lesser evils he liberally cataloged. And why would Ignatieff appear to propose an outright ban on torture when such a ban already exists in current law?

In this regard, in an April 2004 report titled "Human Rights Standards Applicable to the United States Interrogation of Detainees," the New York City Bar Association stated:

> First and foremost, the U.S. obligation to prohibit and prevent the torture and cruel, inhuman or degrading treatment of detainees in its custody is set forth in the Convention Against Torture and Other Cruel, Inhuman, or Degrading Treatment ("CAT"), to which the U.S. is a party.[10]

A federal statute (18 U.S.C. §§ 2340–2340A) codifies procedural mechanisms with which to prosecute under US criminal law violations of the Convention Against Torture.[11]

Furthermore, in a report on Iraq issued in June 2004, the United Nations High Commissioner for Human Rights, in a section titled "International Humanitarian Law," stated:

> 51. The use of torture and other forms of physical and psychological coercion against any detainee to extract confessions of intelligence related information is a violation of international humanitarian law and is prohibited. According to the Third (Art. 17, 87, 99) and the Fourth Geneva Convention (Art. 5, 31, 32), evidence that has been obtained through coercion can never be used as such by the Coalition Forces.
>
> 52. Willful killing, torture or inhuman treatment, if committed against detainees protected by international humanitarian law, constitute a grave breach under the Geneva Conventions and therefore of international humanitarian law and is prohibited at any time, irrespective of the status of the person detained. The above-described acts might be designated as war crimes by a competent tribunal. The requirement that protected persons must at all times be humanely treated is a basic pillar of the Geneva Conventions. . . .
>
> 54. Any practice of torture or other cruel, inhuman or degrading treatment or punishment violates international human rights standards to which both the US and UK are a party, including the International Covenant on Civil and Political Rights (ICCPR) and the Convention against Torture and Other Cruel, Inhuman or Degrading Treatment or Punishment (CAT). There is an absolute prohibition of torture applicable in times of conflict as well as in times of peace. CAT defines torture as any act that is intentional, that causes severe pain or suffering, that is used to obtain information or

confession, to punish, intimidate or coerce, and that has been authorized by someone in an official position. In addition to article 7 of the ICCPR, which prohibits torture and cruel, inhuman or degrading treatment or punishment, article 10 of the ICCPR specifically provides that all persons deprived of their liberty shall be treated with humanity and with respect for the inherent dignity of the human person.[12]

Regarding Ignatieff's prescription for "coercive interrogations," international law prohibits "the use of torture and other forms of physical and psychological coercion against any detainee to extract confessions of intelligence related information." Regarding "keeping prisoners in hoods," international law prohibits "cruel, inhuman or degrading treatment of detainees." Furthermore, Ignatieff's support for hooding detainees as a coercive technique to induce "disorientation" is clearly prohibited, given that "physical and psychological coercion" to extract intelligence related information is prohibited.

Writing in a section of the May 2 article titled "The Necessity of the Lesser Evils," Ignatieff openly acknowledged that his proposal with respect to coercive interrogations (and to indefinite detention of suspects, targeted assassinations, and preemptive war) "strays from national and international law." Ignatieff justifies rejecting so much law because "thinking about lesser evils is unavoidable" in the war against terrorism, because "sticking too firmly to the rule of law simply allows terrorists too much leeway to exploit our freedoms," and because "to defeat evil, we may have to traffic in evils."

Ignatieff's proposals here exhibit characteristics, not of a constitutional democracy, but of a totalitarian democracy, where Soviet-like "free institutions" would be maintained to rubber-stamp the tyrannical power of the president and ceremonially oversee the residue of the Constitution's civil rights and liberties. Ignatieff notes, however, that there would be some perks, such as a transparent national security state that might routinely shoot down its own civilian airliners, which we citizens would somehow appreciate:

> The war [on terrorism] would be less secretive, not more. We need to know more about it, not less, even if what we learn is hard. If it comes to it, we need to know, every time we fly, that in case of a hijacking, the president has authorized our pilots to shoot us down if a crash risks killing still more people. In a war on terror, painful truth is far better than lies and illusions.

Thus, if the war on terrorism transitions to authoritarianism in the United States, we will be the first ones to learn about it, and we'll all be consoled because the "painful truth"—presumably the intended point of Ignatieff's dreadful May 2 piece in the *Times* magazine—would be preferable to any nostalgia for our former democracy.

Three weeks after the *New York Times Magazine* published Ignatieff's torture overture, it published a cover story on May 23 by Susan Sontag renouncing torture.[13] With apparent embarrassment that it had just published the Ignatieff piece, the magazine somewhat self-consciously printed a torture disclaimer across its May 23 cover to the effect that "the photographs are not us." This resembled President Bush's self-serving disclaimer that the torture photographs from Abu Ghraib did not represent the American people.

Unlike Ignatieff, Sontag recited the laws that prohibit torture with precision and respect, including the 1984 Convention Against Torture and Other Cruel, Inhuman or Degrading Treatment or Punishment, which Ignatieff never mentioned in his May 2 article. Sontag also noted that the Convention stipulates "no exceptional circumstances whatso-ever, whether a state of war or a threat of war, internal political instability or any other public emergency, may be invoked as a justifi-cation of torture." This effectively negates on legal grounds Ignatieff's argument that coercive interrogations should be formally integrated into US counterterrorism policy.

In addition, post April 28, Ignatieff's lesser-evil proposals are to the right even of President Bush and Attorney General Ashcroft. For example, on June 10, President Bush stated: "What I have authorized," with regard to the interrogation of detainees, "is that we stay within U.S. law." Bush also said:

> I'm going to say it one more time. In fact, maybe I can be more clear. The instructions went out to our people to adhere to law. That ought to comfort you. We're a nation of law. We adhere to laws. We have laws on the books. You might look at those laws, and that might provide comfort for you. And those were the instructions from me to the government.[14]

Although this statement likely reflected a foxhole conversion by the president to the rule of law, given his political and legal troubles with respect to the torture scandal, and although the president's definition of "law" in this statement almost certainly reflected the diluted legal standards of his government lawyers with respect to torture, it is nevertheless important that the president publicly reaffirmed in principle the rule of law in the United States with respect to US counterterrorism policy and torturing detainees—which, in this instance, is more law-oriented than what Ignatieff proposed.

Ignatieff is also somewhat to the right of the public statements of Attorney General John Ashcroft, who said in congressional testimony on June 8 2004 that, "First of all, this administration opposes torture," and "I condemn torture."[15] Although the administration's unacceptably limited notions of torture are again at issue, this statement, taken at face value, sets a moral and legal standard against which the administration's conduct with respect to torture must be investigated and judged. This is more than what Ignatieff proposed, given his recommendations to stray from national and international law.

Like Bush and Ashcroft—and Kenneth Pollack when no nuclear-weapons program in Iraq was found—Ignatieff was forced to change course after the Abu Ghraib torture scandal broke on April 28. Writing in the *New York Times Magazine* on June 27 as if he had never prescribed coercive interrogations of detainees in US custody, including prolonged hooding, and as if he had not proposed that the US government ignore or violate international and federal law in its war against terrorism, Ignatieff criticized the president's lawyers for neglecting applicable law with respect to torture:

> The memoranda from White House counsel, and from Department of Justice and Department of Defense lawyers, gave new meaning to Robert Lowell's phrase "savage servility." Their argument that "the president's inherent constitutional authority to manage a military campaign" rendered the United States' obligations under the Torture Convention "inapplicable" to interrogations conducted pursuant to his command left you wondering if they had ever heard of the Nuremberg tribunal. You might have thought that after Justice Robert Jackson's great opening speech at the war crimes trials of Nazi leaders in Nuremberg, no American lawyer would ever dare to use obedience to superior authority as justification for inhuman acts of abuse. In the memos that filled the pages of our newspapers, there was more than servility. There was also a terrible forgetting.[16]

This statement is fine when it is read outside the context of (a) Ignatieff's earlier support for the invasion of Iraq, which was a "war of aggression," "a crime against peace," and "the supreme international crime" under the Nuremberg precedent; (b) Ignatieff's proposal that the president be given the power to preventively detain US citizens and coercively interrogate detainees in US custody; (c) Ignatieff's proposal to lay aside international and national laws, including the Torture Convention, that prohibit torture and cruel and inhuman treatment of detainees, and (d) Ignatieff's own "terrible forgetting" of the international and national laws that prohibit much if not most of what he proposed in his three previous cover stories for the *New York Times Magazine* with respect to Iraq and US counterterrorism policy. Read in this context, the passage cited above resembles the post–April 28 public conversions by President Bush and Attorney General Ashcroft.

Commenting on June 27 specifically about Abu Ghraib, Ignatieff wrote:

> At Abu Ghraib, America paid the price for American exceptionalism, the idea that America is too noble, too special, too great to actually obey international treaties like the Torture Convention or international bodies like the Red Cross. Enthralled by narcissism and deluded by servility, American lawyers forgot their own Constitution and its peremptory prohibition of cruel and unusual punishment. Any American administration, especially this one, needs to learn that in paying "decent respect to the opinions of mankind"—Jefferson's phrase—America also pays respect to its better self.

For someone who wrote a little more than a month earlier that to protect ourselves from terrorism we may have to stray from national and international laws in an unprecedented manner, this passage, with its refusal to acknowledge these earlier views, is nothing short of remarkable.

After April 28, the *Times* published a good deal of excellent journalism on Abu Ghraib and the wider practice and policy of the United States toward detainees in its custody. This coverage for the most part to date (June 2004) sought to expose government misconduct and deception, to enlighten the citizenry with respect to such conduct, and favorably referenced laws that prohibited torture and cruel, inhuman, and degrading treatment of detainees.[17] The result generally was sustained high-quality journalism.

To the extent that the *Times* failed to make a serious effort to expose government deception and misconduct, and neglected to incorporate even basic rules and principles of international law into its coverage of Iraq policy before April 28, its coverage was deplorable. The May 2 cover story in the *Times* magazine by Michael Ignatieff, who argued that the US government should "traffic" in the "lesser evils" of preventive detentions, coercive interrogations, preemptive assassinations, and pre-emptive wars in violation of laws that prohibited this conduct, was arguably the low point of the *Times'* coverage of the Bush adminis-tration's post-September 11 foreign policy.

6

INTERVENTIONISM AND DUE DILIGENCE: OVERTHROWING VENEZUELA'S PRESIDENT

On April 11 2002, the democratically elected president of Venezuela was overthrown by a group of military officers who installed a prominent Venezuelan businessman as president. The Bush administration announced that day that it supported the military coup. Two days later, on April 13, the lead editorial in the *New York Times* announced that it also supported the coup, arguing that it was a victory for democracy:

> With yesterday's resignation of President Hugo Chávez, Venezuelan democracy is no longer threatened by a would-be dictator. Mr. Chávez, a ruinous demagogue, stepped down after the military intervened and handed power to a respected business leader, Pedro Carmona. ... Rightly, [Chávez's] removal was a purely Venezuelan affair.[1]

Since nearly every state in Latin America, from Mexico to Chile, denounced the military coup and criticized the Bush administration for supporting it, the *Times* editorial backing the coup was to the right of every official statement given by every government in the Western hemisphere, except the United States.

The *Times* editorial page also accepted without qualification the claim made by Venezuelan military plotters and the Bush administration that Chávez had resigned. However, when Chávez returned to power on April 14—after only three days, and following mass protests and a military counter-coup supporting him—it was clear that he had not resigned, and that the *Times*' April 13 editorial, in addition to supporting an illegal coup attempt, had misreported an important fact pertaining to the status of the elected Venezuelan president.

In a tight spot due to the quick reversal, the *Times* editorial page withdrew its support for the coup in an April 16 editorial, and reversed its claim that Chávez had resigned:

In his three years in office, Mr. Chávez has been such a divisive and demagogic leader that his forced departure last week drew applause at home and in Washington. That reaction, which we shared, overlooked the undemocratic manner in which he was removed. Forcibly unseating a democratically elected leader, no matter how badly he has performed, is never something to cheer.[2]

Thus, the *Times* changed "yesterday's resignation of President Hugo Chávez" (the April 13 editorial) to "forcibly unseating a democratically elected leader" (the April 16 editorial), and changed "democracy is no longer threatened" thanks to the coup to "we ... overlooked the undemocratic manner in which [Chávez] was removed."

The claim in the April 13 editorial that "[Chávez's] removal was a purely Venezuelan affair" is also of interest. Given the long history of US intervention in Latin America, why would the *Times* editorial page let the Bush administration off the hook so quickly, and, after only two days, how would the editorial page know, one way or the other, whether the administration had played a role in the coup or not?

In fact, an April 16 front-page story in the *Times* reported that "senior members of the Bush administration met several times in recent months with leaders of a coalition that ousted the Venezuelan president, Hugo Chávez, for two days last weekend, and agreed with them that he should be removed from office, administration officials said today."[3] The next day, April 17, the *Times* reported that "a senior [Bush] administration official [Otto Reich] was in contact with the man [Pedro Carmona] who succeeded Mr. Chávez on the very day he took office," and that

Mr. Carmona, who heads Venezuela's largest business association, was one of numerous critics of Mr. Chávez to call on [Bush] administration officials in recent weeks. Officials from the White House, State Department and Pentagon, among others, were hosts to a stream of Chávez opponents, some of them seeking help in removing him from office.[4]

And on April 25 the *Times* reported:

In the past year, the United States channeled hundreds of thousands of dollars in grants to American and Venezuelan groups opposed to President

Hugo Chávez, including the labor groups whose protests led to the Venezuelan president's brief ouster this month.[5]

These and other news reports about a US connection to persons and organizations involved in the coup undermine the editorial page's claim that the coup "was a purely Venezuelan affair." The issue here is not whether the editorial page should have known, two days after the coup, about any evidence of US involvement; rather, it's that the editorial page asserted that the United States was not involved in the coup before it could have known whether it was or was not.

The *Times* April 13 editorial also reported that "after the military intervened" it handed power to "a respected business leader, Pedro Carmona." By itself, this is an open-minded description of someone who had just come to power without any constitutional authority as a result of a military coup that had overthrown an elected president. Moreover, the editorial page published this benign portrait of the newly installed president of Venezuela in an editorial on April 13; this was after Carmona had "dissolve[d] the National Assembly and fire[d] all members of the Supreme Court" at 5:45 p.m. the previous day, according to a chronology of events published by the *New York Times*.[6] So many Venezuelans were offended by Carmona's behavior that "the respected business leader" was driven from power almost before the ink had dried on the *Times* April 13 editorial, and fled the country a short time later.[7]

Given these developments, one must ask how it came to pass that the editorial page of the *New York Times* would support a military coup overthrowing an elected president in Venezuela, while reporting prematurely that the ousted president had resigned and that the United States had nothing to do with the coup. Even without knowing the facts at the time, and even if it didn't support Chávez's policies in Venezuela, the principle that should have guided the *Times* April 13 editorial was articulated by many political leaders throughout Latin America, including President Alejandro Toledo of Peru, who stated, while opposing the coup, "I have been and am a critic of many of the characteristics of the government of Hugo Chávez. ... We are not defending the democratic characteristics of a particular government, we are defending the principle of the rule of law."[8]

In this case the rule of law refers to the political inviolability of representative democracy and its constitutional institutions, and the fundamental norm of nonintervention in the domestic affairs of states, as established, for example, in the Charter of the Organization of American

States (OAS Charter),[9] and recently reaffirmed in the Inter-American Democratic Charter (IADC), which was negotiated in part on behalf of the United States by Secretary of State Colin Powell. The very first paragraph of the IADC states that it

> recognizes that representative democracy is indispensable for the stability, peace, and development of the region, and that one of the purposes of the OAS is to promote and consolidate representative democracy, with due respect for the principle of nonintervention.[10]

The editorial page apparently completely overlooked these fundamental legal norms when on April 13 it announced its support of the military coup in Venezuela. It also ignored the apparent contradiction between Secretary Powell reaffirming the principles of representative democracy and nonintervention in the IADC in September 2001, and the recess appointment a few months later by President Bush of Otto Reich as the chief policy maker in the State Department for Latin America.[11]

In the 1980s, Reich ran a secret propaganda operation inside the United States in support of the Reagan administration's efforts to overthrow the Sandinista government in Nicaragua.[12] A government investigation declared that Reich's domestic propaganda operation was illegal under US law, and the US Congress closed it down.[13] Reich then became US ambassador to Venezuela from 1986 to 1989, and knows the country and its major players well. He was also the "senior Bush administration official" reportedly in touch with Carmona on April 11, the day Carmona took office as president of Venezuela.[14]

The recall-election effort in Venezuela to unseat Chávez began with the failed April 2002 coup. Some of the same opposition groups involved in the coup attempt have not stopped trying to remove Chávez from power. To this effect, the *New York Times* reported in August 2003:

> Venezuelan opposition groups today presented election officials with 3.2 million signatures calling for the removal of President Hugo Chávez, the first step in a new effort to oust the leftist leader through a constitutional recall referendum. . . .
>
> The Bush administration has strongly supported a referendum to resolve the political tumult in Venezuela, an oil-rich country of 25 million. Stability in Venezuela is crucial to American policy makers, who see the Andean country as a critical component in the supply chain of oil to the United States.

Under the Venezuelan Constitution, a referendum is allowed halfway through the president's six-year term. Mr. Chávez, who was re-elected in 2000, reached that milestone on Tuesday [August 19].

For an opposition led by a haphazard coalition of big businessmen, labor groups and news organization owners, today's action was the latest stage in a 19-month effort aimed at toppling Mr. Chávez. The opposition failed to remove the president with a coup in April last year and four national strikes that left the economy, Latin America's fourth largest, in tatters.[15]

The Bush administration's interest in Venezuela's oil is nearly as keen as its interest in Iraq's. In an August 2003 op-ed piece in the *New York Times*, Manik Talwani, a professor of geophysics at Rice University, wrote "the largest deposits of oil in the world are not in the Middle East—or in Russia or off West Africa or in the Caspian Sea area. They are in two Western Hemisphere countries: Venezuela and Canada." Talwani wrote that industry analysts estimate that Venezuela has 300 billion barrels of extractable crude oil. By comparison, the United States imports about 4 billion barrels of oil a year, remaining US domestic oil reserves are estimated at 28 billion barrels, and the Arctic National Wildlife Refuge in Alaska has an estimated 4 billion to 12 billion barrels of recoverable oil.[16]

In its editorial supporting the coup attempt against Chávez, the *Times* clearly recognized Venezuelan oil as a key US foreign-policy interest, and came close to justifying an oil-related rationale for the coup: "Washington has a strong stake in Venezuela's [post-Chávez] recovery. Caracas now provides 15 percent of American oil imports, and with sounder policies could provide more."[17] Though the *Times* editorial page bothered to look up the percentage of oil supplied to the United States by Venezuela in the immediate aftermath of the coup, it practiced no such due diligence toward the US State Department Inspector General's report on the Bush administration's involvement in the coup.

The Inspector General's report on the role of the State Department and the US embassy in the brief ouster of President Hugo Chávez renders a picture of Bush administration complicity in the coup—a determination awkwardly avoided by the Inspector General and overlooked altogether by the *Times*.

Issued on July 29 2002, the report was requested by US Senator Christopher Dodd (D–Conn.), who had asked for "a review of U.S. policy and actions during the weekend of April 12–14, 2002, when

Venezuelan president Hugo Chávez was briefly ousted from power, and the six-month period preceding that weekend."[18]

While concluding that the Bush administration "worked to support democracy and constitutionality in Venezuela" and played no role in the coup, the Inspector General, as we shall see, modified a key question from Senator Dodd about the administration's role that redirected the intended focus of the senator's question while relieving the Inspector General of the burden of an honest response. This permitted the Inspector General to insert the stock reply—repeated ritually throughout the report and later in US State Department press releases[19]—that US policy toward Venezuela "supported democracy and constitutionality."

Meanwhile, the Inspector General accepted the statements of Bush administration officials at face value (the Inspector General apparently interviewed no one under oath), and used such statements throughout the report to corroborate his conclusion that the administration sup-ported only "democracy and constitutionality" in Venezuela. In fact, the Inspector General interviewed only US officials from the Bush administration and the National Endowment for Democracy (NED), explaining:

> Purposely, we did not interview any Venezuelans, either supporters or opponents of the Chávez government. We were concerned that doing so could complicate the work of Embassy Caracas [the US embassy in Caracas] in dealing with the Venezuelan government and its opponents, especially at a time when the political situation in Venezuela remains so volatile.

Furthermore, while the Inspector General, Clark Kent Irvin, reported that "OIG [Office of Inspector General] examined almost 2000 docu-ments" and "obtained reams of electronic data from the [State] Department's information systems, including those located at Embassy Caracas and in the Western Hemispheric Affairs (WHA) Bureau in Washington," he also reported:

> We note that there are some apparent gaps in the electronic information. For example, at this time, we are not sure we have all e-mails from the embassy's classified internal system. According to embassy information technology staff, they did not have enough recording tape to back up their systems fully; instead, they used the same tapes over and over again, and as a result, data from that time period may have been lost.

While the Inspector General reported he "was able to obtain some of this information from other sources," it appears that he was referring not to any recovery of the actual erased e-mail messages, but to the acquisition of information from other data sources about the period under review. He also reported no investigation of the erased e-mails, and presumably did not conduct one.

Finally, while the Inspector General reported "it's clear that NED, Department of Defense (DOD), and other U.S. assistance programs provided training, institution building, and other support to individuals and organizations understood to be actively involved in the brief ouster of the Chávez government," he concluded "we found no evidence that this support directly contributed, or was intended to contribute, to that event," and that "OIG found nothing to indicate that assistance programs in Venezuela ... were inconsistent with U.S. law or policy."

Upon review, we will show that the Inspector General's investigation and report were carefully tailored to reach these conclusions, to have these conclusions reported in the executive summary of the report, and to have the same conclusions reported in the US news media based on the customary skimming of such summaries that the news media usually devote to such reports. This is how the *Times* covered the Inspector General's report on the Venezuelan coup—consistent with its non-crusading editorial policy. Despite some good early news reporting on the coup by *Times* reporter Christopher Marquis,[20] its overall coverage suffered from an absence of due diligence to get to the bottom of what happened in Venezuela in April 2002.

In a letter dated May 3 2002, Senator Dodd, who at the time chaired the subcommittee on Western Hemispheric Affairs of the Senate Foreign Relations Committee, submitted a list of questions to the State Department's Inspector General concerning the Bush administration's role in the April coup. Pursuant to these questions, the Inspector General conducted a review of US policy toward Venezuela, and issued a report that was released on July 29 2002.

Each of Senator Dodd's five questions to the Inspector General is reproduced below, as are each of the Inspector General's responses as they were published in the executive summary of his report. Together, these questions and answers constitute the entire substantive portion of the executive summary of the report.

Senator Dodd's First Question: "What actions did Embassy Caracas and the Department of State take in response to the events of April 12–14? Here, I request a detailed chronology of the course of events and the response by [US] Embassy and Department officials, including contacts between Embassy and Department officials and the interim government and its supporters."

The Inspector General's Response: "Throughout the course of the weekend of April 12–14, Embassy Caracas and the [US State] Department worked to support democracy and constitutionality in Venezuela. Based on credible reports that (a) pro-Chávez supporters had fired on a huge crowd of peaceful Chávez opponents, killing some and wounding others; (b) the Chávez government had attempted to keep the media from reporting on these developments; and, bowing to the pressures, (c) Chávez had fired his vice president and cabinet and then resigned, the Department criticized the Chávez government for using violent means to suppress peaceful demonstrators and for interfering with the press. Both the [State] Department and the embassy worked behind the scenes to persuade the interim government to hold early elections and to legitimize its provisional rule by obtaining the sanction of the National Assembly and the Supreme Court. When, contrary to U.S. advice, the interim government dissolved the assembly and the court and took other undemocratic actions, the Department worked through the Organization of American States (OAS) to condemn those steps and to restore democracy and constitutionality in Venezuela."

Our Comments (Friel and Falk): The Inspector General stated throughout the report that the State Department and its embassy in Caracas "worked to support democracy and constitutionality in Venezuela." But this claim is meaningless without a definition of "democracy and constitutionality" as it applies to US policy toward Venezuela, and the Inspector General made no effort to define these terms in the report. Also, by denouncing "the Chávez government for using violent means to suppress peaceful demonstrations and for interfering with the press," the Inspector General situated disputed facts within an excessively narrow narrative to convey a misleading impression of coup-related events. The Inspector General's account, for example, could have mentioned that many witnesses reported that pro- and anti-Chávez forces fired at each other, that the pivotal pre-coup demonstration was organized by US-supported individuals and organizations that wanted Chávez overthrown, and, as the Inspector General reported, many of these people had discussed plans to overthrow Chávez on many occasions for many months in the presence of US State Department and embassy officials prior to April 11.

Facts supporting this account of the coup were widely reported. For example, on April 25, two weeks after the short-lived coup, the *New York Times* reported:

> In the past year, the United States channeled hundreds of thousands of dollars in grants to American and Venezuelan groups opposed to President Hugo Chávez, including the labor groups whose protests led to the Venezuelan president's brief ouster this month. The funds were provided by the National Endowment for Democracy, a nonprofit agency created and financed by Congress. As conditions deteriorated in Venezuela and Mr. Chávez clashed with various business, labor and media groups, the endowment stepped up its assistance, quadrupling its budget for Venezuela to more than $877,000.[21]

Furthermore, the Inspector General reported beyond the executive summary that "during the period in question [the six-month pre-coup period specified by Senator Dodd], the embassy's and Department's contacts were heavily weighted toward individuals and groups known to be opponents of the Chávez government," that "neither the [State] Department nor the [U.S.] embassy [in Caracas] sought out Chávez supporters in or out of government in any aggressive, organized fashion," and that "the opposition's willingness to talk to Embassy Caracas in detail about their plans against President Chávez and the embassy's willingness to listen may have left doubts about the sincerity of our professed opposition to undemocratic and unconstitutional means of removing President Chávez."

Furthermore, while Senator Dodd had requested "a detailed chronology of the course of events" of April 12–14, the Inspector General provided no such chronology in the unclassified published report. Rather, he provided a chronology for the classified unpublished report, "based upon classified or administratively controlled documents, and includ[ing] information and names protected under national security and privacy laws and regulations." In other words, the Inspector General appeared to classify the chronology of a possible US role in the coup as a US national security secret.

The Inspector General also reported that the US State Department and embassy "worked behind the scenes to persuade the interim government to hold early elections and to legitimize its provisional rule." This is what Bush administration officials told the Inspector General. However, at least some of the details about what the administration did behind the scenes to legitimize the provisional rule of the coup plotters were classified by the Inspector General. Furthermore, why were Bush administration officials working behind the scenes with people, who themselves had worked behind the scenes, to overthrow the democratically elected president of Venezuela? Why did the Bush administration seek "to legitimize the provisional rule" of the people who had illegally overthrown the democratically elected president of Venezuela? Furthermore, the provisional, US-backed government that seized power by unconstitutional means also unconstitutionally suspended the Venezuelan Constitution, dismissed the Venezuelan National Assembly, and fired the Venezuelan Supreme Court. This occurred at 5:45 p.m. on April 12 without public criticism from the Bush administration for the next 30 hours of the provisional government's brief existence. This fact alone undermines the Bush administration's claim, repeated by the Inspector General, that it supported democracy and constitutionality in Venezuela.

Finally, once the provisional government had collapsed, the Bush administration claimed it had privately counseled the government's head—Mr Carmona—at a 9 a.m. breakfast meeting on April 13 to reinstate the National Assembly and the Supreme Court. The Inspector General supported this claim. However, even assuming some merit in privately counseling Carmona to this effect in the absence of a public condemnation, the Inspector General conspicuously declined to publish the chronology of coup-related events, including "contacts between Embassy and Department officials and the interim government" that Senator Dodd had requested with the intent of clarifying the role of the Bush administration in the coup.

Senator Dodd's Second Question: "What was U.S. policy toward Venezuela during the six months preceding the weekend in question? By what means was this policy expressed by the embassy and the Department? Were the actions of the U.S. government—both in the six months before the weekend and during that weekend—consistent with U.S. policy in support of the Inter-American Democratic Charter?"

The Inspector General's Response: "In brief, the policy of the United States toward Venezuela during the operative period was support for democracy and constitutionality. The Department and the embassy urged the Chávez government to conduct itself in a democratic and constitutional fashion, and the Department and the embassy urged opponents of the Chávez government to act within the limits of the constitution of Venezuela. This policy was expressed orally in numerous meetings and occasional speeches and press statements throughout the period. The policy was fully consistent with the Inter-American Democratic Charter (IADC), the OAS agreement designed to promote democracy and constitutionality in the Americas."

Our Comments: The ritualistic repetition of this phrase—"support for democracy and constitutionality"—by the Inspector General functions throughout his report as a way of avoiding substantive answers to Senator Dodd's questions. One might ask how the Inspector General knew that "support for democracy and constitutionality" was US policy toward Venezuela during this period. The Inspector General states that he knows this because "this policy was expressed orally in numerous meetings and occasional speeches and press statements [by Bush administration officials] throughout the period." But one must ask about the point of an investigation that simply takes the subjects of that investigation at their word. What if Bush administration officials in Venezuela and Washington were simply repeating a "talking points" policy line to the effect that the United States supported democracy and constitutionality in Venezuela? What if these officials were not telling the truth? Any investigator, obviously, would cross-check such statements with other persons functioning in other capacities who may have been likewise or similarly involved, such as officials within the Chávez administration and other Venezuelans, including those involved in the coup (on both sides), or who were recipients of US political and financial support and who also were involved in the coup. But the Inspector General apparently did no such checking.

What about any documentary evidence to support the claim that US policy toward Venezuela supported "democracy and constitutionality?" Here the Inspector General resorted to a well-worn and not altogether persuasive assertion that he exhaustively reviewed thousands of documents and found nothing. In this regard, the Inspector General wrote: "during the course of this review, OIG examined almost 2,000 documents" and "obtained reams of electronic data from the [State] Department's information systems, including those located at Embassy Caracas and in the Western Hemispheric Affairs (WHA) Bureau in Washington." This review of paper documents and electronic data was meant to support the Inspector General's claim that his investigation was thorough. However, the Inspector General also noted without concern that classified e-mail messages from the US embassy in Caracas had been taped over by embassy employees and "may have been lost." Thus, at least some classified embassy e-mails were intentionally or unintentionally erased, and the Inspector General provided no indication that he investigated the erased e-mails. This is potentially significant. The recovery by congressional Iran–Contra investigators of e-mail messages that Reagan administration officials had attempted to erase revealed illegal US activity in Central America that had been previously denied by those officials.

The notion that US policy in Venezuela supported "democracy and constitutionality" over the six-month period referenced by Senator Dodd is questionable for other reasons. In his expanded response to Senator Dodd's second question, the Inspector General reported:

> Each U.S. diplomatic mission is required to prepare annual Mission Performance Plans (MPP). The MPP covers planning for the fiscal year (FY) two years ahead. These plans set out U.S. national interests in relation to the mission's host country, strategic goals, etc., and identifies the sections and agencies in the mission which are to deal with each area of interest and goal.

The Inspector General noted that "promoting democracy" is a low priority for US diplomatic missions in an already democratic country, and that in the MPP for Venezuela in FY 2002, which was prepared in 2000, that is, during the Clinton administration, "promoting democracy was ranked in fourth place." Because Hugo Chávez was elected president of Venezuela in 1998, the Clinton administration's MPP for its last year in office (2000) ranked promoting democracy as a low priority for its diplomatic mission in Venezuela. However, according to the Inspector General, "In the FY 2003 plan, prepared in 2001, democracy moved to the highest priority." Thus, when the Bush administration and its hard-right cadre of officials assumed power, the so-called "promotion of democracy" agenda for Venezuela went from fourth place to first place.

Rather than consider this priority upgrade as potential evidence that a right-wing US administration might be interested in undermining or overthrowing a left-wing Latin American president, the Inspector General viewed the upgrade through a different lens, and stated: "This dramatic reordering of priorities clearly reflected the growing concern of US officials about the various anti-democratic actions deemed by the United States to have been taken by the Chávez government." This statement provides some indication of what US officials and the Inspector General meant when they argued that US policy supported "democracy" in Venezuela. If the elected president of Venezuela is *a priori* anti-democratic in the minds of Bush administration officials, his overthrow would "support democracy."

While the Inspector General's report is laden throughout with his own finding that US policy toward Venezuela supports "democracy and constitutionality," he refers to identical statements by the Bush administration as "ritualistic," "mantra-like," and a "policy line." Just as Bush administration officials, quoted in the Inspector General's report, hold unwaveringly to the "policy line," so does the Inspector General, despite at least a few critical press reports and evidence in his own report that the Bush administration was involved in Chávez's overthrow.

Referring to the Bush administration's claims that its policy toward Venezuela supported only "democracy and constitutionality," the Inspector General wrote:

> We found no evidence of any deviation from this policy line by U.S. officials, publicly or privately. A New York Times article of April 16, 2002, quoted an unnamed "Defense Department official" as saying, "We were not discouraging people. We were sending informal, subtle signals that we don't like this guy [Chávez]. We didn't say, 'No, don't you dare,' and we weren't advocates saying, 'Here's some arms; we'll help you overthrow this guy.' We weren't doing that." If there was any such DOD official, despite our best efforts, OIG has not been able definitively to identify him or her. If any such unspoken signals of support for removing President Chávez unde-mocratically or unconstitutionally were sent by Department or embassy officials, we found no evidence of it.

This is the only reference to press reports contradicting the policy line, though many other press reports could have been referenced, including a more incriminating quote from a report by Christopher Marquis in the same day's *New York Times* that the Inspector General chose to ignore: "Senior members of the Bush administration met several times in recent months with leaders of a coalition that ousted the Venezuelan president, Hugo Chávez, for two days last weekend, and agreed with them that he should be removed from office."[22] But this report, and other such press reports, were not cited in the Inspector General's report.

Senator Dodd's Third Question: "Did [US] embassy or [US State] Department officials meet with opponents of the Chávez government in the six months preceding the weekend in question? If so, with whom, with what frequency, and at what level? Were any such meetings consistent with normal embassy or Department practice?"

The Inspector General's Response: "Embassy and Department officials frequently met with individuals and groups opposed to President Chávez during the operative period. These meetings took place at all levels of the Department and the embassy. Such meetings are consistent with normal embassy and Department practice throughout the world."

Our Comments: The Inspector General's fuller response to this question not included in the executive summary indicated that "Department and Embassy Caracas officials during this period met frequently, at high levels, with opponents of the Chávez government," and that these meetings "involved figures in the Venezuelan government, the military, political parties, non-governmental organizations, labor organizations, business organizations, the media, and religious groups." In other words, State Department and US embassy officials met "frequently" with virtually every opposition segment involved in the coup.

The Inspector General also reported that "during the period in question, the embassy's and Department's contacts were heavily weighted toward individuals and groups known to be opponents of the Chávez government." While the report states "this is explained in part by the fact that supporters of President Chávez tended to view the U.S. government as unsympathetic to them, and accordingly, they did not seek out contact with U.S. officials," the report also states "it is clear, though, that neither the Department nor the embassy sought out Chávez supporters in or out of government in any aggressive, organized fashion."

The report continues:

> The opposition's willingness to talk to Embassy Caracas in detail about their plans against President Chávez and the embassy's willingness to listen may have left doubts about the sincerity of our professed opposition to undemocratic and unconstitutional means of removing President Chávez. We do not mean to suggest that the embassy should have avoided meeting with the opposition; but the frequency of such contacts, and the relative lack of contact with pro-Chávez elements, may have led some Venezuelans to question whether the United States was really neutral as regards Venezuelan internal politics.

While the Inspector General reported that State Department and US embassy officials met almost exclusively with anti-Chávez individuals and groups, including the Venezuelan military and other organizations that were directly involved in the coup, he chose not to identify these individuals or groups in the unclassified report. Rather, the Inspector General wrote: "So as not to inhibit the [U.S.] embassy in any way in its necessarily ongoing efforts to deal with both the Chávez government and its opponents, and in accordance with U.S. laws and regulations governing the protection of intelligence information, we have limited to the report's classified annex the identities of those with whom U.S. officials met."

One must ask, why would the identities of the individuals and organizations with whom US officials met in support of democracy and constitutionality, which is understood to be an inherently open and non-secretive process, be classified under US laws protecting intelligence information?

Senator Dodd's Fourth Question: "Did opponents of the Chávez government, if any, who met with embassy or Department officials request or seek the support of the U.S. government for actions aimed at removing or undermining that government? If so, what was the response of embassy or Department officials to such requests? How were any such responses conveyed, orally or in writing?"

The Inspector General's Response: "Taking the question to be whether, in any such meetings, Chávez opponents sought help from the embassy or the Department for removing or undermining the Chávez government through undemocratic or unconstitutional means, the answer is no. Chávez opponents would instead inform their U.S. interlocutors of their (or, more frequently, others') aims, intentions, and/or plans. United States officials consistently responded to such declarations with statements opposing any effort to remove or undermine the Chávez government through undemocratic and unconstitutional means. These responses were conveyed orally."

Our Comments: Note that the point of inquiry in Senator Dodd's question is whether Venezuelan opposition groups sought, and whether the Bush administration provided, support for "removing or undermining" the Chávez government. Note also that the Inspector General avoided answering Senator Dodd's question by changing the question. Thus, the Inspector General modified the point of inquiry from whether the Bush administration supported "removing or undermining" the Chávez government to whether it supported "removing or undermining the Chávez government through undemocratic or unconstitutional means." Having changed Senator Dodd's question, the

Inspector General was able to answer the question in a way that fit the administration's alibi—that its policy toward Venezuela supported democracy and constitutionalism. At a minimum, this would appear to be unethical behavior on the part of the State Department's Inspector General. A more disturbing consideration is that the Inspector General changed the question to cover up the Bush administration's illegal involvement in "removing or undermining" the Chávez government in Venezuela.

Senator Dodd's Fifth Question: "Were U.S. assistance programs in Venezuela during the six months prior to the weekend of April 12–14—either through 'normal' assistance channels or through programs funded by the National Endowment for Democracy—carried out in a manner consistent with U.S. law and policy?"

The Inspector General's Response: "OIG found nothing to indicate that U.S. assistance programs in Venezuela, including those funded by the National Endowment for Democracy (NED), were inconsistent with U.S. law or policy. While it is clear that NED, Department of Defense (DOD), and other U.S. assistance programs provided training, institution building, and other support to individuals and organizations understood to be actively involved in the brief ouster of the Chávez government, we found no evidence that this support directly contributed, or was intended to contribute, to that event."

Our Comments: Given (a) that Senator Dodd's line of questioning implicates international law and the norm of non-intervention in the internal affairs of sovereign states, including the OAS Charter and the Inter-American Democratic Charter; (b) that Article VI(2) of the US Constitution states that "all treaties made, or which shall be made, under the authority of the United States, shall be the supreme law of the land"; (c) that the OAS Charter clearly falls within the definition of such treaties under Article VI(2) of the Constitution; and (d) that US obligations and responsibilities under the OAS Charter and IADC are therefore part of "US law" as referred to by Senator Dodd and the Inspector General, it would be the case that any US assistance and NED-funded programs that knowingly went to individuals and groups in Venezuela, who were planning to overthrow President Chávez, would violate the OAS Charter and IADC, the US Constitution and, therefore, US law.

In this context, consider the following obligations of the United States under the OAS Charter in its policy toward Venezuela:

Article 2

The Organization of American States ... proclaims the following essential purposes. ...

b) To promote and consolidate representative democracy, with due respect for the principle of non-intervention.

Article 3

The American States reaffirm the following principles:

a) International law is the standard of conduct of States in their reciprocal relations;

b) International order consists essentially of respect for the personality, sovereignty, and independence of States, and the faithful fulfillment of obligations derived from treaties and other sources of international law;

c) Good faith shall govern the relations between States;

d) Every State has the right to choose, without external interference, its political, economic, and social system and to organize itself in the best way suited to it, and has the duty to abstain from intervening in the affairs of another State.

Given these standards, the Inspector General's assertions that the Bush administration's interventions in Venezuela supported "democracy and constitutionality," and that such interventions were therefore legal under US law, would not be correct if these interventions:

(a) did not "promote and consolidate representative democracy" in Venezuela, which they did not appear to do, given that much of the political and financial assistance given by the Bush administration to individuals and groups in Venezuela were ultimately used to help overthrow the democratically elected president of Venezuela;

(b) did not respect "the principle of non-intervention," which they did not appear to do, given the fact that the Bush administration publicly supported the overthrow of President Chávez;

(c) did not constitute a "good faith" relationship between the Bush administration and the democratically elected Chávez government, which would be difficult for the Inspector General to assert, given his admission that US State Department and embassy officials met exclusively with opponents of the elected president of Venezuela, including individuals and groups admittedly involved in the April 2002 coup;

(d) did not respect Venezuela's "right to choose, without external interference, its political, economic, and social system," and

(e) did not "abstain from intervening" in Venezuela's internal affairs.

In addition to his misleading and inaccurate finding that the Bush administration violated no US law with respect to its involvement in the coup attempt in Venezuela, the Inspector General provided other specific examples of almost certain US violations of the OAS Charter without identifying them as such. For example, the Inspector General reported that the US National Endowment for Democracy awarded $150,000 through the American Center for International Labor Solidarity (ACILS), one of four core NED grantees, to the Confederation of Venezuelan Workers (through FY 2002) to "promote democratic reforms at all levels of government." On April 25, two weeks after the April 11 coup, Christopher Marquis of the *New York Times* reported:

> [T]he Confederation of Venezuelan Workers led the work stoppages that galvanized the opposition to Mr. Chávez. The union's leader, Carlos Ortega, worked closely with Pedro Carmona Estanga, the businessman who briefly took over from Mr. Chávez, in challenging the government.[23]

The Inspector General also reported that the National Endowment for Democracy had awarded $340,000 to the International Republican Institute (IRI), another of the core grantees, to "encourag[e] the development of democratic structures and practices" in Venezuela, and "to develop ... civil society groups and individual citizens that demonstrate a willingness to interact with political parties in planned activities." On April 12 2002, the day after what appeared at the time to be a successful coup in Venezuela, the head of IRI, George Folsom, issued a public statement supporting the coup, that read in part:

> Last night, led by every sector of civil society, the Venezuelan people rose up to defend democracy in their country. ... The Institute has served as a bridge between the nation's political parties and all civil society groups to help Venezuelans forge a new democratic future, based on accountability, rule of law and sound democratic institutions. We stand ready to continue our partnership with the courageous Venezuelan people.[24]

On April 25, the *New York Times* reported that "the institute [IRI] has close ties to the Bush administration, which had also embraced the short-lived takeover," and, "in an interview, Mr. Folsom said discussions at the institute on Venezuela involved finding ways to remove Mr. Chávez by constitutional means only."[25]

Thus, while the Inspector General reported finding "no evidence that NED funds were intended to contribute to the events of that weekend

[April 12–14]," the head of a core grantee of NED funds stated shortly after the coup that his institute had sought Chávez's removal.

The *Times*' total coverage of the Inspector General's report consisted of 158 words, reprinted in full below:

Venezuela Inquiry Clears U.S. Aides

By The New York Times

Washington, July 29—The State Department's inspector general has concluded that department officials did not act inappropriately during the brief ouster of the Venezuelan president, Hugo Chávez, in April.

Clark Kent Irvin, the inspector general, released preliminary findings today that department officials sent a consistent message of support for democracy in Venezuela and discouraged talk of removing Mr. Chávez by force. "The department and the embassy urged the Chávez government to conduct itself in a democratic and constitutional fashion," and they urged government opponents "to act within the limits of the Constitution of Venezuela."

Senator Christopher J. Dodd, a Connecticut Democrat, requested the report after administration officials set off an outcry by appearing to embrace Mr. Chávez's ouster and establishing contacts with his self-declared successor.

"I requested this report because questions surrounding this matter continued to be raised, and I believe a full and accurate accounting of administration actions would help put them to rest," Mr. Dodd said in a statement.[26]

Like its reports from Iraq in April 2003 that barely mentioned the cluster-bombing of Hilla and Baghdad, foreign news coverage at the *Times* seems designed at critical moments to ignore important stories rather than to cover them. For example, nearly two years after the *Times* simply repeated what the Inspector General said in its coverage of his report, the British newspaper the *Independent* reported:

Washington has been channeling hundreds of thousands of dollars to fund the political opponents of Venezuelan President Hugo Chavez—including those who briefly overthrew the democratically elected leader in a coup two years ago.

Documents obtained under the Freedom of Information Act reveal that, in 2002, America paid more than a million dollars to those political groups in what it claims is an ongoing effort to build democracy and "strengthen political parties". Mr Chavez has seized on the information, telling Washington to "get its hands off Venezuela."

Jeremy Bigwood, a Washington-based freelance journalist who obtained the documents, yesterday told *The Independent*: "This repeats a pattern started in Nicaragua in the election of 1990 when [the US] spent $20 per voter to get rid of [the Sandinista President Daniel] Ortega. It's done in the name of democracy but it's rather hypocritical. Venezuela does have a democratically elected President who won the popular vote which is not the case with the US."

The funding has been made by the National Endowment for Democracy (NED), a non-profit agency financed entirely by Congress. It distributes $40m (£22m) a year to various groups in what it says is an effort to strengthen democracy.

But critics of the NED say the organisation routinely meddles in other countries' affairs to support groups that believe in free enterprise, minimal government intervention in the economy and opposition to socialism in any form. In recent years, the NED has channeled funds to the political opponents of the recently ousted Haitian president Jean-Bertrand Aristide at the same time that Washington was blocking loans to his government.[27]

Reporting on the same set of documents, the *Times* reporter in Venezuela, Juan Forero, wrote:

Under United States pressure to allow a recall referendum against his rule, President Hugo Chávez has in recent days counterattacked, charging that the Bush administration is trying to oust him by aiding his adversaries, including those who briefly overthrew him in a 2002 coup.

Mr. Chávez has seized on the information in reams of United States government documents, made public by a pro-Chávez group in New York that show Washington is trying to strengthen political parties and other antigovernment groups that want to remove the populist firebrand through a recall.

Aid to opposition groups by the National Endowment for Democracy, a nonprofit agency financed by the United States Congress, is not new. Nor is the $1 million spent here last year excessively high for an organization that spends $40 million a year to finance hundreds of organizations in 81 countries.

But the unearthing of 2,000 pages of documents has provided details of how the Bush administration considers the rehabilitation of Venezuela's battered political parties the best way to counter a leader Washington views as erratic and authoritarian.[28]

Like Burns, who would not report the facts of the Baghdad-market bombing without first tying the bombing itself to Saddam Hussein, Forero also seems unable to report the facts in this instance without first tainting them with anti-Chávez innuendo or downsizing their significance. Thus, Chávez "has seized" on the evidence that Washington has been seeking his overthrow; the evidence itself, which consists of US government documents, nevertheless was produced by a "pro-Chávez group in New York"; and NED aid to opposition groups such as those in Venezuela is neither new nor excessively high—all distractions from the facts at hand. On the other hand, Forero writes without any such encumbrances about the ultimate US objective of replacing Chávez in Venezuela for reasons of oil and economic connections: "For the United States, which is dependent on Venezuelan oil supplies and has close economic ties to the country, the possibility that the [Chávez-recall] referendum could be scrapped would be a serious blow to a carefully calibrated policy aimed at building feasible political alternatives to Mr. Chávez."[29]

Looking at the news and editorial-page coverage of these two stories—Iraq and Venezuela—over the course of only two years (April 2002 to March 2004), the record of that coverage does not reflect what one might expect from the leading newspaper in the world's most important democracy. The *New York Times* editorial page (a) lent its support to an attempted military coup in Venezuela seeking the overthrow of a democratically elected president; (b) inaccurately reported, in the context of its support for the coup, that President Hugo Chávez had resigned; (c) argued that the coup was a victory for democracy in Venezuela; and (d) claimed that the Bush administration had no involvement in the coup without evidence to support this claim. We found that the *Times* covered a 95-page report on the coup in Venezuela by the State Department Inspector General by simply repeating in a 150-word blurb the report's conclusion that the Bush administration had not engaged in inappropriate or illegal conduct. And we found that the editorial page supported the Bush administration's Iraqi WMD claims without question, supported on principle the threat and use of force against Iraq based on those claims, and never considered the legality of an Iraq invasion—whether unilateral or with "broad international support"—under international law.

By any measure, this negligent coverage of major US foreign-policy issues by the paper's editorial page, veteran foreign correspondents, and top editors represents a crisis of credibility at the *Times*, far exceeding in magnitude and seriousness the damage done to the country by Jayson Blair—a lone inexperienced reporter who had never been assigned to cover issues involving war and peace, international law, the future of world order, and whether thousands of people might live or die. This crisis of credibility is not generated by an errant reporter but by the bedrock editorial policy of the *Times*, which has elevated "non-crusading" journalism to the point of evading due diligence in its coverage of issues of major importance to the United States and the world.

7

A DODGY DISSENT: NICARAGUA V. UNITED STATES AT THE WORLD COURT

On July 1 1986, the *New York Times* published an editorial on the decision in *Nicaragua v. United States* by the International Court of Justice (the World Court) at The Hague. The Court, which is the highest judicial body of the United Nations, ruled that by arming and financing the *contras*, attacking Nicaraguan territory, and laying explosive mines in the territorial waters of Nicaragua, in addition to other offenses, the United States had violated international law. The Court also ordered the United States to cease and refrain from such actions and to pay reparations to Nicaragua.[1]

Despite the careful and authoritative reasoning by which the Court reached its decision, the *Times* editorial page denounced the ruling. It wrote: "Predictably, the World Court has found the United States guilty of violating international law by supporting the 'contra' war against Nicaragua." The editorial page asserted that "the Court's judgment was deplorably broad" and described the Court as "a hostile forum" that issued "hostile judgments" against the United States. It also denounced "the Court's tendentiousness" and deplored "the presence of Communist judges, and those of other incompatible ideologies" at the Court.

The editorial page meanwhile commended the judge from the United States for his dissenting opinion in the case and support for the United States:

On a dozen other counts, it was left to the American judge, Stephen Schwebel, to make the case and amass the evidence that the United States should have brought to court. Had it done so, it might have restrained the hostile judgments and emphasized the world's deep disagreements about what constitutes aggression. But who will now read Judge Schwebel's voluminous dissent—his demonstrations of Court prejudice in not even hearing El Salvador's claims against Nicaragua or his condemnation of the Court's double-standard in justifying only "anti-colonial" interventions across frontiers?[2]

By the end of this chapter, we will have reviewed several paragraphs of this editorial because virtually every paragraph misled the nation with respect to the majority's decision and Judge Schwebel's dissent.

The *Times* editorial was important, however, not only because it misrepresented the facts and law in a landmark case and historic milestone in international law, which was bad enough, but also because it demonstrated that the editorial page of the *New York Times*—even after Vietnam and well into the tenure of an administration that used and threatened force frequently—had developed no editorial policy integrating international law into its analysis of US foreign policy.

Finally, while the editorial badly misrepresented the process and outcome of the case, it was nevertheless a model of *New York Times* editorial policy, given that it balanced its criticism of the Court for being "predictable" and "hostile" with criticism of the Reagan administration for being "predictable" and "petulant" in its behavior in the case, and to question whether the Reagan administration's support of the *contras* was wise.

While "balancing" reporting or commentary in this fashion is the gold standard of journalistic objectivity in the United States, it is not only inadequate by itself as a standard of due diligence, but can be easily undermined by balancing for balancing's sake and by the more sophisticated positioning strategy of the *Times*. Thus, while the *Times* is credited professionally for "balance" in its coverage of US foreign policy, such coverage is pegged to no standard of law or even factually accurate news reports or editorials. The fact is the *New York Times* has failed to reconcile the use of American global power with any existing law. An equally troubling fact is that this failure has easily coexisted with the reverential regard for the *Times*' coverage of US foreign policy throughout the political and journalistic establishments.

Whereas the previous chapter on the 2002 coup attempt in Venezuela functioned as a case study on the absence of due diligence at the *Times* editorial page with respect to its "non-crusading" analysis of US foreign policy, this chapter will function as a case study of similar inadequacies two decades earlier. This examination will also lead to familiar results with respect to our analysis of Iraq policy and the *Times* in earlier chapters: (a) phony US weapons claims against another state supported by the editorial page; (b) the illegal US use of force against that state supported on principle by the editorial page on the basis of the weapons claims; and (c) a badly flawed editorial policy at the nation's leading editorial page that failed to analyze clearly an illegal foreign policy and the government lies that supported it.

As we move backward to Vietnam in the next chapter, to the origins of US military involvement and escalation there, we will have shown a record of serious US violations of international law in the conduct of its foreign policy over the past half-century—a period in which the *Times* criticized none of those policies on international law grounds. This is a record of journalistic malfeasance with far-reaching implications for constitutionalism in the United States and the rule of law for our country and the world.

On April 9 1984, the Sandinista government of Nicaragua formally initiated legal proceedings at the World Court against the US government, charging that the Reagan administration's military and paramilitary activities in and against Nicaragua violated a number of international laws. Not coincidentally, the Reagan administration, anticipating Nicaragua's initiative, had informed the Court three days earlier that it would not recognize the World Court's jurisdiction for the next two years in disputes involving Central America. It seems that the administration had received confidential intelligence reports that formal charges against the United States were imminent. A US State Department official, commenting on this abrupt refusal to recognize the Court's jurisdiction to address the merits of Nicaragua's claims under international law, stated "We had to do it very rapidly ... if they filed before we moved, we'd be stuck. We did not want to turn the World Court into a big propaganda forum that would allow the Sandinistas to try to focus attention away from their own actions in El Salvador and in their own country."[3]

Despite the absence of the United States, the Court was obliged nevertheless to maintain standards of fairness that guaranteed the equality of both parties before the Court. According to Article 53 of the World Court statute, "[w]henever one of the parties does not appear before the Court ... the Court ... must satisfy itself ... that the claim is well-founded in fact and law."[4] To comply with this mandate, and despite the refusal of the Reagan administration to make a formal submission of evidence or witnesses, the Court accepted material that was informally presented by the administration, such as documents from the US State Department's Office of Public Diplomacy on Latin America and the Caribbean (LPD) and its Bureau of Public Affairs. In accepting such documents, the Court stated that "it is valuable for the Court to know the views of both parties in whatever form those views may have been expressed," that "where one Party is not appearing it is especially incumbent upon the Court to satisfy itself that it is in full possession of all the available facts," and that "the equality of the parties to the dispute must remain the basic principle for the Court."[5]

What the Court did not know at the time was that LPD was a joint US Central Intelligence Agency/US National Security Council propaganda agency that was only nominally based at the State Department, and was set up to justify in US public opinion the administration's attacks against Nicaragua. A year after the Court issued its final judgment, the Comptroller General of the United States found the LPD to be an illegal domestic propaganda arm of the US government.[6] Though the *Times* supported the dissenting opinion of Judge Schwebel, who relied to a significant extent on LPD documents in his opinion, as we shall see, the *Times* ignored the Comptroller General's report on the LPD.

The Court's decision to make use of LPD documents—such as "Revolution Beyond Our Borders: Sandinista Intervention in Central America"—was made over the objections of Nicaragua's lawyers, who argued that such documents "do not constitute evidence in this case."[7] The Court ruled, however, that "in view of the special circumstances of this case"—that is, US non-participation—"it may, within limits, make use of information in such a publication."[8] The fact that the Court accepted materials of this sort seems more than fair, considering the US refusal to participate in the case.

The Court's willingness to consider documents published by the Reagan administration as evidence, over the objections of the government of Nicaragua, does not support the claim by the *New York Times* editorial page that the Court was "a hostile forum" that rendered "hostile judgments" against the United States. Nor did the Court's more substantive rulings on evidence, which we itemize below.

Did the United States Government "Create" the Contras? The Court's initial assessment of the facts focused on substantiating or rejecting Nicaragua's factual claims against the United States. We will examine each of these claims, and indicate whether the Court accepted or rejected them. For example, Nicaragua charged that the United States had "conceived, created and organized a mercenary army, the *contra* force."[9] In rejecting Nicaragua's claim, however, the Court noted that "some armed opposition to the Government of Nicaragua existed in 1979–80, even before any interference or support by the United States," and that the first US presidential finding authorizing CIA covert actions in Nicaragua was dated March 9 1981, which was months after some of the armed groups had already formed.[10] The Court also cited the affidavit of Edgar Chamorro, former *contra* leader and witness for the Nicaraguan government, which refers to the "ex-National Guardsmen who fled to Honduras when the Somoza government [in Nicaragua] fell and had been conducting sporadic raids on Nicaraguan border positions ever since."[11]

The Court also pointed to other statements in Chamorro's affidavit that described "a political opposition to the Nicaraguan Government, established outside Nicaragua, from the end of 1979 onward."[12] In August 1981, according to Chamorro, the political opposition in exile merged with diffuse but previously existing bands of Nicaraguan armed opposition. This merger of political and armed opposition groups, which took place under the direction of the CIA, was the organizational origin of what would become the main *contra* group—the National Democratic Front (FDN).[13] The Court argued, however, that even if it could be shown that the CIA assembled the FDN from smaller, pre-existent opposition groups, Nicaragua did not allege in the Court's proceedings that the United States was involved in the formation of the other major armed opposition group, the *Alianza Revolucionaria Democratica* (ARDE), which was formed in 1982 by Alfonso Robelo Callejas (a former member of the original 1979 junta that replaced Somoza) and Eden Pastora Gomez (a former Sandinista military commander).[14]

Thus, based on (a) admissions by Nicaragua's own witness that armed bands of ex-National Guardsmen existed prior to a March 1981 US presidential finding authorizing covert actions against Nicaragua; (b) the existence of a Nicaraguan political opposition group prior to the March 1981 presidential finding; and (c) the absence of claims by Nicaragua that the United States was involved in the formation of the ARDE armed opposition group, the Court rejected Nicaragua's claim, and ruled that "even on the face of the evidence offered by the Applicant [Nicaragua] . . . the Court is unable to find that the United States created an armed opposition in Nicaragua."[15]

The Court's conclusion here is hardly evidence of an evaluation of facts that is biased against the United States, as Judge Schwebel and the *New York Times* had charged. The Court could have argued, at least as plausibly, pursuant to a more liberal interpretation of Chamorro's affidavit, that the United States had in fact "conceived, created and organized" the *contras* as the government of Nicaragua had claimed. For instance, although it was generally accepted that armed bands of opposition to the Nicaraguan government existed prior to the March 1981 presidential finding, Chamorro stated that these bands "were poorly armed and equipped, and thoroughly disorganized." At their inception and soon afterward, these disorganized "ineffectual" bands had no affiliation with the exiled Nicaraguan political group living in Miami, who themselves were doing little more than writing letters to the US Congress. It was not until US General Vernon Walters "himself arranged for all bands to be incorporated within the 15th of September Legion," or until "the merger of the UDN with the 15th of September Legion was accomplished in August 1981" when "the name of the organization [FDN], the members of the political junta, and the members of the general staff were all chosen or approved by the CIA," that the *contras*—as an organized, armed and supplied army—was created. It was not until after the CIA had organized the *contras* that "a special unit was created for sabotage," that the "first combat units were sent into Nicaraguan territory," and that "the first military successes of the organization came."[16] It is difficult to sustain the view that this is not creating the *contras* as the *contras* existed and functioned throughout the 1980s, and as they were identified and discussed in the case at the World Court.

Rejecting Nicaragua's claim that the United States created the *contras* was questionable for another reason: The first presidential finding that authorized US covert assistance to Nicaraguan opposition groups was not the March 1981 finding cited by the Court; rather, the first such presidential finding was signed by President Jimmy Carter approximately fourteen months before the March 1981 finding. In his book, *Veil: The Secret Wars of the CIA, 1981–1987*, Bob Woodward wrote:

> [William] Casey was intrigued to find that within six months of the Sandinista takeover [which occurred in July 1979], President Carter had signed a top-secret finding authorizing the CIA to provide political support to opponents of the Sandinistas—money and backing to encourage and embolden the political opposition, newsprint and funds to keep the newspaper *La Prensa* alive. Designed to work against one-party rule, the opposition was a standard political action program to boost the democratic

alternative to the Sandinistas—to develop alternatives to parties and people thought to be close to the Soviet Union and its line.[17]

The *Report of the Congressional Committees Investigating the Iran–Contra Affair* also dated the Carter finding "in the fall of 1979," when Carter "signed a Finding authorizing support to the democratic elements in Nicaragua because of the concern about the effect of the Sandinista takeover."[18]

Both sources on the Carter finding—Woodward's book and the *Iran–Contra Report*—were published a year after the Court issued its judgment on the merits in June 1986; thus, the Court did not know at the time about President Carter's earlier finding. In short, the Court was again more than fair to the United States when it rejected the government of Nicaragua's fundamental claim that the United States had created the *contras*.

Did the United States Provide "Direct Combat Support" to the Contras? Nicaragua claimed that the United States "provided direct combat support" to the *contras* for attacks in and against Nicaragua, and that the United States "devised the strategy and directed the tactics of the *contra* force."[19] To support this claim, Nicaragua cited the sequence between congressional funding of the *contras* and the *contra* military offensives that followed. Moreover, Edgar Chamorro testified that the CIA had consistently "ordered" or "instructed" the *contras* with respect to military strategy and tactics.[20]

Summarizing Nicaragua's evidence in support of this charge, the Court said:

> There is considerable material in press reports of statements by FDN officials indicating participation of CIA advisers in planning and the discussion of strategy or tactics, confirmed by the affidavit of Mr. Chamorro. Mr. Chamorro attributes virtually a power of command to the CIA operatives: he refers to them as having "ordered" or "instructed" the FDN to take various actions. The specific instances of influence of United States agents on strategy or tactics which he gives are as follows: the CIA, he says, was at the end of 1982 "urging" the FDN to launch an offensive designed to take and hold Nicaraguan territory. After the failure of that offensive, the CIA told the FDN to move its men back into Nicaragua and keep fighting. The CIA in 1983 gave a tactical directive not to destroy farms and crops, and in 1984 gave a directive to the opposite effect. In 1983, the CIA again indicated that they wanted the FDN to launch an offensive to seize and hold Nicaraguan territory. In this respect, attention should also be drawn to the statement of Mr. Chamorro that the CIA supplied the FDN with intelligence, particu-

larly as to Nicaraguan troop movements, and small aircraft suitable for reconnaissance and a certain amount of supply-dropping.[21]

Despite Chamorro's testimony on US involvement in the strategy, tactics, and supply of the *contras*, the Court ruled that it could not warrant a finding that the United States gave "direct and critical combat support," at least, "if that form of words is taken to mean that this support was tantamount to direct intervention by the United States combat forces, or that all *contra* operations reflected strategy and tactics wholly devised by the United States."[22] Thus, the Court ruled that unless the United States had intervened with combat troops to "direct" and "support" the *contras*, Nicaragua's charge on this count could not be sustained.

As in the previous question regarding the creation of the *contras,* the Court denied one of Nicaragua's main claims against the United States by defining the claim in narrow terms for the purposes of the case, then ruling that Nicaragua's evidence did not support the narrowed claim. Also, as in the previous instance, the Court's decision here certainly does not support the charge by Judge Schwebel and the *New York Times* that it was a "hostile forum" issuing "hostile judgments" against the United States.

Is the United States Legally Responsible for Contra Atrocities? Nicaragua charged that atrocities committed by the *contras* against Nicaraguan civilians were the product of US-directed military tactics, including "the spreading of terror and danger to non-combatants as an end in itself with no attempt to observe humanitarian standards and no reference to the concept of military necessity."[23] As before, the Court decided against supporting Nicaragua's allegations, stating that "the Court does not consider that the assistance given by the United States to the *contras* warrants the conclusion that these forces are subject to the United States to such an extent that any acts they have committed are imputable to that State."[24]

What the Court had to investigate, it said, was not complaints related to alleged violations of humanitarian law by the *contras*, "but rather unlawful acts for which the United States may be responsible directly in connection with the activities of the *contras*."[25] In this respect, according to the Court, "the material facts are primarily those connected with the issue in 1983 of a manual of psychological operations."[26]

Was the US Government Responsible for the Manual of "Psychological Operations in Guerrilla Warfare" Issued to the Contras? The preface of the manual describes its purpose as "for the training of insurgents in psychological operations, and its application to the concrete case of the Christian and democratic crusade waged in Nicaragua by the Freedom Commandos [the *contras*]."[27] The Court confirmed US authorship of this manual based on a January 1985 report by the US House Intelligence Committee that specifically referred to the manual's publication by the CIA.[28]

In view of the manual's existence, its content, and its CIA authorship as documented by the US House Intelligence Committee, the Court concluded that

> in 1983 an agency of the United States Government supplied to the FDN a manual on psychological guerrilla warfare which, while expressly discouraging indiscriminate violence against civilians, considered the possible necessity of shooting civilians who were attempting to leave a town; and advised the "neutralization" for propaganda purposes of local judges, officials or notables after the semblance of a trial in the presence of the population.[29]

In this instance, then, the Court supported Nicaragua's factual claim that the US government had written and issued a manual of psychological operations in guerrilla warfare to the *contras* on grounds that a US congressional committee had already established the CIA's authorship of the manual. This finding, citing an official US government source as evidence to support it, resembled the findings below by the Court that were supported by official US government sources as evidence.

Did the United States Finance, Supply, and Support the Contras? The Court supported this claim by noting that "the financing by the United States of the aid to the *contras* was initially undisclosed, but subsequently became the subject of specific legislative provisions and ultimately the stake in a conflict between the legislative and executive organs of the United States."[30] After citing numerous instances of US financial assistance to the *contras* authorized by the Reagan administration and the US Congress from 1981 to 1985, the Court concluded that "from 1981 until 30 September 1984 the United States government was providing funds for military and paramilitary activities by the *contras* in Nicaragua, and thereafter for 'humanitarian assistance.' "[31]

Did the United States Lay Explosive Mines in the Territorial Waters of Nicaragua? In supporting this claim, the Court noted "it was announced in the United States Senate on 10 April 1984 that the Director of the CIA had informed the Senate Select Committee on Intelligence that

President Reagan had approved a CIA plan for the mining of Nicar-aguan ports."[32] The Court also noted that "the British government indicated to the United States that it deeply deplored the mining, as a matter of principle," and that "Nicaragua has also submitted evidence to show that the mining of ports caused a rise in marine insurance rates for cargo to and from Nicaragua, and that some shipping companies stop-ped sending vessels to Nicaraguan ports."[33]

Did the United States Attack Oil Facilities, Ports, and Other Facilities in Nicaragua? Nicaragua had accused the United States of attacks on its territory in a number of incidents.[34] On this count the Court rejected the claims that could not be established by official US government sources, and accepted as factual the claims that were supported by such sources. For example, Nicaragua had claimed that the United States was behind an airplane attack on Sandino International Airport in Managua on September 8 1983. Because Nicaragua presented little more than a news account of this incident—in which the *contra* group ARDE was reported to have claimed responsibility for the September 8 attack on the airport and to have purchased the plane used in the attack from the CIA—the Court declined to attribute the September 8 attack to any agency of the US government. Thus, the Court rejected Nicaragua's charge on grounds of insufficient evidence.[35]

Considering the Court's rejection of this claim, it is worth noting evidence of CIA involvement in the attack, as Nicaragua had charged, and as described by Bob Woodward in *Veil*:

Early on the morning of Thursday, September 8, [Senator William] Cohen, [Senator Gary] Hart and a Marine escort officer left [Washington, DC] on an Air Force C-140, due to land in Managua [Nicaragua] about 9:15 a.m.

About an hour outside the Nicaraguan capital, the pilots were told that the Augusto César Sandino Airport was closed. There had been some kind of air attack. A propeller-driven twin-engine Cessna with a 500-pound bomb strapped under each wing had been shot down, crashing into the control tower and the terminal building. ...

After they finally arrived at the Managua terminal, in the early afternoon, Hart was astonished at the destruction. Smoke damage was everywhere and the center of the terminal was wiped out. Broken glass and oil were scat-tered all about. And the fuselage of the downed plane was cut in half. The pilot and co-pilot were both dead. Forty people waiting for flights had run for their lives. One worker had been killed. The VIP room where the senators were to have given their press conference had also been hit. Cohen calculated that if they had arrived before schedule that morning, they might be dead.

The Nicaraguan news media was there to ask questions.

One reporter said that the bombing attack was obviously a CIA-supported *contra* raid.

"The CIA is not that dumb," Cohen said.

The Nicaraguan officials had produced a briefcase which had been retrieved from the plane. Cohen and Hart peered inside. There was a manifest instructing the pilot to meet someone in Costa Rica at a certain restaurant, a bill of lading from Miami and the pilot's Florida driver's license, a U.S. Social Security card and American credit cards.

And there was more, including some code identifications for the operation and the contract. Both Cohen and Hart recognized them as authentic CIA paperwork.[36]

Thus, it seems that in this case, as well as others, the Court rejected a factual assertion by Nicaragua that appears to have been true. The Court also rejected two other claims by Nicaragua of US attacks on its territory.[37] But the Court accepted others based on a classified CIA memorandum reproduced in the US press that specifically referred to the attacks, and based as well on the sworn testimony given by Edgar Chamorro, who stated that many of the attacks were the work of UCLAs (Unilaterally Controlled Latino Assets of the CIA) dispatched from a mother ship. Given the US government documentation on the attacks, the Court concluded "the imputability to the United States of these attacks appears therefore to the Court to be established."[38]

By now it should be clear that the Court applied a consistently high standard of evidence to Nicaragua's charges against the United States—the Court accepted those charges when they could be confirmed by official US government sources.

Did the United States Violate Nicaragua's Airspace? Nicaragua charged that the United States had directed or authorized overflights of Nicaraguan territory for military and intelligence purposes. The Court summarized Nicaragua's claim as follows: "This claim refers to overflights by aircraft at high altitude for intelligence reconnaissance purposes, or aircraft for supply purposes to the *contras* in the field, and aircraft producing 'sonic booms.' "[39]

With regard to reconnaissance flights, the Court stated: "During the proceedings on jurisdiction and admissibility, the United States government deposited with the Court a 'Background Paper' published in 1984, incorporating eight aerial photographs of ports, camps, an airfield, etc., in Nicaragua, said to have been taken between November 1981 and June 1984."[40] The Court also noted that "in the course of a [United Nations] Security Council debate on 25 March 1982, the United States representative said that 'it is true that once we became aware of Nicaragua's intentions and actions, the United States Government undertook overflights to safeguard our own security and that of other States which are threatened by the Sandinista government.' "[41] On the basis of this evidence—the existence of US reconnaissance photographs of Nicaragua and the public admission by a US government official—the Court found that "the high-altitude reconnaissance flights" are "imputable to the United States."[42]

Regarding the November 1984 incidents of US overflights of Nicaragua to make sonic booms, the Court stated that these incidents "are to some extent a matter of public knowledge," given the numerous press reports, charges by Nicaraguan government officials, and the failure of the United States government to deny either the press reports or the charges by the Nicaraguan government.[43] About overflights for supply purposes, the Court ruled that these "were carried out generally, if not exclusively, by the *contras* themselves" and the Court therefore did not consider them as acts imputable to the United States government.[44]

Did the United States Enact a Trade Embargo Against Nicaragua? Nicaragua claimed that the United States had imposed a trade embargo against it. The Court cited several US government documents that verified Nicaragua's claims. For example, the Court cited an executive order of the president of the United States dated May 1 1985. The executive order declared a national emergency—which the Reagan administration described as Nicaragua's threat to the national security of the United States—in order to establish a total trade embargo on Nicaragua that prohibited all exports from and imports to Nicaragua, barred Nicaraguan vessels from United States ports, and excluded Nicaraguan aircraft from entering the United States. On the basis of President Reagan's May 1 1985 executive order, the Court established that the United States had enacted a trade embargo against Nicaragua.[45]

These were the totality of Nicaragua's charges against the United States. Rather than exhibit an anti-American bias, the Court rejected Nicaragua's most serious charges against the United States—that it had "created" the *contras*, gave "critical and direct combat support" to the *contras*, and was responsible for atrocities committed by the *contras*—and accepted as evidence only those charges against the United States that were substantiated by US government sources.

Contrary to what the *New York Times* editorial page had asserted, the World Court showed no indication of an anti-US bias in its determination of the facts as declared by Nicaragua. Nor did the Court exhibit an anti-American bias in its assessment of the facts in the context of international law, as the following sections show.

The Court's decision on the merits included a total of sixteen counts.[46] In the first count the Court, on behalf of the United States, invoked the multilateral treaty reservation of the United States.[47] The Court invoked the reservation even though the United States itself was not present during the merits phase of the proceedings to invoke the reservation on its own behalf. The US multilateral treaty reservation prevented the Court from citing US violations of multilateral treaties, including the UN Charter and the OAS Charter. This explains why the Court cited only US violations of customary international law and a bilateral treaty between the United States and Nicaragua without also citing US violations of the UN Charter, the OAS Charter, or other multilateral treaties.

In the second count the Court rejected the US claim that it had attacked Nicaragua in collective self-defense with El Salvador.[48] We address this count separately below. Count 16 "recall[ed] to both Parties their obligation to seek a solution to their disputes by peaceful means in accordance with international law."[49] Thus, counts 3 to 15, then, applied basic principles of customary international law to the facts, as the Court established them, to rule that the United States had violated its obligations under customary international law not to intervene in the affairs of another state, not to use force against another state except in self-defense, and not to violate the sovereignty of another state.[50] The Court also ruled that the United States violated the 1956 Treaty of Friendship, Commerce and Navigation between the United States and Nicaragua when it declared a general embargo on trade with Nicaragua in 1985, and the Court ordered the United States to pay reparations to Nicaragua to compensate it for its economic losses as a result.[51]

We note the degree to which Judge Schwebel dissented from the majority on these counts: He dissented eleven of thirteen times in counts 3 to 15, disagreeing with the majority, for example, that the United States had violated customary international law not to intervene in the affairs of another state, not to use force against another state, and not to violate the sovereignty of another state when the United States had supplied and financed the *contras*, attacked Nicaraguan territory, laid explosive mines in the internal or territorial waters of Nicaragua, and directed or authorized overflights of Nicaraguan territory.[52]

Judge Schwebel's disagreement with the Court included important issues in addition to its determination of the facts and law. This section will examine one of those disputes—whether the Court treated the government of El Salvador fairly in an early phase of the case—while also identifying another problematic aspect of the *New York Times'* endorsement of his dissent.

The *Times* argued in its editorial of July 1 1986 that the Court demonstrated its anti-American "prejudice in not even hearing El Salvador's claims against Nicaragua."[53] This reference to "El Salvador's claims against Nicaragua" is actually to El Salvador's Declaration of Intervention, which the government of El Salvador issued to the Court in August 1984 during the jurisdiction phase of the proceedings. The purpose of El Salvador's declaration was stated in the declaration itself:

> El Salvador makes this declaration for the sole and limited purpose of arguing that this Court does not have jurisdiction over Nicaragua's Application or the claims set forth herein, that for multiple reasons the Court should declare itself unable to proceed concerning such Application and claims, and that such Application and claims are inadmissible.[54]

Thus, what the *New York Times* referred to as "El Salvador's claims against Nicaragua" was more precisely a claim against the Court's jurisdiction to hear Nicaragua's case.

El Salvador's arguments on jurisdiction were presented essentially as follows: Because Nicaragua charged the United States with violating multilateral treaties, such as the UN Charter and the OAS Charter, because El Salvador is a party to those treaties, and because El Salvador is a victim of armed attack from Nicaragua and US actions against Nicaragua are aimed at defending El Salvador as permitted by such treaties, a judgment from the Court against the United States would adversely affect El Salvador's right to collective defense.[55]

The Court responded that, because its jurisdiction was established on the basis of Nicaragua's claims with respect to customary international law, El Salvador's claims with respect to multilateral treaties did not affect the Court's jurisdiction. However, rather than reject El Salvador's intervention outright, the Court invited El Salvador to appear in the merits phase to present its claim that it was the victim of armed attack by Nicaragua requiring collective defense with the United States.[56]

El Salvador, however, refused the Court's invitation to participate in the merits phase. Thus, contrary to what the *New York Times* editorial page charged, the Court did not refuse to hear "El Salvador's claims against Nicaragua"; rather, El Salvador refused the Court's invitation to present its substantive claims against Nicaragua in the merits phase of the proceedings, where such claims are appropriately presented.

Given the facts in this case, the United States and El Salvador chose not to appear in the merits phase because both governments almost certainly knew the evidence would show that Nicaragua was not engaged in an armed attack against El Salvador, and that US military and paramilitary actions against Nicaragua could not be justified under international law as a defense of El Salvador. Judge Schwebel, however, chose an alternative explanation of El Salvador's refusal to appear in the merits phase. He argued that the Court's handling of El Salvador's declaration in the jurisdiction phase was so unfair that El Salvador's dignity justifiably led it to refuse participation in the merits:

> It may reasonably be assumed that the procedures of the Court's treatment of El Salvador's Declaration of Intervention influenced El Salvador's decision not to exercise its right of intervention at the stage of the merits—a decision which necessarily had great impact on the content and tenor of the proceedings of the merits, and which may have had like impact on the shaping of the Court's Judgment (as surely as the absence of the United States).
>
> Nicaragua has contended that, by reason of El Salvador's failure to intervene at the stage of the merits, an inference should be drawn against the truth of the facts which El Salvador alleges in its Declaration of Intervention. In my view no such inference can reasonably be drawn, particularly because of the manner in which the Court treated El Salvador's Declaration.[57]

Schwebel's argument that the government of El Salvador was unfairly treated in the jurisdiction phase of the proceedings is simply not credible. Furthermore, would a government choose not to appear in the merits phase of a major case when the defense of its country is reputed to be at stake because the Court had hurt that government's feelings in a ruling on jurisdiction? Note, however, that Judge Schwebel, unlike the *Times* editorial page, at least acknowledged that El Salvador rejected the Court's invitation to participate in the case.

In its Declaration of Intervention submitted to the Court during the jurisdiction phase in August 1984, El Salvador made substantive allegations against Nicaragua, including the charge that "we [El Salvador] are the victims of aggression and armed attack from Nicaragua and have been since at least 1980." With respect to this claim, El Salvador alleged that "terrorists" seeking the overthrow of the Salvadoran government were "directed, armed, supplied, and trained by Nicaragua," and, "although the quantities of arms and supplies, and the routes used, vary, there has been a continuous flow of arms, ammunition, medicines, and clothing from Nicaragua to our country." The declaration also alleged that Nicaragua's foreign minister, Miguel D'Escoto Brockmann, in July 1983 "admitted [Nicaragua's] direct involvement in waging war on us."[58]

Nicaragua responded to these charges as follows:

> The Court should know that [El Salvador's submission of its Declaration of Intervention] is the first time El Salvador has asserted it is under attack from Nicaragua. None of these allegations, which are properly addressed to the merits phase of the case, is supported by proof or evidence of any kind. Nicaragua denies each and every one of them, and stands behind the affidavit of its Foreign Minister, father Miguel d'Escoto Brockmann, in which the Foreign Minister affirms that the Government of Nicaragua has not supplied arms or other materials of war to groups fighting against the Government of El Salvador or provided financial support, training or training facilities to such groups or their members.[59]

Nicaragua argued that the US claim of collective self-defense with El Salvador was a "pretext" to justify US objectives in Nicaragua to destabilize and overthrow the leftist Sandinista government.[60]

While both the United States and El Salvador made these claims to the Court in the jurisdiction phase, both countries declined the Court's invitation to appear in the merits phase to substantiate them with evidence and witnesses. In contrast, Nicaragua presented two witnesses to refute the claims made by the United States and El Salvador: Edgar Chamorro, a former political leader of the *contras*, and David MacMichael, a former senior analyst in the US Central Intelligence Agency. Chamorro's testimony was limited to a sworn affidavit he gave in Florida because the US State Department refused to issue him a travel visa to The Hague to testify. Meanwhile, MacMichael appeared before the Court and gave extensive, sworn testimony that contested US charges of an arms flow from Nicaragua to Salvadoran rebels.

In his affidavit, Chamorro testified:

[T]he CIA Agents instructed us that, if asked, we should say that our objective was to interdict arms supposedly being smuggled from Nicaragua to El Salvador. If any of us ever said anything publicly about overthrowing the Nicaraguan government, we would be visited immediately by a CIA official who would say, "That's not the language we want you to use." But our goal, and that of the CIA as well (as we were repeatedly assured in private), was to overthrow the government of Nicaragua, and to replace the Sandinistas as a government. It was never our objective to stop the supposed flow of arms, of which we never saw any evidence in the first place. The public statements by United States government officials about the arms flow, we were told by the CIA agents with whom we worked, were necessary to maintain the support of the Congress and should not be taken seriously by us.[61]

Chamorro's responsibilities as a political leader of the *contras* primarily involved the dissemination of CIA-generated information throughout Central America as part of a Reagan administration campaign to discredit the Sandinistas and generate support for the *contras*.[62]

David MacMichael, a US citizen, was free to travel to The Hague to testify and did so. MacMichael was employed by the CIA as a senior estimates officer with the analytic group of the CIA's National Intelligence Council from March 6 1981 to April 2 1983. The National Intelligence Council consists of CIA senior staff who work for the director of central intelligence. In his capacity as senior estimates officer, MacMichael had, in his words, a "top-secret clearance with an additional type of clearance which enabled me to go out of the boundaries of what is known as 'special compartmented intelligence.' "[63]

As a member of the analytic group, MacMichael specialized in Latin America. His first assignment was to analyze the Salvadoran insurgency, as he described it in his testimony to the Court: "My concern, as I have expressed, was about the proper design of an arms interdiction system, which led me as a matter of professional responsibility, and working with the approval of the National Intelligence officer at large who controlled our actions, to continue to make a close study of intelligence relating to the alleged arms flow from Nicaragua to El Salvador."[64]

In short, as Nicaragua's lawyer, Abram Chayes—Harvard Law School professor and former legal adviser to the Secretary of State in the Kennedy administration—stated: "It was part of [MacMichael's] responsibility to be familiar with and analyze the intelligence collected by the United States government on the subject of delivery of arms or other war materials from Nicaragua to rebels in El Salvador."[65]

Throughout the course of his work, MacMichael had access to "raw intelligence," including reconnaissance photographs, records of communications, intercepts, and reports of interrogations, as well as "finished intelligence," that is, summaries and reports based on analyses of raw intelligence. MacMichael also discussed the arms-flow issue with other intelligence officials operating in the field, never made a request to see or review intelligence material pertaining to the alleged arms flow that was denied, and, in general, was familiar with the intelligence information that the US government collected with regard to arms trafficking between Nicaragua and the insurgents in El Salvador.[66]

MacMichael's testimony was important also because it corroborated Edgar Chamorro's testimony that there was no evidence of an arms flow from the Nicaraguan government to the Salvadoran rebels. MacMichael's testimony is also relevant to assessing Judge Schwebel's dissent, which supported the arguments of the Reagan administration with respect to a Nicaraguan arms flow.

In his testimony, MacMichael described in detail the following aspects of US policy toward Nicaragua: (a) that the purpose of the 1981 US covert-action plan to field and supply the *contras* was to bring about a "state of emergency [in Nicaragua] generated by these [*contra*] attacks" such that "the Nicaraguan government would clamp down and eliminate civil liberties," whereby such a scenario would "help justify in United States public opinion actions which the United States might take against Nicaragua"; (b) that despite official US justifications citing "arms interdiction" as the reason for fielding and supplying the *contras*, no US arms interdiction plan had been formulated or existed; (c) that despite the deployment of US intelligence capabilities "of a very high order," the United States was unable to detect or collect evidence of a Nicaraguan arms flow to El Salvador from early 1981 to April 1983; and (d) that from "late 1980 to very early 1981," evidence surfaced that arms were going to Salvadoran rebels from Nicaragua, but that such evidence "did not come in anymore after very early 1981."[67]

MacMichael's testimony to this effect was supported by the testimony of former *contra* leader, Edgar Chamorro, who reported in his affidavit: "it was never our objective to stop the supposed flow of arms, of which we never saw any evidence in the first place."[68] Both MacMichael and Chamorro, then, undermine Judge Schwebel's principal factual assertion—endorsed by the *New York Times* editorial page—that "the Nicaraguan government, despite its denials, in fact has acted as the principal conduit for the provision of arms and munitions to the Salvadoran insurgents from 1979 to the present day [June 27 1986]."[69]

In his dissenting opinion, Judge Schwebel did not challenge the Court's factual findings that the United States had armed the *contras*, mined Nicaraguan territorial waters, and attacked Nicaraguan oil facilities. Instead, Schwebel argued that, in light of his own exhaustive examination of the facts, these actions were justified under international law in the collective self-defense of El Salvador, which was the victim of armed attack from Nicaragua by virtue of the arms flow that he claimed to have established in his dissenting opinion.[70]

The factual and legal logic of Schwebel's dissent, then, is the following: Because Nicaragua had been sending weapons to Salvadoran insurgents, Nicaragua had engaged in an armed attack against El Salvador; if Nicaragua had engaged in an armed attack against El Salvador, then El Salvador was entitled to individual and collective self-defense under international law; if El Salvador was entitled to collective defense, then it had a right under international law to ask the United States to assist in its defense; if international law permitted the United States to help defend El Salvador, then it was permissible for the United States, in a response proportionate to Nicaragua's aggression against El Salvador, to arm the *contras* and conduct paramilitary and military activities of its own in and against Nicaragua.

Conversely, and putting aside for now the legal problems with this argument, a failure by Schwebel to substantiate his fundamental factual claim of a Nicaraguan arms flow would invalidate his argument as follows: If there is no evidence of a Nicaraguan arms flow to Salvadoran insurgents, there can be no claim that Nicaragua had engaged in an armed attack against El Salvador, no claim by El Salvador to individual or collective self-defense, and no sound factual or legal basis for the United States to attack Nicaragua—or for Schwebel's dissent. Thus, Judge Schwebel's pivotal assertion is his claim to have established persuasive evidence of a Nicaraguan arms flow to Salvadoran insurgents. However, Schwebel established no such evidence, as we show below.

In part because the Salvadoran government accused Nicaragua of sending weapons to rebels in El Salvador, Judge Schwebel argued that the United States had a right to arm the *contras* and attack Nicaragua on grounds that the United States was defending El Salvador. However, El Salvador did not claim to be the victim of attack by Nicaragua until it issued its Declaration of Intervention on August 15 1984—three years after the CIA had organized and armed the FDN, the main *contra* group. Prior to this date, El Salvador had not notified the UN Security Council that Nicaragua was arming anti-government rebels in El Salvador or that it needed to exercise its rights to individual or collective self-defense, as the UN Charter requires.[71]

For his part, Judge Schwebel attempted to explain El Salvador's failure to fulfill its formal notification requirements under the Charter:

> If El Salvador has seemed restrained, if it has not protested quite as soon as and as loudly and formally as it otherwise might have, if it has not itself attempted to attack the warehouses, safehouses, training sites, and command-and-control facilities which Salvadoran insurgents have enjoyed in the territory of Nicaragua, has not that been not because of El Salvador's lack of legal standing but its lack of power?[72]

In addition to Schwebel's admission that El Salvador failed to fulfill the notification requirements, his defense of El Salvdor's silence on the issue up to 1984 is based on supposition. If we also indulged in supposition, wouldn't the reverse explanation make more sense? That is, if in fact El Salvador was under attack by Nicaragua, wouldn't El Salvador move quickly to be legitimately and legally defended? Wouldn't El Salvador seek to comply with the straightforward procedures of international law in order to avail itself of its legal right to individual and collective self-defense?

Despite the speculative nature of his argument, Schwebel continued:

> [I]n the Court's view, apparently the only kind of declaration that a State is under armed attack which counts is one formally and publicly made; and the only kind of request for assistance that appears to count is one formally and publicly made. But where is it written that, where one State covertly promotes the subversion of another by multiple means tantamount to an armed attack, the latter may not informally and quietly seek foreign assistance.[73]

According to Schwebel, El Salvador did not publicly and formally announce it was under armed attack from Nicaragua, but did so "informally and quietly." But under international law, "informal and quiet" declarations do not "count" because the purpose of a public and formal declaration is to allow the Security Council to fulfill its obligation under UN Charter Article 39, that is, to "determine the existence of any threat to the peace, breach of the peace, or act of aggression." Indeed, one purpose of Article 39 is to foreclose the possibility of "informal and quiet" declarations, thus preventing individual states from initiating unauthorized, unilateral military action under the pretext of individual or collective self-defense.

While Judge Schwebel cited allegations from El Salvador as evidence of a Nicaraguan arms flow, the sources he relied on most, and which he considered unimpeachable, were documents published by the Reagan administration. For example, Schwebel described the US State Department's 1981 white paper on El Salvador, and the documents on which the white paper was based, as "provid[ing] graphic and substantial support for United States allegations concerning Nicaraguan, Cuban, Vietnamese, Ethiopian and other provisions of arms and ammunition in great quantities to the Salvadoran insurgents."[74] Schwebel also described the State Department's "Revolution Beyond Our Borders" as "contain[ing] a wealth of data, much of it documented, supporting the claims of the United States that Nicaragua has been and is engaged in activities subverting the Government of El Salvador, and to a lesser extent, Honduras and Costa Rica."[75] Schwebel also relied heavily on documents published by the Office of Public Diplomacy on Latin America and the Caribbean (LPD), the Reagan administration propaganda agency that targeted US citizens. And Schwebel accepted the claims of US-processed defectors at face value—"defectors" who either were first captured by the Salvadoran military and detained for several weeks before making public statements, or who were paid large sums of money, in some instances hundreds of thousands of dollars, by the US government. The sections below examine Schwebel's use of sources from the Reagan administration to support his foundational claim that Nicaragua was arming the Salvadoran insurgency, and thus deserved to be subjected to paramilitary and military actions by the United States under international law.

The White Paper on Communist Interference in El Salvador. The State Department's white paper, "Communist Interference in El Salvador," was based on documents allegedly captured from Salvadoran insurgents. These documents, the white paper claimed, supplied evidence for Reagan administration claims that the Soviet Union, Cuba, and Nicaragua were supplying weapons to insurgents in El Salvador. In describing the value of the white paper and the documents upon which it was based, Judge Schwebel wrote that "they provide graphic and substantial support" for the claim of a Nicaraguan arms flow to Salvadoran insurgents.[76]

There were, however, several press reports that challenged not only the white paper's interpretation of the documents, but the authenticity of the documents themselves. With regard to these reports, published years before the majority and dissenting opinions in *Nicaragua v. United States*, Schwebel wrote:

> The authenticity of these captured documents, and, more, the accuracy of a State Department White Paper construing them, generated controversy in the press soon after their publication in 1981. The United States Government refuted that criticism in detail and maintains that the documents are authentic.[77]

This is the extent of Schwebel's response to press investigations of the white paper and the captured documents. Thus, Schwebel simply rejected these press reports as inconsequential and accepted at face value the administration's claims that the documents were genuine and that the white paper was accurate. By writing these press reports off with a single sentence, however, Schwebel ignored the evidence in them that rendered the white paper and its supporting documents without any credibility as a source of facts or evidence of a Nicaraguan arms flow.

For example, a front-page article in the *Wall Street Journal* by Jonathan Kwitny on June 8 1981 raised some difficult questions about the captured documents and the white paper. Kwitny quoted the State Department's principal author of the white paper, Jonathan Glassman, who conceded that parts of the white paper are possibly "misleading" and "over-embellished." Kwitny reported: "Glassman freely acknowledges that there were 'mistakes' and 'guessing' by the government's intelligence analysts who translated and explained the guerrilla documents, which were written in Spanish with code names."[78]

With regard to the captured documents, Kwitny wrote:

> Several of the most important documents, it's obvious, were attributed to guerrilla leaders who did not write them. And it's unknown who did. Statistics of armament shipments into El Salvador, supposedly drawn directly from the documents, were extrapolated, Mr. Glassman concedes. And in questionable ways it seems. Much information in the white paper can't be found at all [in the captured documents]. This information now is attributed by the State Department to other, still secret sources.[79]

According to Kwitny, the Salvadoran National Police found fifteen of the "captured" documents in a Salvadoran grocery store. Doubting the authenticity of the documents himself, Glassman told Kwitny that once the documents were in his hands, one of the first things he did was to satisfy himself that they were genuine. In this regard, Kwitny reported:

> There was the possibility that the Salvadoran military might have fabricated them or that they had been planted by the Central Intelligence Agency. Says Glassman: "I submitted all of the documents to them [the CIA], and I asked, 'Did you fabricate any of the documents, or is there any indication they were fabricated by anyone else?' And the answer was no to both."[80]

Glassman, at the time a mid-level State Department official, was not in a position to challenge CIA denials, and his attempt to authenticate the documents in this manner, though perhaps laudable, was inconsequential.

The day after the *Wall Street Journal* published Jonathan Kwitny's analysis of the white paper in 1981, which Schwebel never mentioned, the *Washington Post* published a front-page article on the white paper by Robert Kaiser—a report that Schwebel also ignored. Kaiser began by writing:

> The State Department's white paper on El Salvador, published in February [1981], contains factual errors, misleading statements and unresolved ambiguities that raise questions about the administration's interpretation of participation by communist countries in the Salvadoran civil war. ...
>
> When the white paper was published, the major news media tended to accept the document at face value, but it has subsequently been challenged in several analyses, primarily by individuals and journals critical of American policy in El Salvador. Yesterday, The Wall Street Journal added its reservations in a front-page story that said the white paper was flawed by errors and guesses.
>
> The Journal's article prompted a statement from the State Department yesterday defending "the conclusions of the white paper," without replying to specific criticisms.[81]

It seems that Judge Schwebel's position on the white paper was identical to the State Department's: both defended the white paper's conclusions without addressing specific criticisms. Given the nature of the specific criticisms, it is hard to imagine how Schwebel managed to ignore them. For example, Kaiser wrote:

> The contention of the white paper that the Salvadoran rebels were enjoying the benefits of "nearly 200 tons" of communist-supplied arms and materiel is not supported anywhere in these documents, and is implicitly refuted by many of them. In document after document there are reports of rebels short

of arms, or exhorting comrades to produce home-made arms, or plotting to kidnap wealthy Salvadorans thought to have access to private arsenals.[82]

One document contained a description of arms and equipment available to the Salvadoran guerrillas at the time the documents were discovered. A US official who read and evaluated this document wrote: "from this it would appear they [the Salvadoran rebels] had only 626 weapons for more than 9,000 men."[83] Kaiser reported: "this document was omitted from the collection released to the press with the white paper."[84]

Though the Kwitny and Kaiser articles on the white paper were written years before the *Nicaragua* case, Judge Schwebel ignored them while arguing that the white paper "provide[s] graphic and substantial support for United States allegations" of a Nicaraguan arms flow to Salvadoran rebels.

This doesn't mean, however, that Schwebel ignored what some prominent US journalists had to say about the white paper. Rather than cite Kwitny or Kaiser, Schwebel wrote that Christopher Dickey, a *Washington Post* journalist and author of *With the Contras: A Reporter in the Wilds of Nicaragua,*

[who] evidences an intimate knowledge of elements of the facts at issue in the current case, concludes that "the source documents themselves appear very much in line with what Salvadoran insurgent leaders and representatives as well as Sandinistas told me privately in Managua [the capital of Nicaragua] in October *1983* and May *1984*" and treats the documents as genuine.[85]

By quoting Dickey to this effect, Schwebel presumably would have us believe that this passage supports Schwebel's claim of a Nicaraguan arms flow. Once Dickey's words are produced in full, however, the meaning they confer is actually quite different. In the quote above from Dickey's book, Schwebel omitted the italicized portion below from the full passage, which, when included, modifies the meaning of Dickey's text:

Yet the source documents themselves appear very much in line with what Salvadoran insurgent leaders and representatives as well as Sandinistas told me privately in Managua in October *1983* and May *1984, especially insofar as the frictions between the Salvadorans and the Nicaraguans were concerned.*[86]

In this passage, "Salvadorans" refers to the Salvadoran rebels and "Nicaraguans" refers to the Sandinistas. The captured documents, then, appear genuine to Dickey in this passage, not because they describe an arms flow from the Nicaraguan government to the Salvadoran rebels, but because they describe "frictions" between the Nicaraguan government and the Salvadoran rebels.

Rather than demonstrating any intimate knowledge about the arms-flow issue, Dickey in fact displayed little knowledge or interest about the white paper, the captured documents, or the arms-flow issue itself. Whenever Dickey mentioned the arms-flow issue, he simply reiterated the administration's claims and cited administration sources. Yet Schwebel, as he did again below, used Dickey as a source to support the existence of a Nicaraguan arms flow:

> Equally informed critics of United States policy in Central America, such as Christopher Dickey, author of With the Contras, A Reporter in the Wilds of Nicaragua, 1985, conclude that:
> "as the [1980] election result came in, with Reagan and his Republican platform the obvious winners, the Sandinistas opened the floodgates for the Salvadoran rebels. By the middle of November [1980] the Salvadorans were complaining they couldn't distribute so much matériel.
> You couldn't hide that many arms. Some were caught. Others were tracked through radio intercepts. And from that point on, the new Reagan administration could present proof that ... the battle for El Salvador and the battle for Nicaragua were one and the same."[87]

According to the only footnote to this quoted passage from Dickey's book, Dickey's sole source is the State Department's white paper on El Salvador.[88] In other words, Dickey simply cited the State Department's white paper and its claims against Nicaragua as his source, while also ignoring the previously published analysis of his journalistic colleagues that discredited the great body of those claims. Furthermore, Schwebel omitted an incriminating portion of this quote, shown in italics below, from Dickey's book:

> And from that point on, the new Reagan administration could present proof that *the judgment of its ideologues had been right*, the battle for El Salvador and the battle for Nicaragua were one and the same.[89]

Apparently, Schwebel was uncomfortable having the lynchpin argument in his dissenting opinion associated with the beliefs of Reagan administration ideologues; thus, he omitted these eight words in his quote from Dickey's book. Schwebel omitted another awkward portion of another passage from Dickey's book. Here is the passage as Schwebel quoted it:

As to whether the arms flow stopped in 1981, Dickey concludes that in 1982: "In fact arms to the Salvadorans ... had not stopped. They had increased."[90]

Here is what Dickey actually wrote, with the italicized words being the ones omitted by Schwebel:

In fact arms to the Salvadorans, *such as they were*, had not stopped. They had increased.[91]

Schwebel omitted "such as they were" because these words appear to downgrade the scale of an arms flow that Schwebel claimed was vast.

As standards of evidence go, the fact that Schwebel cited unsubstantiated and uninformed assertions about the Nicaraguan arms flow is not impressive. With respect to Dickey's use of the white paper as his arms-flow source, Schwebel would have done better to invoke the standards of evidence used by the Court, that "widespread reports of a fact may prove on closer examination to derive from a single source, and such reports, however numerous, will in such case have no greater value as evidence than the original source."[92]

While Schwebel used Dickey's book as a source to support his claims of a Nicaraguan arms flow, he ignored Raymond Bonner's book, *Weakness and Deceit: U.S. Policy in El Salvador*, published one year before Dickey's book. In his analysis of the white paper, Bonner, a former *New York Times* correspondent in Central America, did not simply repeat the white paper's claims; rather, he analyzed the white paper from a broader historical and factual perspective:

The newly elected administration issued a white paper, charging that "aggression has been loosed against an independent people who want to make their own way in peace and freedom." The "brutal campaign of terror and armed attack" was "inspired, directed, supplied and controlled" by a neighboring Communist nation. The white paper contained what the State Department described as "massive evidence" establishing "beyond question" that the Communists were carrying out the aggression against an "established government."

The date [of this white paper] was February 27, 1965. The country seeking peace and freedom was South Vietnam. The Communist aggressor was North Vietnam. Sixteen years later, on February 23, 1981, the newly elected administration of Ronald Reagan issued a similar-sounding white paper. "Communist Interference in El Salvador" was the title. Only the names and dates seemed to have changed much.[93]

Referring to the 1981 white paper's claim that it provided "definitive evidence of the clandestine military support given by the Soviet Union, Cuba, and their communist allies to Marxist–Leninist insurgents now fighting to overthrow the established government of El Salvador," Bonner wrote:

> The evidence was said to be contained in some eighty captured guerrilla documents, weighing eighteen pounds. There were journals of international travels, minutes of meetings within guerrilla councils, statements of political philosophy.
>
> The white paper concluded that these documents proved that the Salvadoran insurgency was a "textbook case of indirect aggression by Communist powers through Cuba."...
>
> But the evidence, it turned out, wasn't quite so "definitive." And the "textbook case" of Communist aggression turned out to resemble instead a textbook case of distortion, embellishments, and exaggeration. The State Department had provided reporters with nineteen documents at the time it released the white paper. As the department almost certainly knew would happen, most reporters wrote their stories from the white paper, not having time to read the thick pile of documents, which were written in Spanish anyway. ...
>
> The documents, it turns out, didn't even weigh eighteen pounds: that was the total weight of Glassman's suitcase, which also contained his personal belongings. Moreover, many of the documents weren't even written by the guerrilla leaders that the administration claimed had written them; there is still doubt about who did write them.
>
> A major white paper claim was that the Salvadoran insurgents had been promised "nearly 800 tons of the most modern weapons and equipment" by Communist nations and that "200 tons of those arms" had already been delivered, "mostly through Cuba and Nicaragua." But neither figure—800 or 200—was found anywhere in the documents. An intelligence source told me that there was no basis for the 200-ton figure, other than "wild guesses."[94]

While ignoring Bonner's book, Schwebel cited a book by Robert F Turner, author of *Nicaragua v. United States: A Look at the Facts*.[95] Turner wrote much of this book, as he acknowledged, while under contract to the US State Department,[96] which published the white paper on El Salvador. While citing Turner's book, and acknowledging that it was "based in part upon research done under contract to the Department of State,"[97] Schwebel wrote:

> A supporter of United States policy towards Nicaragua, who has produced a detailed, documented study of the extent of what he views as aggression by

the Nicaraguan Government against El Salvador, Honduras and Costa Rica, treats the captured documents as genuine and draws much illuminating detail from them showing the pervasive involvement of the Nicaraguan Government in the arming, supply, training and direction of the insurgency in El Salvador. . . . Turner's study contains a wealth of additional factual data in support of his conclusions, among them that the Nicaraguan Government has played and continues to play the pivotal role in sustaining the Salvadoran insurgency, acting as the chief conduit for funds, ammunition, and supplies as well as a training and command centre.[98]

Turner's book makes a number of additional claims. For example: "the Vietnamese communists succeeded in defeating the United States not through armed struggle on the battlefield but by political struggle inside the United States"; "to further their image as the 'victim' in the current controversy, the Sandinistas went so far as to file suit before the International Court of Justice alleging that the United States was guilty of unprovoked aggression" which "was a clever strategy, and the refusal of the United States to participate actively in the case led many to believe that the U.S. charges of Nicaraguan aggression were unfounded"; and that key portions of the manual of "Psychological Operations in Guerrilla Warfare" authored by the CIA "may have been a Sandinista 'dirty trick' aimed at discrediting the Contras."[99] This is the level of analysis that Judge Schwebel viewed as credible enough to cite favorably in his dissent while ignoring the work of Kwitny, Kaiser, and Bonner.

In addition to the State Department's white paper, the Reagan administration's outlawed propaganda agency— the LPD—was also a principal source for Judge Schwebel in his dissenting opinion. In the 160 paragraphs of section H in Schwebel's factual appendix—the section that Schwebel claimed provides the factual evidence of a Nicaraguan arms flow—he cited domestic public diplomacy sources in thirty of those paragraphs.[100]

"Public diplomacy" is a euphemism for state propaganda. Under its standard formulation, US public diplomacy targets the hearts and minds of audiences outside US borders. The Reagan administration took the additional and illegal step of explicitly targeting the US Congress, the US news media, and the American people with an organized propaganda effort in support of the administration's policies toward Central America.[101]

The domestic propaganda operation was officially conducted under the auspices of the State Department but in fact was operated out of the

White House. A year and a half after Judge Schwebel featured LPD as a factual source in his dissenting opinion in *Nicaragua v. United States*, the US Comptroller General found that LPD had been running an illegal domestic propaganda operation.[102]

Referring to the domestic LPD effort, Robert Parry and Peter Kornbluh wrote in the *Washington Post* that the White House created a sophisticated apparatus that mixed propaganda with intimidation and consciously misled the American people.[103] The LPD campaign, according to Parry and Kornbluh, involved CIA covert operatives who were assigned to the White House to conduct covert domestic propaganda. In addition to the CIA operatives, "five other psy war specialists from the 4th Psychological Operations Group at Fort Bragg, North Carolina" were recruited for the LPD office.[104]

The LPD document, "Revolution Beyond Our Borders: Sandinista Intervention in Central America," has a featured place in Judge Schwebel's dissenting opinion—an entire section of his factual appendix is devoted to it. Schwebel wrote: " 'Revolution Beyond Our Borders' contains a wealth of data, much of it documented, supporting the claims of the United States that Nicaragua has been and is engaged in activities subverting the Government of El Salvador, and, to a lesser extent, Honduras and Costa Rica."[105]

Other analysts had different things to say about "Revolution Beyond Our Borders." For example, Morris Morley and James Petras described the basic public-diplomacy function of the document:

> The argument and evidence presented in this *Report* constitute the most comprehensive effort by the Reagan administration to justify U.S. policy toward the Sandinista government in Nicaragua. ... The *Report* was intended not only to provide a public defense of its war against Nicaragua, but also to counter any adverse publicity that might flow from the change in U.S. policy toward the World Court and weakened support for the precepts of international law.[106]

Simply stated, "Revolution Beyond Our Borders" served as a public-diplomacy substitute for US participation in *Nicaragua v. United States* at the World Court.

The document also followed the familiar pattern of unsupported charges, beginning with its title and imputed meaning, as Morley and Petras wrote:

> The title of the *Report*, starting with "Revolution Beyond Our Borders," refers to a speech by [Sandinista Interior Minister] Tomás Borge which has

been misrepresented time and again, as the State Department does here. Borge used the phrase "this revolution transcends national boundaries." The *Report* mistranslates this into "this revolution goes beyond our borders." The context of Borge's speech clearly indicates that he was referring to the Nicaraguan revolution serving as a moral example—not to Nicaragua militarily intervening in other countries' internal affairs. Borge himself made this point in the same speech when he stated: "All the revolutionaries and particularly all the people of Latin America know that our people's hearts are with them and beat with them. Latin America is within the heart of the Nicaraguan revolution and the Nicaraguan revolution is also within the heart of Latin America. This does not mean that we export our revolution. It is sufficient—and we cannot avoid this—that they take our example."[107]

Another claim made in the document is that an offensive Nicaraguan military buildup "threatens Nicaragua's neighbors"—El Salvador, Honduras, and Costa Rica. This claim was made in September 1985, the publication date of the document. Yet, according to the *Wall Street Journal*, a classified US intelligence report prepared in late 1984 concluded that "the overall [Sandinista] buildup is primarily defense-oriented, and much of the recent [Sandinista] effort has been devoted to improving counter insurgency capabilities" to fight the US-backed *contras*.[108] Similarly, in early 1985 US Secretary of State George Shultz repeated the charge of a destabilizing Sandinista military buildup: "We see a government that is being armed by the Soviet Union, developing an army—including reserves—that far exceeds anything remotely needed for defense in Central America." The same *Wall Street Journal* article, citing Shultz's testimony, said that it

> seems designed mainly to inflame the public debate and influence Congress. The classified U.S. intelligence report prepared late last year contradicts Secretary Shultz. And figures in the report suggest the increase in Soviet aid to Nicaragua may have been prompted by the escalation of the CIA-backed contra war.[109]

Schwebel also cited defectors from the Salvadoran rebels and the Sandinista government as sources supporting the arms-flow claim. Referring to published reports about defectors, Judge Schwebel wrote that evidence of a Nicaraguan arms flow received "explicit and emphatic support in declarations of defectors from [Salvadoran insurgents] and from the Sandinistas."[110] Schwebel also inferred that defectors in the hands of the United States have high credibility because they would have nothing to fear if their revelations ran counter to what the United

States might wish them to say.[111] But Schwebel failed to mention that one of the first Sandinista "defectors" to support the Nicaraguan arms-flow claim—Orlando José Tardencillas Espinosa, who was captured by the Salvadoran military before "defecting"—later recanted and stated that he had been coerced by the United States and the Salvadoran military:

> At the press briefing [in Washington, DC], Mr. Tardencillas said, "An official of the U.S. Embassy told me that they needed to demonstrate the presence of Cubans in El Salvador." He added: "They gave me an option. They said I could come here [to the United States] or face certain death. All my previous statements about training in Ethiopia and Cuba were false."[112]

This statement, reported in the *New York Times* in May 1982, was published four years before Judge Schwebel's dissent in the *Nicaragua* case; however, Schwebel never mentioned the Tardencillas incident—a significant omission since it bears witness to the process behind the revelations of "defectors" who made statements supporting the Reagan administration's position.

Following the publication of Judge Schwebel's dissent, congressional committees released documents showing US government payments to *contra* leaders involving millions of dollars. For example, Arturo Cruz, a former Sandinista ambassador to the United States, defected in the early 1980s and became a *contra* political leader. Cruz reportedly received substantial payments from the CIA and Oliver North from at least 1984 to 1986, including when he was a presidential candidate in the 1984 Nicaraguan elections.[113]

Judge Schwebel also cited reports from the US House Intelligence Committee, issued in 1982, 1983, and 1985, as supporting his claim of a Nicaraguan arms flow. For example, Schwebel cited a passage from the March 1982 report by the committee:

> There is further persuasive evidence that the Sandinista government of Nicaragua is helping train insurgents and is transferring arms and financial support from and through Nicaragua to the insurgents. They are further providing the insurgents bases of operation in Nicaragua. Cuban involvement—especially in providing arms—is also evident.
>
> What this says is that, contrary to the repeated denials of Nicaraguan officials, that country is thoroughly involved in supporting the Salvadoran insurgency. That support is such as to greatly aid the insurgents in their struggle with government forces in El Salvador.[114]

Schwebel also cited a passage from the May 1983 report by the committee asserting that the insurgency in El Salvador

> depends for its life-blood—arms, ammunition, financing, logistics and command-and-control facilities—upon outside assistance from Nicaragua and Cuba. The Nicaraguan-Cuban contribution to the Salvadoran insurgency is longstanding. ... It has provided the great bulk of the military equipment and support received by the insurgents.[115]

And Schwebel cited a June 1985 text by former Congressman Lee Hamilton, who at the time chaired the US House Intelligence Committee:

> [T]he Nicaraguan Government appears to have committed itself to a policy of support for the insurgencies in other Central American countries. The most important example of this policy is the assistance provided by Nicaragua to the Salvadoran guerrillas. It seems clear that the Nicaraguan commitment to the Salvadoran guerrillas stems from FMLN support to the Sandinistas during their efforts to overthrow Somoza and is a matter of revolutionary pride and solidarity.
>
> The flow of arms from Nicaragua to the Salvadoran guerrillas continues. The network used for this purpose is run by Salvadorans with Nicaraguan support.[116]

These are the charges, cited by Judge Schwebel, but there is little evidence to support them. In fact, Judge Schwebel, while continuing to quote Congressman Hamilton, provided additional information that undermined his case:

> There have been no appreciable interdiction of arms shipments by the Salvadoran armed forces and none at the point of entry into El Salvador. The capture of supplies of arms in the past have been in Honduras while in transit or in safehouses. ...
>
> The inability of the Salvadoran or Honduran forces to interdict shipments by water routes alone is a factor of their corruption or lack of proficiency and of what must either be an extremely effective guerrilla network or a very small volume of shipments. ...
>
> The judgments made above concerning assistance to the Salvadoran insurgents are inferential and based on substantial, but circumstantial information.[117]

Thus, even as Congressman Hamilton stated that "the flow of arms from Nicaragua to the Salvadoran insurgents continues," he also stated in the same document that "there have been no appreciable interdiction of arms shipments by the Salvadoran armed forces and none at the point of entry into El Salvador," and that the lack of interdicted arms may be the result of "a very small volume of shipments." Schwebel ignored the obvious significance of these qualifications: If in 1985 evidence of a Nicaraguan arms flow into El Salvador, according to the chair of the House Intelligence Committee, was only "inferential" and "circumstantial," and if by 1985 no weapons had been interdicted in the supposedly massive flow of arms from Nicaragua to Salvadoran insurgents, and if one possible conclusion in 1985 from the lack of evidence is that the flow of weapons might be "very small," then what was the evidentiary basis for the arms-flow claims in the 1982 and 1983 House Intelligence Committee reports?

This lack of evidence is consistent with the accounts of the arms-flow's evidentiary status provided by Bob Woodward's *Veil*, published in 1987, and in former CIA analyst David MacMichael's testimony at the World Court. Woodward wrote that "the [US] National Security Agency communications intercepts were not yielding the evidence [CIA Director William] Casey wanted to demonstrate that Nicaragua was supporting the arms flow to the Salvadoran rebels" and that many officials in the CIA were "not so sure this proof [of a Nicaraguan arms flow] existed."[118] And MacMichael testified that there was no evidence of an arms flow after early 1981.[119]

Meanwhile, congressional legislation in 1982 authorizing funds to interdict a Nicaraguan arms flow provided the legal pretext Congress sought in order to comply with Reagan administration funding requests for the *contras*. In 1982, the first Boland Amendment[120] prohibited Congress from appropriating funds to the *contras* to overthrow the Sandinista government; however, a loophole in the law did not expressly prohibit Congress from appropriating funds for US interdiction of an alleged Sandinista arms flow to Salvadoran rebels. Yet, as both David MacMichael and Edgar Chamorro pointed out in their testimony to the Court, at that time neither the *contras* nor the US government had an arms interdiction program in place anywhere in Central America. Moreover, the country alleged by the United States to be the victim of armed attack as a result of the arms flow—El Salvador—had not requested interdiction assistance, nor had it claimed at the time to be the victim of an armed attack from Nicaragua. Thus, Congress officially appropriated funds to the *contras* in 1982 for an arms interdiction program that almost certainly did not exist. Indeed, the congressional *Iran–Contra Report* made this same point a few years after the House Intelligence Committee had issued their reports:

With the first Boland Amendment, then, came a temporary compromise between the Administration and Congress. But it was an inherently uneasy compromise, based more on semantics than substance: The Contras were not in the field to stop Sandinista arms flowing to El Salvador; they were in the field to overthrow the Sandinistas.[121]

If the Congress knew in 1982 that "the Contras were not in the field to stop Sandinista arms flowing to El Salvador," why would Congress appropriate funds to the *contras* to stop Sandinista arms flowing to El Salvador? The *Iran–Contra Report* simply explained that the congressional rationale for funding the *contras* was a "contradiction inherent in the new law" because Congress was unwilling to bear responsibility for the loss of Central America to what it saw as communist military and political forces.[122] Thus, it appears the House Intelligence Committee, chaired at the time by Congressman Edward P Boland of Massachusetts, misstated its intentions in 1982 when it supported the appropriation of funds to interdict a Nicaraguan arms flow into El Salvador.

The fact that the US Congress appropriated money to the *contras* apparently for publicly announced reasons that it knew were false is not surprising, since there were many other such instances of "contradictions" in the early 1980s, as the *Iran–Contra Report* itemized:

- The public policy was to ban arms shipments to Iran and to exhort other Governments to observe this embargo. At the same time, the United States was secretly selling sophisticated missiles to Iran and promising more.

- The public policy was to improve relations with Iraq. At the same time, the United States secretly shared military intelligence on Iraq with Iran and [Oliver] North told the Iranians in contradiction to United States policy that the United States would help promote the overthrow of the Iraqi head of government.

- The public policy was to observe the "letter and spirit" of the Boland Amendment's proscriptions against military or paramilitary assistance to the Contras. At the same time, the NSC staff was secretly assuming direction and funding of the Contras' military effort.

- The public policy, embodied in agreements signed by [CIA] Director [William] Casey, was for the [Reagan] Administration to consult with the Congressional intelligence oversight committees about covert activities in a "new spirit of frankness and cooperation." At the same time, the CIA and the White House were secretly withholding from those Committees all information concerning the Iran initiative and the illegal Contra supply network.[123]

Similar to what the Reagan administration itself had done, the Congress failed to identify the real mission of the *contras* that it was funding—to destabilize and overthrow the Sandinista government. And rather than challenge the arms-flow claims of the administration, it leveraged those claims to circumvent its own proscriptions against funding the *contras*.

There were other reasons for doubting the arms-flow claims of the House Intelligence Committee cited by Judge Schwebel. In making determinations with regard to intelligence matters, the congressional intelligence committees are dependent to a large extent on the quality of intelligence they receive from the intelligence agencies of the executive branch, in this case President Reagan's intelligence agencies. One of the central findings of the Iran–Contra investigation was the extent of the administration's lying to Congress. In fact, well before the *Iran–Contra Report* was published, a 1982 report by staff members of the House Intelligence Committee titled "US Intelligence Performance on Central America: Achievements and Selected Instances of Concern"[124] warned of questionable intelligence from the Reagan administration to Congress.

As the staff report noted, "a major intelligence briefing" was provided in 1982 "by the intelligence community" to high officials in Congress and the executive branch about Nicaragua and El Salvador. Members of the House Intelligence Committee were given the same briefing on March 4 1982. Following this briefing, Congressman Boland's Committee issued the statement alleging a Nicaraguan arms flow that is quoted above from the committee's 1982 report, and was used by Judge Schwebel in his dissenting opinion. Yet there were numerous areas of concern among the committee's staffers about the intelligence briefing to Boland's committee concerning the Nicaraguan arms flow, as the staffers explained in their report:

> The [intelligence] briefing stated that "lots of ships have been traced" from the Soviet Union, through various countries, and on to Nicaragua, but when the [House Intelligence] Committee asked how many ships had been traced along this route and when, the written response indicated that intelligence could show only a very few examples. Another [intelligence briefing] statement was that, "You don't plan an operation like what is being run in El Salvador if you haven't gone to somebody's command and general

staff college." Subcommittee staff understood this statement to mean that the [Salvadoran] insurgency was being commanded by graduates of schools comparable to the U.S. Army Command and General Staff College—presumably in the Soviet Union or bloc countries. The Committee asked about the evidence, and the written response explained the comment as "a figure of speech meant simply to emphasize the greater sophistication and training of the Salvadoran insurgents compared to the Sandinistas at the time they overthrew Somoza."

A slide titled "Guerrilla Financing (Non-Arms)" indicated that Salvadoran guerrillas were receiving money in addition to weapons, showing a total of some $17 million annually. This resulted from an extrapolation which, as outlined by the briefer, seemed particularly tenuous. It was based on a single piece of evidence indicating the monthly budget for the commander of one faction on one front. The extrapolation would have required that figure to be representative of the budgets of the other four factions and all five factions to be equally active on each of the five fronts. In a question for the record, the Committee asked about these assumptions. In its response, the intelligence community said it was unable to comment on whether the original monthly figure was representative, and instead explained that the bottom line of the $17 million which appeared in the briefing slide "was not an estimate," but was intended only to indicate that "relatively large sums of currency" were going to the insurgents.[125]

The same intelligence briefing also included a section on Salvadoran guerrilla propaganda. This presentation, according to the staff report, focused on a slide that contrasted the way a counterinsurgency sweep by the Salvadoran military was reported in the *Washington Post* with what was known from available intelligence. The *Post* article reported that the US-backed Salvadoran military attacked insurgents and civilians indiscriminately. The briefer from the intelligence community presented the *Post* article as an example of guerrilla propaganda reaching the US public. The intelligence community asserted that *Washington Post* reporter Philippe Bourgois "was with an FMLN [Salvadoran guerrilla] fighting unit," a challenge to Bourgois' claim that he was with civilians when attacked. When committee staffers requested evidence that Bourgois was with the FMLN fighting unit, the intelligence briefers responded that its claim was an "analytic judgment" based on a certain body of intelligence. Upon reviewing this intelligence, the committee staff discovered that, in their words, "no intelligence existed to contradict Bourgois' claim that he was with noncombatants," and "it was misleading to present the [Bourgois] article as an example of guerrilla 'propaganda': no fraudulent media manipulation has been shown."[126]

In short, the House Intelligence Committee made a policy decision to support the notion of a Sandinista arms flow despite an absence of supporting evidence and credible intelligence from the Reagan administration's intelligence agencies. Although Judge Schwebel cannot be faulted for disseminated deceptions by the administration's intelligence agencies and congressional oversight failures in the 1980s, he nevertheless ignored the staff report by the House Intelligence Committee, and the committee's own words in its 1985 report that indicated that the arms-flow findings in the committee's reports were issued with political expediency rather than established facts in mind.

Even if Judge Schwebel had found evidence of a Nicaraguan arms flow to Salvadoran rebels, his argument that such a finding would justify the Reagan administration's policy of arming the *contras* and attacking Nicaragua was not sound. In its decision on the merits, the Court's 12–3 majority stated:

> Even assuming that the supply of arms to the opposition in El Salvador could be treated as imputable to the Government of Nicaragua, to justify invocation of the right of collective self-defence in customary international law, it would have to be equated with an armed attack by Nicaragua on El Salvador. As stated above, the Court is unable to consider that, in customary international law, the provision of arms to the opposition in another State constitutes an armed attack on that State.[127]

Schwebel disagreed with this formulation of "armed attack." He argued that the Court had applied a double standard disadvantageous to the United States when it ruled that a US arms flow to the *contras* was an illegal use of force while failing to rule that a Nicaraguan arms flow to Salvadoran guerrillas was an illegal armed attack against El Salvador.

On its face Schwebel's argument has no validity. There is a distinction in international law between the broad concept of "use of force" and the narrow concept of "armed attack." Whereas "use of force" encompasses various intensities and magnitudes of force, from indirect aggression to armed attack, an "armed attack" is understood to mean a sustained military assault by one state across the territorial borders of another. Thus, while an "armed attack" can be described as a "use of force," a "use of force" is not necessarily an "armed attack." It was, therefore, reasonable for the Court to find that a US arms flow to the *contras*—a proven factual assertion that neither the United States nor Judge Schwebel denied—violated the prohibition on the use of force, while also arguing that a Nicaraguan arms flow to Salvadoran rebels would not constitute an armed attack under international law.

Rather than clarify the distinction between "use of force" and "armed attack," Schwebel confused it, fostering the impression of a Court favorably disposed to Nicaragua and unfavorably disposed to the United States. Consistent with this effort, Schwebel reproduced a passage from Ian Brownlie's *International Law and the Use of Force,* quoting Brownlie:

> There can be little doubt that "use of force" is commonly understood to imply a military attack, an "armed attack", by the organized military, naval, or air forces of a state; but the concept in practice and principle has a wider significance. ... governments may act by means of completely "unofficial" agents, including armed bands, and "volunteers", or may give aid to groups of insurgents on the territory of another State.[128]

While a superficial reading appears to indicate that Brownlie equates "use of force" and "armed attack," a careful reading indicates that Brownlie simply incorporated the narrower concepts of "armed attack" and "aid to groups of insurgents" within the broader concept of "use of force." Had Schwebel cited another passage in Brownlie's text, titled "What is an Armed Attack," he would have revealed a construction of "armed attack" that is clearly consistent with the Court's decision:

> Since the phrase "armed attack" strongly suggests a trespass it is very doubtful if it applies to the case of aid to revolutionary groups and forms of annoyance which do not involve offensive operations by the forces of a state.[129]

In summary, by confusing the legal meaning of "armed attack" and "use of force" while also accusing the Court of an anti-American bias, Schwebel's legal argument in his dodgy dissent was just as flawed as his factual presentation.

Having reviewed the Court's decision and Judge Schwebel's dissent, we can now review the *New York Times* editorial on the case. The first paragraph is a model of editorial writing at the *Times,* given that, "predictably," the first two sentences are balanced like entries in a double-entry accounting ledger:

> Predictably, the World Court has found the United States guilty of violating international law by supporting the "contra" war against Nicaragua. Just as predictably, the Reagan administration feels vindicated for not bothering to defend itself; it scorns this frail institution as irredeemably hostile.

The appearance through such balancing is that the *Times* is scrupulously fair—it criticizes the Court and the Reagan administration on identical grounds. The third sentence is equally well balanced, again with pejoratives on both sides of the ledger:

> The Court's judgment was deplorably broad, but America's response was damagingly petulant.

The fourth sentence is also balanced, with a mild rebuke for the administration's non-participation and an allusion to the Court's supposed antagonism toward the United States:

> The "laws" the Court seeks to articulate are more accurately values, rooted in traditions that America should honor even in a hostile forum.

By balancing its editorial in this way, the editorial page essentially entered false entries in the ledger. For one thing, the editorial asserted that international law, including presumably the Charter of the United Nations—the most important US-ratified treaty—is more accurately a set of "values" and is not real law. However, to repeat once again, Article VI(2) of the US Constitution states that "all treaties made, or which shall be made, under the authority of the United States, shall be the supreme law of the land." Thus, citing no legal authority and having none, the *Times* editorial page simply declared null and void what the Constitution has made "the supreme law of the land." Also, there was no factual or legal basis to declare the Court's opinion against the United States "deplorably broad." If anything, the Court factually and legally narrowed the case against the United States to the disadvantage of Nicaragua. Furthermore, any predictability in the case was a function of the case's merits, and not any anti-American bias at the Court. Both the facts and law strongly supported Nicaragua's main legal arguments, explaining why the government leadership in Managua initiated expensive legal proceedings in a distant venue.

The fifth and sixth sentences in the editorial continued the balanced but misleading analysis:

> As the Nicaragua case shows, the absence of effective rebuttal only aggravates the Court's tendentiousness. Worse, for America not to defend its policy leaves the impression the policy is indefensible.

There was no tendentiousness at the Court toward the United States. In fact, rather than "aggravate" the Court, the US absence prompted the Court to invoke the US multilateral treaty reservation on behalf of the

United States, which significantly narrowed the severity of its judgment on the administration's illegal policies toward Nicaragua. Having established the Court's bias in the reader's mind, however, the editorial page sets up its conjured criticism of the administration for exacerbating that prejudice by not appearing before the Court. Thus, the editorial appeared to criticize both parties; thus, it appeared to be balanced and fair.

By establishing an appearance of balance at the outset, the editorial page presented itself with opportunities to discredit the Court's decision while still maintaining a facade of fairness. This resulted in a complete distortion of the Court's decision within the guise of a fair and balanced editorial. Thus, in addition to what the editorial had already reported, the ninth sentence of the editorial stated:

> But even the majority acknowledged that prior attacks against El Salvador from Nicaragua made "collective defense" a possible justification for America's retaliation.

In order for this statement to be true, it would have been necessary for the Court to rule that El Salvador had been the victim of "prior attacks" by Nicaragua. But the Court made no such statement. While the Court stated it "is satisfied that, between July 1979, the date of the fall of the Somoza regime in Nicaragua, and the early months of 1981, an intermittent flow of arms was routed via the territory of Nicaragua to the armed opposition in El Salvador," it stated in the next sentence that, "on the other hand, the evidence is insufficient to satisfy the Court that, since the early months of 1981, assistance has continued to reach the Salvadoran armed opposition from the territory of Nicaragua on any significant scale, or that the Government of Nicaragua was responsible for any flow of arms at either period."[130] Thus, the Court could not have ruled, and did not rule, that El Salvador had been the victim of "prior attacks" by Nicaragua.

Nor did the Court make "collective self-defense" a possible justification for "America's retaliation," as the Court itself indicated:

> Even assuming that the supply of arms to the opposition in El Salvador could be treated as imputable to the Government of Nicaragua, to justify invocation of the right of collective self-defence in customary international law, [the arms flow] would have to be equated with an armed attack by Nicaragua on El Salvador. As stated above, the Court is unable to consider that, in customary international law, the provision of arms to the opposition in another State constitutes an armed attack on that State. Even at a time

when the arms flow was at its peak, and again assuming the participation of the Nicaraguan government, that would not constitute such armed attack.[131]

Nor did the Court describe US military and paramilitary actions against Nicaragua as "retaliation" by the United States; nor were there any grounds to describe the American paramilitary and military actions against Nicaragua as "retaliation."

Sentences thirteen through fifteen of the *Times* editorial endorsed Judge Schwebel's dissenting opinion as follows:

> On a dozen other counts, it was left to the American judge, Stephen Schwebel, to make the case and amass the evidence that the United States should have brought to court. Had it done so, it might have restrained the hostile judgments and emphasized the world's deep disagreements about what constitutes aggression. But who will now read Judge Schwebel's voluminous dissent—his demonstrations of Court prejudice in not even hearing El Salvador's claims against Nicaragua or his condemnation of the Court's double standard in justifying only "anti-colonial" interventions across frontiers.

Here, the editorial page expresses its disappointment that the Reagan administration did not bring Judge Schwebel's presumably excellent factual and legal arguments with it to the Court, while continuing its character assassination of the World Court as an inherently "hostile" and "prejudiced" forum against the United States. And it accused the Court of refusing to hear El Salvador's case against Nicaragua, even though it was El Salvador that turned down the Court's invitation to appear in the merits phase to make that case.

In its unbounded balancing act, the *Times* concludes with this finale:

> Despite the presence of Communist judges, and those of other incompatible ideologies, the Court is the only body that even pretends to search for rational guidelines of international conduct. In such a forum, and doubly so when it feels wronged, Americans should never be silent.

Perhaps it is significant, for the purposes of deconstructing this slur against the Court, that Article 9 of the World Court's statute requires the distribution of the Court's judges to reflect "the main forms of civilization and of the principal legal systems of the world." This explains the presence of judges from the Soviet Union and China on the bench. In any event, whether Communist judges contributed to the majority opinion or not was immaterial to the factual and legal merits of the opinion itself, which clearly was of no concern to the *Times* editorial page. Even so, despite what the editorial page described as anti-American hostility at the Court and incompatible ideologies among the judges, the editorial page admonished the Reagan administration again for not participating in the case, given that we all felt "wronged" as "Americans" by the fundamental unfairness of the process and judgment of the Court.

Up to this point we have tried to demonstrate that the various subtle permutations of editorial policy at the *New York Times*—from Ochs' "impartiality" to Sulzberger's "non-crusading" journalism, to Rosenthal's political "centrism" to everyone's gold standard of objective "balancing"—by themselves do not satisfy the fundamental journalistic requirement of due diligence with respect to facts and law and public accountability, are susceptible to abuse, and have been exploited to facilitate the corrupt positioning strategy of the *Times*. In the next chapter on Vietnam and in our brief conclusion, we propose an alternative editorial policy with higher journalistic standards than these for the US press to apply to its coverage of US foreign policy.

8

THE VIETNAM SYNDROME: FROM THE GULF OF TONKIN TO IRAQ

At 11:37 p.m. on August 4 1964, President Lyndon Johnson announced on national television that US air attacks against North Vietnam were underway in response to "open aggression on the high seas against the United States of America" in the Gulf of Tonkin. The president was referring to North Vietnamese PT-boat attacks on two American destroyers—the *USS Maddox* and *USS Turner Joy*—that he said had occurred earlier that day, and to his decision to order a reprisal bombing of North Vietnam.[1] Minutes later, Secretary of Defense Robert S McNamara reported that the US military reprisal was an "appropriate action in view of the unprovoked attack in international waters on United States naval vessels."[2]

The next day, August 5, the eight-column headline on the front-page of the *New York Times* reported:

U.S. PLANES ATTACK NORTH VIETNAM BASES;

PRESIDENT ORDERS 'LIMITED' RETALIATION

AFTER COMMUNISTS' PT BOATS RENEW RAIDS[3]

The lead front-page story on the incident said that the president's order to bomb North Vietnam "followed a naval battle in which a number of North Vietnamese PT boats attacked two United States destroyers with torpedoes."[4]

A second front-page story reported that McNamara "said that the [US air] attacks had been directed against the bases used by the North Vietnamese PT boats that attacked two United States destroyers in international waters yesterday."[5]

In a third front-page story that day on the Tonkin Gulf incident, the *Times* reported that "the Defense Department announced tonight that North Vietnamese PT Boats made a 'deliberate attack' today on two United States destroyers patrolling international waters in the Gulf of Tonkin off North Vietnam."[6] Throughout its news coverage of the Tonkin incident that day and the days that followed, the *Times* reported the North Vietnamese attacks on the *Maddox* and *Turner Joy* on August 4 as established events as claimed by top Johnson administration officials.

The *Times* editorial page, on August 5, in effect confirmed those events, arguing that President Johnson had presented "the American people last night with the somber facts." The editorial, referring also to the first attack on the *Maddox* on August 2 in the Tonkin Gulf, also gave its support to the reprisal bombing of North Vietnam:

> The attack on one of our warships that at first seemed, and was hoped to be, an isolated incident is now seen in ominous perspective to have been the beginning of a mad adventure by the North Vietnamese Communists. After offensive action against more vessels of our Navy the President has backed up with retaliatory fire the warnings that North Vietnam chose frequently to ignore.[7]

The editorial also echoed President Johnson's claim that he sought "no wider war," though the decision to bomb targets inside North Vietnam clearly signaled a major US military escalation in Vietnam.[8]

We know today that the charges issued by Johnson and McNamara —that North Vietnamese boats had attacked the *Maddox* and *Turner Joy* on August 4—were almost certainly not accurate. We also know that the *Times'* headlines, news reports, and editorial on August 5 about an August 4 Tonkin incident—tied as they all were to official claims made by the Johnson administration—also were not accurate. We also know that, rather than seeking "no wider war" in its reprisal bombing of North Vietnam, the Johnson administration had already authorized secret military and paramilitary actions inside North Vietnam with the aim of provoking an incident that the administration could exploit as a pretext for escalating US military involvement in Vietnam.

We know these things in part because, nearly seven years after the Tonkin Gulf affair, the *New York Times* published on June 13 1971 the first article in its series on the Pentagon Papers, the Defense Department's 43-volume classified study "of how and why the United States had become so deeply involved in Vietnam."[9] When he was defense secretary, McNamara had ordered Pentagon analysts to conduct a classified history of the Vietnam War, of which only a few copies of the massive study were ever printed, all of which were kept in secret locations.[10]

With regard to the Johnson administration's clandestine military and paramilitary campaign against North Vietnam, the *Times* reported:

> What the Pentagon papers call "an elaborate program of covert military operations against the state of North Vietnam" began on Feb. 1, 1964, under the code name Operation Plan 34A. . . .
>
> Through 1964, the 34A operations ranged from flights over North Vietnam by U-2 spy planes and kidnappings of North Vietnamese citizens for intelligence information, to parachuting sabotage and psychological warfare teams into the North, commando raids from the sea to blow up rail and highway bridges and the bombardment of North Vietnamese coastal installations by PT boats.[11]

With regard to the two US destroyers that supposedly were attacked without provocation by North Vietnamese PT boats in early August 1964, the *Times* reported:

> The [US] destroyer patrols in the Gulf of Tonkin, code-named DeSoto patrols, were the third element in the covert military pressures against North Vietnam. While the purpose of the patrols was mainly psychological, as a show of force, the destroyers collected the kind of intelligence on North Vietnamese warning radars and coastal defenses that would be useful to 34A raiding parties or, in the event of a bombing campaign, to pilots. . . .
>
> But the [Pentagon] study makes it clear that the physical presence of the destroyers provided the elements for the Tonkin clash. And immediately after the reprisal air strikes, the Joint Chiefs of Staff and Assistant Secretary of Defense [John T.] McNaughton put forward a "provocation strategy" proposing to repeat the clash as a pretext for bombing the North.[12]

This information from the Pentagon Papers, reported by the *Times* in June 1971, not only contradicted what the Johnson administration had claimed in August 1964, it, ironically, exposed serious problems in the *Times'* August 1964 coverage of the Tonkin incident and its aftermath, given that the *Times* reported that North Vietnam's attacks on the *Maddox* and *Turner Joy* were unprovoked and, for this reason, the US reprisal bombing of North Vietnam was justified. Furthermore, the *Times* reported without question the Johnson administration's assertions that it sought no wider war in Vietnam, despite the *prima facie* escalation of the bombing itself.

Embracing these assumptions not only infected news reports and editorials in its coverage of the Tonkin incident, it also exposed serious flaws in the editorial policy of the *Times*. For example, how should the *Times* mediate competing factual claims between designated enemies of the United States and its own government in the midst of serious conflict or war? In this case, President Johnson announced that North Vietnam had attacked US ships without provocation in the Gulf of Tonkin on August 4. Hanoi denied that it had attacked the ships at all. Hanoi was right. Forty years later, Saddam Hussein denied having WMD, and apparently he was right too. Yet in both cases the *Times* reported and supported misleading US charges that led the United States to catastrophic wars in Vietnam and Iraq.

What, if anything, could the *Times* have done to expose US government deception prior to full-scale war in Vietnam and Iraq? And how can it modify its editorial policy to expose government deception prior to the onset of other such unwarranted wars in the future? In this chapter we propose changes to editorial policy at the *New York Times* that would improve the quality of its journalism, align its editorial mission with its constitutional mandate "to expose government deception"[13] and "enlighten the citizenry"[14] in its coverage of US foreign policy, and allow it to adopt international law as a standard to assess the legality of future threats of force and recourse to war by the United States.

So what could the *Times* have done differently in its news and editorial pages that would have allowed it to cover the late-night August 4 announcements from President Johnson and Defense Secretary McNamara with journalistic independence and integrity? There were, after all, no independent observers in the Tonkin Gulf or aboard the *Maddox* or *Turner Joy* on August 4 that could have confirmed or denied the administration's claim of an attack. And North Vietnamese PT boats apparently had attacked the *Maddox* two days earlier—though with no casualties to the crew or damage to the American ship. Furthermore, on August 7, the US House of Representatives voted 416–0 and the US Senate voted 88–2 to support President Johnson's decision to bomb targets inside North Vietnam in response to the reported August 4 attacks on the *Maddox* and *Turner Joy*, and to authorize the "Commander in Chief, to take all necessary measures to repel any armed attack against the forces of the United States and to prevent further aggression."[15] Thus, at the time, a near unanimous consensus existed in the US government that the *Maddox* and *Turner Joy* had been attacked on August 4 and that the US military reprisal against North Vietnam was justified.

In contrast, the government of North Vietnam had denounced the American claim that two US destroyers had been attacked by North Vietnamese boats on August 4 as "a sheer fabrication by the United States imperialists,"[16] and the governments of the People's Republic of China and the Soviet Union denounced the US bombing of North Vietnam as "deliberate armed aggression"[17] and "armed aggression."[18] In short, given the absence of any evidence to contest the Johnson administration's claim that US ships had been attacked on August 4, the preponderance of American opinion that the *Maddox* and *Turner Joy* had been attacked on August 4, and that the reprisal bombing of North Vietnam was justified, there were few evidentiary opportunities or political incentives for the *Times* to oppose the consensus view of its government with respect to the Tonkin incident without appearing to position itself (without evidence) with North Vietnam's claim that the incident was fabricated by American imperialists.

Variations on this clash between not wanting to support the claims of US enemies in opposition to official US claims would present themselves to the *Times* and its editors for decades to come after August 1964. Whether the clash involved US assertions with respect to Iraqi WMD possession and Saddam Hussein's denials, US claims of a Sandinista arms flow and Sandinista denials, or implausible US claims of non-involvement in the attempted overthrow of Hugo Chávez in Venezuela and Chávez' claims to the contrary, or any of the many other such clashes, the *Times* has never resolved or acknowledged this long-time vulnerability of its editorial policy.

This journalistic point between a rock and hard place—between on the one hand not wanting to be seen giving aid and comfort to the real or fictitious enemies of the United States and on the other fulfilling the paper's mission to "enlighten the citizenry" and "expose government deception"—identifies a major challenge not just to the *Times* but to the US news media in general. This particular dilemma also identifies a major defect in the modern scheme of US constitutionalism. Namely, editorial policy is essentially undifferentiated throughout the US news industry, although derivative to a large extent of the gold standard of objectivity supposedly embodied by the *Times*. Because this flaw in editorial policy is common throughout the industry, the *Times* and the press in general have ceded an excess of constitutional power to the president to initiate illegal and costly military adventures that the authors of the Constitution did not intend and that the Constitution itself clearly prohibits.

So how might the *Times* address this defect, assuming any interest or desire to do so? To answer this question, it is helpful to revisit the events of August 4 1964 and the *Times'* coverage of those events the following day.

Most critics of the Johnson–McNamara announcements near midnight on August 4 have focused their attention on the likelihood that the *Maddox* and *Turner Joy* had not been attacked that day by North Vietnamese boats. One of the best accounts is by Daniel Ellsberg, who begins his excellent book on the Pentagon Papers affair by describing his own involvement with events that day:

> On Tuesday morning, August 4, 1964, my first full day on my new job in the Pentagon, a courier came into the outer office with an urgent cable for my boss. He'd been running. The secretaries told him Assistant Secretary John McNaughton was out of the office; he was down the hall with Secretary of Defense Robert McNamara. They pointed him to me, his new special assistant. The courier handed me the cable and left. It was easy to see, as I read it, why he had been running.[19]

Although most people know Daniel Ellsberg as the former Pentagon official who leaked the Pentagon Papers to the *New York Times*, he is less well known for being the person at the Pentagon on August 4 1964 who first read the cables that Captain John J. Herrick—the commanding officer of the *Maddox* and *Turner Joy* mission in the Tonkin Gulf—had frantically sent as the *Maddox* was being attacked by North Vietnamese PT boats. Or so Herrick thought.

Ten minutes after receiving the first cable, Ellsberg read a second cable from Herrick. "Am under continuous torpedo attack," Herrick wrote. The cables from Herrick kept coming. "The messages were vivid," wrote Ellsberg:

> Herrick must have been dictating them from the bridge in between giving orders, as his two ships swerved to avoid torpedoes picked up on the sonar of the *Maddox* and fired in the darkness at targets shown on the radar of the *Turner Joy*. "Torpedoes missed. Another fired at us. Four torpedoes in water. And five torpedoes in water. . . . Have . . . successfully avoided at least six torpedoes."

Nine torpedoes had been fired at his ships, fourteen, twenty-six. More attacking boats had been hit; at least one sunk. This action wasn't ending after forty minutes or an hour. It was going on, ships dodging and firing in choppy seas, planes overhead firing rockets at locations given them by the *Turner Joy's* radar, for an incredible two hours before the stream of continuous combat updates finally ended. Then, suddenly, an hour later, full stop. A message arrived that took back not quite all of it, but enough to put everything earlier in question.[20]

That message from Herrick said:

Review of action makes many reported contacts and torpedoes fired appear doubtful. Freak weather effects on radar and overeager sonarmen may have accounted for many reports. No actual visual sightings by *Maddox*. Suggest complete evaluation before any further action taken.[21]

In later cables that day, Herrick expressed doubts that a prolonged confrontation with hostile boats and torpedoes had taken place, "except for apparent attempted ambush at beginning."[22] Ellsberg concluded that afternoon, "along with everyone else I spoke to, that there probably had been an attack of some sort" on the *Maddox* and *Turner Joy*,[23] though he also wrote: "As negative evidence accumulated, within a few days it came to seem less likely that any attack had occurred on August 4; by 1967 it seemed almost certain there had been no second attack, and by 1971 I was convinced of that beyond a reasonable doubt."[24]

It is generally accepted today that no second attack in the Gulf of Tonkin on August 4 1964 had occurred, and that the confusion on board the *Maddox* and *Turner Joy* was due to the misinterpretation of radar effects by crewmen.[25] However, for our purposes, we need to focus on another question regarding the events of August 4, "one that went unasked in Washington in August 1964"[26] and in the *New York Times* as well: "Whether there were one or two attacks by North Vietnamese boats [between August 2 and August 4], was the U.S. reprisal strike justified"?[27] In his memoirs, published in 1995, McNamara answered, "Probably."[28] However, shortly after his memoirs were published, McNamara initiated and participated in a series of conferences with former North Vietnamese government officials "to review the decision-making of both sides" throughout the war in Vietnam.[29] The book that was the product of those conferences, coauthored by McNamara, and that analyzed the significance of the meetings and recorded exchanges among the participants, concluded "the reprisal, in retrospect, was clearly a mistake as originally conceived."[30] This is because of two major findings that resulted from the McNamara-sponsored conferences.

With regard to the first finding, McNamara relates how General Vo Nguyen Giap, North Vietnam's defense minister during the US war in Vietnam, told McNamara that the August 4 attack did not occur, to which McNamara responded, "I have no reason to believe he is in error."[31] Regarding the second finding, McNamara relates how General Nguyen Dinh Uoc, director of North Vietnam's Institute of Military History, confirmed that an August 2 attack on the *Maddox* had occurred in response to Operation Plan 34A attacks on North Vietnam. Furthermore, McNamara learned that the decision to attack the *Maddox* on August 2 "was not ordered by the central authority in Hanoi but rather by the commander of the torpedo boat squadron in the Tonkin Gulf" and that, therefore, "Hanoi could not read the signal" that McNamara intended to send with the US reprisal bombing "because it did not order the attack."[32]

Thus, one of McNamara's objectives in convening the meetings with former North Vietnamese officials—to determine whether the US military reprisal had contributed to the "misperceptions, misjudgments, and misunderstandings" that led to "the spiral of escalation toward a U.S.-Vietnam war"—had been achieved.[33] He concluded that bombing North Vietnam in response to the Tonkin incident was an unnecessary escalation toward a wider war in Vietnam.[34]

Though McNamara, in our view, identifies the key question with respect to the events that occurred in early August 1964—that is, whether the US reprisal bombing of North Vietnam was justified—and though we also conclude that it was not, we cite different reasons. We argue that, even if the North Vietnamese had attacked US ships in the Gulf of Tonkin on August 2 and August 4, and even if North Vietnam had ordered the attacks, under international law the US reprisal bombing nevertheless would have been illegal and unjustifiable.

A military reprisal involves a unilateral use of force by one state against a second state in response to a prior infliction of injury by the second state. In the context of the Tonkin incident, the United States bombed targets inside North Vietnam in response to a presumptive North Vietnamese attack on US ships on August 2 and 4. However, as the US Lawyers Committee on Vietnam argued in 1967, "in the present system of world order, injured states may take actions short of violence, but a general consensus prohibits the use of force in reprisal in view of the categorical prohibitions of the United Nations Charter."[35]

The Lawyers Committee cited a number of authoritative commentators, with a few cited here, showing a legal consensus with respect to the illegality of military reprisals. A study issued under the auspices of the British Royal Institute of International Affairs concluded: "It is now generally considered that reprisals involving the use or threat of force are illegal."[36] In April 1964, a UN Security Council resolution, in reference to British raids against Yemen in reprisal to Yemen's attacks on the British Protectorate of Aden, condemned "reprisals as incompatible with the purposes and principles of the United Nations."[37] In its decision on the merits in the *Corfu Channel Case* (1949), the International Court of Justice unanimously determined that a British mine-sweeping operation in Albanian territorial waters (after mines exploded there had caused the death of forty-seven British seamen) was an illegal military response by the British government, despite the fact that the Court found the mines had been illegally emplaced by Albania. The Court argued that military reprisal is impermissible because "from the nature of things, it would be reserved for the most powerful states, and might easily lead to perverting the administration of international justice itself."[38]

In the extended debate in the UN Security Council on April 6 1964, prior to the Council's resolution on the British–Yemen incident cited above, US Ambassador to the United Nations, Adlai Stevenson, stated: "My government has repeatedly expressed its emphatic disapproval of provocative acts and retaliatory raids, wherever they occur and by whomever they are committed."[39] Given the date and context of Ambassador Stevenson's statement, recall that Operation Plan 34A was already underway and that the US reprisal bombing of North Vietnam would be launched exactly four months later. Thus, the "repeatedly expressed emphatic" position of the US government recognized, in principle, the illegality of its own provocative Operation Plan 34A actions inside North Vietnam in addition to its reprisal bombings against North Vietnam.

With respect to the *New York Times'* coverage of the Tonkin incidents, its editors and reporters did not have until 1967 and 1971, as in the case of Daniel Ellsberg, or more than thirty years, as in the case of Robert McNamara, to determine for the purposes of its August 5 1964 edition whether the *Maddox* and *Turner Joy* had been attacked on August 4 or not. However, as the most important newspaper in the most important democracy and most powerful nation in the world, and given the major significance of the US reprisal attack inside North Vietnam, the *Times* should have elevated its coverage to a higher level of scrutiny to consider whether the reprisal bombing of North Vietnam was or was not consistent with international law. Furthermore, any decision to resort to force by the United States—given its immense military power, its standing in the international community as the world's premier democratic state, and its official, repeated, announced commitment over two centuries to the rule of law—clearly merits the strictest scrutiny by the leading newspaper in the United States as an expression, affirmation, and symbol of that commitment. This highest level of journalistic scrutiny would include an analysis of whether a use of force by the United States was consistent with international law or not.

Instead of raising its level of journalistic review to match the seriousness of the occasion, however, the *Times* neglected on August 5 1964 to report the *prima facie* illegality of the US reprisal bombing of North Vietnam, or to raise any questions at all with respect to legality. This negligence was due then, as today, to the *Times*' refusal to incorporate international law into its editorial policy. Without international law as a component of editorial policy in any major US news outlet, the Johnson administration was completely free to operate illegally toward Vietnam. Given that the US Congress had also disregarded international law in its consensus support for the Tonkin Gulf resolution, the constitutional system of checks and balances had completely broken down, as it would in the future under similar conditions. Had the press and the Congress invoked international law at that critical moment, a debate about the legality of the president's decision to bomb North Vietnam might have ensued, the Constitution might have been strengthened (rather than weakened), the world might have been spared the full catastrophe of the Vietnam War that followed, and a journalistic precedent might have been established as a check against any future president's inclination to launch illegal military attacks based on faultily asserted factual claims.

One irony with respect to the *Times*' coverage of the Tonkin incident in August 1964 is that it reflected the *Times*' standards of non-crusading journalism, including an excessive deference to a deployment of executive power beyond the Constitution's limits, while its series on the Pentagon Papers, which in effect corrected the record of the Tonkin incident as reported by the *Times*, was a departure from those standards. Furthermore, even though the *Times*' series on the Pentagon Papers exposed retroactively a major weakness in its editorial policy, evident in its earlier rubber-stamping of official facts and conduct during the Vietnam War, the *Times* apparently never reviewed its coverage of the Tonkin incident and the reprisal bombing of August 1964 in light of its

Pentagon Papers revelations. Not only is there no public evidence of such a review, but the *Times* proceeded for the next four decades to apply the same uncorrected standards of editorial policy to what became a repetitive characteristic of US foreign policy—the use and threat of force, often in flagrant violation of international law and with official justifications citing unverifiable or inaccurate representations of fact.

In the wake of the Tonkin Gulf incident, the Johnson administration increased its troop commitment, and by February 1965 there were 23,000 US soldiers in Vietnam.[40] Since at least 1961, the United States had been waging a major counterinsurgency campaign in South Vietnam against guerrillas of the South Vietnamese National Liberation Front (NLF), dubbed "Vietcong" by the United States. According to a *New York Times* report, by February 1965, 376 Americans had been killed (263 in combat and 113 in accidents) in Vietnam since January 1 1961.[41] In comparison, by early 1965, the US counterinsurgency war in South Vietnam had killed more than 150,000 Vietnamese.[42]

This was the war context of a February 7 1965 early-morning NLF attack on the US airbase at Pleiku in northern South Vietnam, and on a US helicopter base a short distance away. The attacks were reported on the front page of the *Times* later that day: "Communist guerrillas killed at least seven United States soldiers and wounded 80 others, two of these critically, this morning in two swift attacks on major Vietnamese Army installations in the central highlands."[43] The next day, the *Times* reported "United States aircraft struck at North Vietnam early today" in reprisal for the attacks on the American airbases.[44] In a statement issued by the White House, President Johnson said:

> Today's action by the U.S. and South Vietnamese Governments was in response to provocations ordered and directed by the Hanoi regime. . . . To meet these attacks the Government of South Vietnam and the U.S. Government agreed to appropriate reprisal actions against North Vietnamese targets.[45]

In its report, the *Times* observed that the NLF attack at Pleiku and the US reprisal bombing represented "the most threatening crisis in Southeast Asia since the Gulf of Tonkin clash last August."[46] Indeed, the US response to the Pleiku attack, like the US response to the Tonkin incident, not only fatefully escalated US military involvement in Vietnam, but the official factual assertions justifying the US response to the Pleiku attack were nearly as flawed as those asserted to justify the US response to the Tonkin incident. While President Johnson announced at the time that the NLF attacks at Pleiku were "ordered and directed by the Hanoi regime," McNamara wrote more than thirty years later that the Pleiku attack "was not ordered by Hanoi."[47] Moreover, the US military reprisal against North Vietnam in response to the Pleiku attacks would have violated international law even if Hanoi had ordered and directed those attacks.

Like its coverage of the Tonkin incident, the *Times'* coverage of the Pleiku attacks published, featured, and supported the factual assertions of President Johnson while neglecting to address the legality of the US reprisal bombing of North Vietnam. In its editorial on the Pleiku incident, titled "Reprisal in Vietnam," the *Times* editorial page, arguing in clear disregard of international law, said "that when the other side strikes in the way that it did, there is no alternative for the United States but to strike back in reprisal," and that "the strike at North Vietnam was understandable and justifiable as a tactical response in a war situation."[48]

For one thing, these remarks apparently regard North Vietnam and the NLF as synonymous and interchangeable entities, given the conflated reference here to "the other side" that consumes at once the NLF (the entity that attacked the airbase at Pleiku) and North Vietnam (the entity that was attacked in retaliation). Furthermore, the editorial does not explain how a South Vietnamese attack on the airplanes and helicopters that at the time were the principal instruments used in killing over 150,000 South Vietnamese is less "understandable and justifiable [as a] tactical response in a war situation" than a US military reprisal that is viewed as illegal under international law.

This logic reflects the insidious influence of excluding international law as a criterion of review in an assessment of war situations and claims, evident also in the *Times'* coverage of the Tonkin incident. The *Maddox* and *Turner Joy* were powerful US destroyers belonging to the US Seventh Fleet, a 100-ship flotilla based in the western Pacific Ocean, and including up to thirty destroyers and three US aircraft-carrier groups —the *USS Ticonderoga*, the *USS Constellation*, and the *USS Yorktown*—which together carried hundreds of attack planes and bombers, including F-4 Phantoms, A-4 bombers, and A-3 heavy attack bombers.[49] In contrast, the North Vietnamese navy in 1964 was "understood to have consisted of about fifty patrol boats of various types, including modernized junks."[50] The US air strikes on August 4 and August 5 destroyed with ease twenty-five of these boats, "about half of the North Vietnamese navy."[51] And given that neither the *Maddox* nor *Turner Joy* sustained any damage or casualties on either August 2 or August 4, that by August 1964 "the United States ha[d] sent [Seventh Fleet] warships into the Gulf of Tonkin from time to time for nearly two years,"[52] and that the Gulf of Tonkin borders the entire coastline of North Vietnam (which is 10,000 miles from the United States), the North Vietnamese had very little capability and few opportunities to militarily injure the United States even as an initial provocation.

Thus, not only did international law escape the *Times'* attention in its coverage of the Tonkin incident, the evident logic of the situation did as well; as it did even in the following instance when the *Times* editorial page, while citing the presence of overwhelming US military power in the Tonkin Gulf, nevertheless offered little more than a senseless warning to Hanoi:

> North Vietnam's capability of injuring the Seventh Fleet is small. The power of the Seventh Fleet to damage North Vietnam is incalculable. Since this must be evident, nothing is more vital than for Hanoi to be left in no doubt about the American intention to remain in the Tonkin Gulf and to continue supporting South Vietnam's effort. The President's action should convey this message clearly.[53]

Though the legal arguments against the US reprisal attacks in response to the Tonkin Gulf and Pleiku incidents were compelling, they required *a fortiori* some ability to independently assess the basic military parameters of the situation. With respect to the NLF attacks at Pleiku, both the Johnson administration and the *Times* appeared to assume that the NLF had no right to attack US positions in South Vietnam, and that the United States, by bombing North Vietnam in a reprisal attack, had a right to retaliate against whomever it wished. In this regard, the Lawyers Committee on Vietnam argued:

> To begin with, no explanation [from the Johnson administration] was offered why the guerrilla attack at Pleiku on February 7, 1965, constituted a "provocation," or in what manner it differed, in law or fact, from previous skirmishes in South Vietnam. "Deliberate surprise" is a normal aspect of hostilities, and the United States had for years prior to that incident, planned and otherwise participated in "deliberate surprise attacks" on a much larger scale against the [NLF] guerrillas. It is, therefore, not possible that the United States suffered a legal wrong by the attack on Pleiku.[54]

Henry Steele Commager made a similar point in a letter that the *Times* published but did not heed:

We are already falling into the pattern of a two-level vocabulary so familiar in Communist dispatches, and in "1984."

Secretary McNamara spoke of the first Vietcong attack as a "sneak" attack; the President's statement of Feb. 11 characterized Vietcong warfare as "murder" and "assassination"; even your own correspondent speaks of "terrorist" attacks.

Are we to suppose that our own attacks on the Vietcong are announced in advance, that they are not designed to spread terror or to kill?

Surely it is not so much guerrilla attacks on military installations which deserve these terms as air bombardment which kills civilian and combatant alike. If we are to have the agony of war may we at least be spared the humiliation of double-talk.[55]

Because an editorial policy that incorporated international law would require some ability to fairly assess facts and context, and apply them logically to government conduct, the *Times* would also need to begin reporting and processing facts independently of what US government officials say, while also evaluating them within the framework of international law.

By early February 1965, the *Times* was referring to the US air strikes against North Vietnam in response to the Pleiku and Tonkin incidents as a "a policy of retaliation." By February 10, however, the Johnson administration had already transitioned to "a policy of greater flexibility," which removed even the pretext of retaliation as a rationale for bombing North Vietnam. "Greater flexibility" was simply a broad, open-ended assertion of an American entitlement to bomb North Vietnam. The *Times* duly noted the administration's transition, but neglected to note the escalating conflict between US policy and international law. For example, in the beginning paragraphs of a front-page article on February 10, *Times* reporter Tad Szulc wrote:

The United States has adopted a policy of greater flexibility in any further retaliatory strikes against North Vietnam, officials reported today.

Future [US] counterstrikes, they said, would not necessarily be limited to those in response to attack on United States forces, as in the Gulf of Tonkin and Pleiku incidents.

Air retaliation might be ordered in response to Vietcong or North Vietnamese assaults upon South Vietnam's troops or installations, even if no United States men or facilities are involved, the officials said.

"There is nothing fixed or absolute about this policy," an official said. "We may strike again whenever it is justified in our view."[56]

The Johnson administration had no legal claim under international law to bomb North Vietnam "whenever it is justified" in its view. North Vietnam had not engaged in an armed attack against South Vietnam—the only possible legal justification at the time for the United States to bomb North Vietnam—nor had the Johnson administration argued that it had. The administration implicitly conceded this point shortly before February 10 when it justified bombing North Vietnam on February 7 as a "reprisal" to the Pleiku incident, not as "collective self-defense" with South Vietnam. Nor had the Johnson administration, prior to February 10 1965, attempted to justify any US military actions in Vietnam as "collective self-defense" with South Vietnam. Furthermore, by February 1965, the United States had reported no North Vietnamese troops south of the 17th parallel—the temporary demarcation line separating the north and south zones of Vietnam—thus making any claim of collective self-defense with South Vietnam nearly impossible, given also the absence of a North Vietnamese air force or navy to speak of. In short, the Johnson administration made virtually no attempt by February 10 to justify under international law a "policy of greater flexibility" to bomb North Vietnam. And the *Times* made no attempt to evaluate within the context of international law the US claim of a discretionary option to bomb North Vietnam.

Meanwhile, by February 1965, uneasiness about the administration's Vietnam policy began to set in, and the see-saw, centrist template of editorial-page commentary—recognizable nearly forty years later in the *Times* editorials on Iraq—commenced in earnest. Thus, in an editorial on February 10, the *Times* on the one hand championed a principled American right to wage and escalate a war in Vietnam while questioning whether the "exemplary" US war mission in Vietnam was achievable:

> There is no cause to quarrel with the sentiments of President Johnson in commenting to his Boy Scout visitors on the American reprisals against North Vietnam:
> "We love peace," he said, "...but we love liberty the more and we shall take up any threat, we shall pay any price to make certain that freedom shall not perish from this earth."
> The people of the United States do love peace; they love freedom; they will fight for it. Mr. Johnson was on completely safe ground, even to a little forgivable plagiarism from Abraham Lincoln.

Having expressed its support for President Johnson's statement of principles, the editorial page then questioned whether the president's principled goals were attainable:

> The motives [for the US war in Vietnam] are exemplary and every American can be proud of them, but the crucial questions are: Can it be done? Is the price too high? Was the military decision in the Kennedy Administration to increase American forces in Vietnam mistaken? Are the dangers of escalation too great? Is this a good battleground of the cold war on which to fight? Is the United States losing more than it is gaining? All lead up to the basic question that some Senators are asking: Is this war necessary?[57]

Although it was already evident at the time that the US war in Vietnam was not about "peace, freedom, and liberty" as President Johnson told the Boy Scouts, other motives were revealed a few years later. In the first installment of the Pentagon Papers series published on June 13 1971, the *Times*' Neil Sheehan reported that the Pentagon study "reveals a deeper perception among the President and his aides that the United States was now the most powerful nation in the world and that the outcome in South Vietnam would demonstrate the will and the ability of the United States to have its way in world affairs."[58] Sheehan also unearthed a memo written by Assistant Defense Secretary John McNaughton to Defense Secretary McNamara that "capsulized" US war aims in Vietnam as follows (the words in parentheses are McNaughton's):

> 70 pct.—To avoid a humiliating U.S. defeat (to our reputation as a guarantor).

> 20 pct.—To keep SVN (and then adjacent) territory from Chinese hands.

> 10 pct.—To permit the people of SVN to enjoy a better, freer way of life.

> Also—To emerge from crisis without unacceptable taint from methods used.[59]

The memo then asserted that the US mission in Vietnam was "NOT—to help a friend," that is South Vietnam, further undermining any notion that bombing North Vietnam had anything to do with the collective self-defense of South Vietnam.

Even if we were to exclude consideration of the consistently hawkish reporting and commentary on Vietnam by Hanson Baldwin and Arthur Krock, and feature only well-articulated criticism of the war to the extent that the *Times* published such criticism, the *Times'* coverage would still be weighted toward an unwarranted principled support of US war aims in Vietnam.

In an important opinion piece on February 14 1965, the *Times* Washington bureau chief, James Reston, wrote that "very few people here" in Washington "question the necessity for a limited expansion of the war by U.S. bombers into Communist territory," given that "the American and South Vietnamese position was crumbling fast, and the political and strategic consequences of defeat would have been serious for the free world all over Asia." Thus, by his own count and by implication, Reston and nearly everyone else in Washington overlooked the obvious illegality involved in bombing North Vietnam. Reston went on, however, to criticize the war effort, arguing that "nobody has made [US goals in Vietnam] clear to the American people"; "President Johnson has not made a major speech on the details of this war since he entered the White House"; and "we are in a war that is not only undeclared and unexplained, but that has not been widely debated in the Congress or the country."

In addition, Reston underscored the potential dire consequences should the US bombing campaign eventually engage "Red Chinese MIG fighters" and bases near the Chinese border. He was also concerned that bombing North Vietnam might prompt the North Vietnamese government to send its armed forces into South Vietnam:

> This is a delicate and highly dangerous situation. The United States has the air and naval power to wipe out North Vietnam and the Chinese Air Force, if it comes into the battle. But the North Vietnamese have a quarter of a million men under arms who have never been committed to the battle at all, and few observers in Washington believe this force could be stopped without the intervention of a very large American army on the ground.

Reston concludes by appealing to the consensus position in Washington to reconsider its indifference toward the war:

> Somebody, however, has to make a move to reverse the trend and stop the present crooked course. For the moment, we seem to be standing mute in Washington, paralyzed before a great issue, and merely digging our thought deeper into the accustomed military rut.[60]

Some of these criticisms were important. However, by accepting in principle the administration's right to bomb North Vietnam—a concession that Reston blandly gives the administration even in the context of its "undeclared and unexplained war"—Reston and other such critics failed to offer for consideration the strong legal and rational case against the bombing and further US escalation, thus relieving the administration of the burden of showing that its war actions in Vietnam were legal or rational. With little opposition to its threats to bomb North Vietnam with "greater flexibility," the Johnson administration initiated in late February 1965 the "Rolling Thunder" US bombing campaign against North Vietnam, which would "remain in effect for the next three and a half years," according to former Defense Secretary McNamara. McNamara also wrote that on February 26 1965, "the president approved the dispatch of two U.S. Marine battalions to Danang as a security force to protect the U.S. airbase there" and that "those Marines would be only the first installment of what would become approximately 2 million U.S. combat personnel who would serve, at one time or another, in South Vietnam during the next decade."[61]

Although the uncontested US bombings of North Vietnam in 1964 and 1965 began the major escalation of US military involvement, the origins of direct US military involvement in Vietnam date back at least to 1954. The signing ceremony of the Geneva Accords on Vietnam in the early morning hours of July 21 1954 marked the official end of the French colonial war in Vietnam. During that war, more than 300,000 Vietnamese were killed by the French from 1946 to 1954, with $2 billion of assistance from the United States, which accounted for most of the French costs of the war in its final years.

The Geneva Accords of 1954 consisted of three agreements on the cessation of hostilities in Vietnam, Laos, and Cambodia, five unilateral declarations issued by the governments of Laos, Cambodia, and France, and a "Final Declaration of the Geneva Conference" that, in the words of the declaration, "takes note of the agreements ending hostilities in Cambodia, Laos, and Vietnam and organiz[es] international control and the supervision of the provisions of these agreements."[62] The Final Declaration was signed by representatives of the United Kingdom, France, the Soviet Union, and the People's Republic of China. Though the United States participated in the conference, it did not sign the Final Declaration.

At the closing session of the Geneva Conference, the United Kingdom's Anthony Eden, who served as the conference chairman, asked his colleagues to vote on the Final Declaration, which would bind each of the participants to the requirements of the agreements. The representatives of France, the People's Republic of China, the United Kingdom, and the Soviet Union signed the Final Declaration with the following pronouncements:

> Mr. Mendes–France (France): "Mr. Chairman, the French delegation approves the terms of the Declaration."
> Mr. Chou En'lai (China): "We agree."
> Mr. Eden (United Kingdom): "On behalf of Her Majesty's Government in the United Kingdom, I associate myself with the Final Declaration of this conference."
> Mr. Molotov (Soviet Union) : "The Soviet Delegation agrees."[63]

With respect to the legal status of the 1954 Geneva Accords, the Lawyers Committee on Vietnam wrote:

> While the Charter of the United Nations, as the most comprehensive basis of world legal order, is of course applicable to the Vietnam situation, the particular situation in Vietnam is governed by a series of compacts, namely, the Geneva Accords of 1954. Under a general principle of international law, special compacts prevail over general rules, insofar as they do not violate them in letter or spirit. The Geneva Accords, carefully designed to restore peace to a war-torn area, fulfill the highest aim of the Charter.[64]

In contrast to this assessment, *New York Times* reporter Hanson Baldwin, in describing the Geneva Accords as a "national defeat" for the French, wrote that "the Geneva peace also represented a defeat for the United States, for despite massive aid to the French our policies were ineffective." Baldwin continued: "If the Allied nations had formed a Southeast Asia alliance, if Britain and the United States had been willing to pay the high price of military intervention in Indochina, if France had given her expeditionary force wholehearted support, if the Allies had stuck together, the answer might have been different."

Referring to US and European colonial interests, Baldwin lamented further that "widespread repercussions are to be anticipated, unfavorable to the United States point of view in Asia and Africa," including "increased Nationalist and Communist-sponsored agitation in French North Africa, important to the French economy and French military strength, and to the United States for air bases." With respect to the specific terms of the treaty, Baldwin wrote: "the military problem is further sharpened by the provision that would require the withdrawal of all 'foreign troops.' About 75,000 Frenchmen, 18,000 French Legionnaires, and 50,000 to 60,000 Africans [who] have been the heart and soul of the Vietnamese defense." "Moreover," Baldwin wrote, "the provision for a general election to reunite Vietnam may mean political communization of the whole area." In short, given the Geneva Accords and the Final Declaration, "the Communists have scored another major victory in the struggle for the world with a cease-fire attained in the Indochinese War."[65]

The *Times* editorial page was more tactful than Baldwin—for example, neglecting to mention that 50,000 to 60,000 Africans had been fighting in Vietnam on behalf of the French with US support—but it reached similar conclusions. While it noted that "the Geneva conference reached agreement last night on an armistice ending more than seven years of armed conflict in Indochina," for which "the whole world can give grateful thanks," the editorial page also argued that the Geneva settlement "in many respects runs contrary to the principles for which we stand," and supported the American decision to disassociate itself from the Accords by refusing to sign the Final Declaration.

The editorial criticized the terms of the Accords on the grounds that they would "turn over more than half of [Vietnam's] 22 million people to Communist rule," would "give the Communist sector a great advantage in the elections scheduled to be held two years hence," which could "end in Vietnam's 'unification' under Communist domination," and that Vietnam could not "express its real choice" in the elections because of "the presence ... of a Communist member with veto power"[66] in the International Control Commission (ICC), the independent commission charged with monitoring compliance to the accords.

However, the Pentagon Papers, which "reviewed U.S. policy toward Indochina during and immediately following World War II," also reviewed "the refusal by the United States to extend assistance to Ho Chi Minh" after the war "despite his requests." They also "make clear the fact that Ho was acknowledged to be a genuine nationalist, as well as a communist, who was intent on maintaining his independence from the Soviet Union and China."[67] Also, "as is generally recognized, the two-year transition period [toward unification elections] and the obligation to withdraw behind the 17th parallel was accepted by the Viet Minh under Soviet and Chinese pressure and constituted a considerable concession" to the French, British, and Americans by the Viet Minh.[68] Furthermore, Article 6 of the Final Declaration stipulated "that the military demarcation line is provisional" pending the unification elections "and should not in any way be interpreted as constituting a political or territorial boundary."[69]

In any event, while "both the French and the Vietnam People's Republic [North Vietnam] properly withdrew to their respective sides of the 17th parallel, as attested to by the ICC" as the required prelude to unification elections, "the refusal of South Vietnam, with United States backing, to hold the elections for unification, violated the provisions of the Geneva Accords that had made them acceptable to the Viet Minh."[70] The US-supported refusal by South Vietnam to participate in or even discuss the unification elections—which would have been won by Ho Chi Minh with "possibly 80 percent" of the vote according to President Dwight Eisenhower,[71] and which denied the Vietnamese people their fundamental right of self-determination under international law—led to the development of the NLF insurgency in South Vietnam, and to the interventionary spiral of US involvement.

In addition to sponsoring South Vietnam's refusal to comply with the most salient feature of the Geneva Accords on Vietnam—that is, the unification elections—the United States systematically violated the second most important feature of the Accords, which prohibited any foreign military buildup in Vietnam. The Lawyers Committee on Vietnam wrote "it is common knowledge that ever since 1954 the United States engaged in a systematic and ever-increasing modernization and military build-up in South Vietnam" and that "the reports of the ICC are filled with statements about the clandestine character of those operations and describe some of the subterfuges used."[72] The contents of ICC reports from August 1955 to April 1957, which itemized US violations of the Geneva agreement, were summarized by the Lawyers Committee as follows:

- Failure to request previous ICC authorization for introduction of "replacements" of foreign personnel or war materials; "facing the Commission with a *fait accompli*," to which "the Commission takes exception," by introducing 290 United States Army service corps personnel called TERM (Temporary Equipment Recovery Mission) before the ICC had acted on the application;

- Failure to submit manifests and other documents to the ICC;

- Failure to furnish advance notification to the ICC (for example, regarding United States Navy planes that "were visiting Saigon airport regularly");

- Failure to reply to ICC inquiries, for example, with regard to the establishment of two new United States military missions—TRIM

(Training Reorganization Inspection Mission) in March 1955, and CATO (Combat Arms Training Organization) in May 1956;

- Claims "in many instances" that incoming war materials and military personnel were "in transit"; but failure to notify the ICC "about their exit, if any";

- Preventing the ICC from physical access to incoming United States military planes and their cargo, by having them taxi directly to the military part of the Saigon airport, from which, contrary to the Accords, the ICC teams were excluded; or by claiming that certain United States "military and other planes" are "United States Embassy planes"; ... or preventing the ICC's reconnaissance of eight areas where, contrary to the Accords, new military airfields were allegedly being constructed.[73]

By disavowing the 1954 Geneva Accords through withholding its signature from the Final Declaration, and then proceeding systematically to violate the two most important features of the Accords, the United States tragically reignited war in Vietnam. By bombing North Vietnam, beginning in 1964 and 1965, in violation of the international law prohibition against the international use of force, the United States unnecessarily escalated its already illegal involvement in Vietnam. Thus, from at least 1954 (when the United States violated the Geneva Accords on Vietnam) to 2004 (when American armed forces in Iraq were found to have violated the Geneva Conventions with respect to detainees and civilians in Iraq), the United States has persistently violated vital and essential rules of international law in the conduct of its foreign affairs, with virtually no journalistic oversight exercised by the *New York Times* with respect to these violations. This absence of oversight and serious debate, including the failure to recognize the relevance of international law to its editorial policy, combined with its repetitive record of unwarranted deference to executive claims of an extraordinary and extra-legal right to wage war and overthrow governments, has in our minds profoundly damaged the credibility of the *Times'* coverage of US foreign policy. It has also contributed to a downward spiral of insult and injury to the US Constitution and the foundational commitment to the rule of law in the United States, especially in the setting of foreign policy.

In an attempt to bring about the end of the Vietnam war, Daniel Ellsberg gave most of the Pentagon's 43-volume secret history of the war to Neil Sheehan, a reporter at the *Times* with whom Ellsberg was acquainted. People involved in the Pentagon Papers project at the *Times* soon realized that the contents of the classified papers "established that the U.S. government had systematically deceived the American people during several administrations about the purpose of American involvement in South Vietnam, the risks of involvement, and the likely duration, destruction, and costs of the war."[74]

A heated debate ensued among top corporate and editorial personnel at the *Times* about whether it should publish an analysis of the documents and even portions of the secret documents themselves. Despite being counseled by a prominent New York City law firm that the *Times'* publisher and the paper's top editors might be imprisoned for violating the espionage laws, the publisher, Punch Sulzberger, and the *Times'* top editor, Abe Rosenthal, decided to publish a ten-part series on the secret papers and to publish portions of key documents. Although the *Times* made a very significant effort to avoid publishing information that might damage US national security, President Nixon's attorney general, John Mitchell, sent Punch Sulzberger a telegram on June 14 that read:

> I have been advised by the Secretary of Defense that the material published in the *New York Times* on June 13, 14 1971 captioned "key texts from Pentagon Vietnam Study" contains information relating to the national defense of the United States and bears a top secret classification.
>
> As such, publication of this information is directly prohibited by the provisions of the Espionage law, Title 18, United States Code, Section 793.
>
> Moreover, further publication of information of this character will cause irreparable injury to the defense interests of the United States.
>
> Accordingly, I respectfully request that you publish no further information of this character and advise me that you have made arrangements for the return of these documents to the Department of Defense.[75]

Also on June 14, Assistant Attorney General Robert Mardian telephoned Harding Bancroft, the *Times* executive vice-president, to say that the government would sue the *Times* if it published other installments on the Pentagon Papers.

Most of the newspaper's reporters and editors supported the newspaper's decision to publish the series, given the importance to the country of what the documents revealed about the conduct of the war in Vietnam. But the publisher—along with Bancroft and Sydney Gruson, the publisher's executive assistant, as well as Abe Rosenthal and James Goodale, the *Times'* in-house attorney—had to decide how to respond to the government's threat. When these four without

Sulzberger, who was in London, "got together in the *Times* executive offices on the fourteenth floor they disagreed over how to reply to the government's request." Rosenthal and Goodale "argued that the *Times* had to publish the series," while Bancroft and Gruson wanted to "suspend publication."[76] David Rudenstine describes what happened:

> Bancroft telephoned Sulzberger, who was asleep in his London hotel, and summarized the telegram Attorney General John Mitchell had sent the newspaper that evening and the position taken by Mardian during Bancroft's call with him. Bancroft also told Sulzberger that [Louis] Loeb [a prominent attorney in New York close to the *Times*] opposed further publication. Rosenthal could contain himself no longer. He shouted into the speaker phone: "Punch, this is Abe. I think you should talk to Goodale." Goodale strongly urged that the *Times* continue to publish the series as planned. Sulzberger asked Goodale if further publication would increase the newspaper's legal liability, and Goodale answered, "Not by five percent." The publisher told them to "go ahead" with the next installment.
>
> Rosenthal went to the city room on the third floor. Over 150 people were waiting to learn whether the *Times* would publish the next installment. Rosenthal announced, "Go ahead," and the crowd cheered.[77]

The Nixon administration's suit against the *New York Times* in the Pentagon Papers case quickly made it to the US Supreme Court. On June 30 1971, the Court voted 6–3 to permit the *Times* (and the *Washington Post*) to continue publishing their respective series on the Pentagon Papers. The majority, finding no violations of the espionage laws and no threat to US national security, argued in an unsigned opinion that "any system of prior restraints of expression comes to this Court bearing a heavy presumption against its constitutional validity" and that the Government "thus carries a heavy burden of showing justification for the imposition of such a restraint."[78]

In a separate opinion, Justice Hugo Black, a 34-year veteran of the Court and in poor health, who had "worked intensely, even feverishly, on his opinion over the four days between the oral argument and the announcement of the Court's judgment," and who "may have sensed that this might be his last opinion," wrote the "most passionate and uncompromising" opinion in favor of the *Times*.[79] The night before the decisions by the justices were due, Black wrote till 4 a.m., in part to overcome a criticism of an earlier draft from his wife. Three months later, Black suffered a stroke, and six days after that, on September 25, he died.[80]

In a separate opinion (quoted earlier, but it bears repeating), his last as a Supreme Court justice, Black wrote:

In the First Amendment the Founding Fathers gave the free press the protection it must have to fulfill its essential role in our democracy. The press was to serve the governed, not the governors. The Government's power to censor the press was abolished so that the press would remain forever free to censure the Government. The press was protected so that it could bare the secrets of government and inform the people. Only a free and unrestrained press can effectively expose deception in government. And paramount among the responsibilities of a free press is the duty to prevent any part of the government from deceiving the people and sending them off to distant lands to die of foreign fevers and foreign shot and shell.[81]

When we read the *New York Times,* especially today, we don't see the spirit of the Pentagon Papers project at the *Times,* or that of Hugo Black, in its news and editorial pages. Instead, the *Times* seems content to serve the governors more and the governed less, often simply repeating what the president says, and publishing his picture in staged settings, as front-page news. It bares few government secrets and exposes little government deception. However, even assuming that the *Times,* one day, would decide to honor Black's mandate, it would need to incorporate international law into its coverage of US foreign policy, while also ending its reliance, to the extent that it cites international law at all, on the right-wing and pro-government international law experts that have dominated even that small space of coverage in recent years.

The fifty-year habit at the *Times* of undermining or ignoring international law in its coverage of US foreign policy not only can be marked by its coverage of the 1954 Geneva Accords on Vietnam and the reprisal bombings of North Vietnam in 1964–65, but also can be seen today as a syndrome that afflicts not only the *Times* but, by extension and in no small part, the nation and its Constitution, the world and its legal Charter, and quite possibly the future of global civilization and life on earth.

CONCLUSION:
STRICT SCRUTINY

In Robert S. McNamara's memoirs, *In Retrospect*, the last chapter is titled "The Lessons of Vietnam." Nearing the end of his book, McNamara summarized the lessons he takes from Vietnam, and of a war-ridden world, as follows:

> In sum, we should strive to create a world in which relations among nations would be based on the rule of law, a world in which national security would be supported by a system of collective security. The conflict prevention, conflict resolution, and peace-keeping functions necessary to accomplish these objectives would be performed by multilateral institutions, a reorganized and strengthened United Nations together with new and expanded regional organizations.[1]

McNamara writes that "such a vision is easier to articulate than to achieve" and though "the goal is clear, how to get there is not."[2]

One way to get to the rule of law among states is to apply this vision, not in retrospect, but today while we still have an opportunity to prevent future wars (including nuclear war), end the retaliatory spiral of state and non-state terrorism, forestall global environmental disaster, and end the human-rights catastrophes of poverty, hunger, and genocide. Incorporating basic standards of international law into the planning and implementation of the foreign policy of the United States—the wealthiest and most powerful nation on earth—and into the editorial policy of its leading news organization, would establish powerful precedents for other countries and news organizations to follow.

Having said this, however, concern remains about how "to get there," with respect to both foreign policy and editorial policy, on a practical level. McNamara himself unintentionally highlighted the practical difficulties when, while issuing a fine statement in support of the rule of law among states, he undermined that goal in practice with his retrospective analysis of the Tonkin Gulf incident in 1964. While posing "the key questions and answers" about "the nine days from July 30 to August 7, 1964," McNamara writes:

> In response to the attacks [on US ships in the Tonkin Gulf], the president ordered a strike by U.S. naval aircraft against four North Vietnamese patrol boat bases and an oil depot. Was the strike justified?
> Answer: Probably.[3]

Thus, even though McNamara argued in principle that the world should strive toward the rule of law, he nevertheless undermined this principle by signaling, even thirty years after the fact, his support of a critical US transgression of international law that led to the fateful American escalation in Vietnam and the full-blown calamity of the war. Furthermore, McNamara never mentioned international law in his other "key questions and answers" about Vietnam, nor did he list international law among his eleven lessons about war in the 2003 movie *The Fog of War.*

The paradox of publicly supporting the rule of law among states in principle while undermining or ignoring it in practice also roughly describes the state of affairs in the United States and at the *New York Times.* Top officials of the US government have routinely expressed their support publicly for the rule of law in principle, while also routinely violating the UN Charter and US Constitution. Likewise, there is most likely a presumption among board members, top management, and editorial staff at the *New York Times* that it upholds the rule of law, even though editorial policy at the *Times* has no practical capability to support that mission.

Furthermore, given that the *Times* has not seriously reconsidered Ochs in light of the post–World War II capability to destroy the world (whether with nuclear weapons or through environmental devastation), it is evident that "impartiality" (as interpreted in practice at the *Times*) is at best obsolete. In other words, how might the *Times* or any other news organization remain impartial or objective about the possibility of total nuclear war or environmental destruction, and still retain any legitimate claim to work in the public interest? Finally, despite the post-war global dominance of the United States, and the counterbalancing complementarity of the UN Charter and the US Constitution, the *Times* apparently has made no attempt to fashion a post-war legal framework with which to assess the exercise of US military, economic, and political power—another indication of Ochsian obsolescence at the *Times*.

We suggest an alternative approach to editorial policy that would update Ochs and permit the *Times* to refine its foundational standard of impartiality while also improving its coverage of US foreign policy. To present this approach, we have borrowed a small portion of terminology and methodology from the US federal judiciary. For example, the judiciary applies its highest standard of judicial review—"strict scrutiny"—when it considers executive or legislative limits on a fundamental constitutional right, such as speech. On the other hand, it applies a lower standard of review to such limits on rights that it does not view as fundamental to the Constitution, such as the so-called right to bear firearms. For example, the US Supreme Court applied a strict scrutiny standard to Attorney General John Mitchell's order to the *New York Times* to stop the publication of its series on the Pentagon Papers, because the case implicated a fundamental First Amendment right. Likewise, the judiciary historically has applied a lower "rational basis" test in its review of gun-control laws, where the courts have largely deferred to an executive or legislative intent to protect public health and safety. These differentiated standards of judicial review make sense because, for one thing, they make it very difficult—both in principle and in practice—for the government to deprive the American people of their fundamental constitutional rights, while also giving the government broader discretion to act in the public interest by limiting rights, if necessary, that are not deemed to be fundamental to the Constitution.

In contrast, it makes no sense for the press to apply the same uniform standard of journalistic review to issues involving war and peace and the survival of the planet as it does to the local town meeting. As a former reporter and a former editor at the *Times* have pointed out, the *Times* applied its "non-crusading" standard of editorial policy equally to housing corruption in New York City[4] and to Hitler's campaign in Europe.[5] Likewise, the *Times* applied, at best, only a "rational basis" test to whether the United States should bomb North Vietnam in response to the reported attacks on US ships in the Tonkin Gulf, when a "strict scrutiny" test would have showed that bombing North Vietnam violated international law under these circumstances. Applying a strict scrutiny standard journalistically to the US involvement in Vietnam, beginning at least since 1954, might have prevented, or at least discouraged, the full-blown war in Vietnam that followed, because it might have made the government's twenty-year record of violating international law and misrepresenting important facts with respect to Vietnam impossible to sustain, or even initiate.

In short, an editorial policy of "strict scrutiny" would apply the most rigorous standards of journalistic review to news events and conditions that implicate war and peace, human survival, human rights, the global environment, and fundamental principles of the UN Charter and US Constitution. The application of this rigorous standard of editorial policy would be justified by the public's compelling interest to avoid and prevent illegal and unnecessary wars, to ensure human survival, to protect human rights and the environment, and to promote the rule of law under the Charter and the Constitution. These "value-oriented" journalistic standards would, paradoxically, update and enhance Ochsian impartiality, because they would exist in principle, independently, and in advance of their application journalistically to the *Times'* coverage of US foreign policy. Furthermore, a strict scrutiny standard would support the US Supreme Court's mandate for the press to "expose government deception" and to "enlighten the citizenry," given that public justification of the illegal use of force historically has involved serious government deception in the vast majority of cases, and because an American citizenry is not enlightened without basic knowledge of basic rules of international law that apply to the global conduct of its government.

Even when we consider a basic function of a newspaper—to report facts—an editorial policy of strict scrutiny would give the *Times* a new capability to report contentious facts with more accuracy than it has in the past. For example, recall that Johnson and McNamara charged that North Vietnamese boats had attacked US destroyers in the Gulf of Tonkin on August 4 1964, and that the North Vietnamese government denied this charge. Also recall that the Reagan administration charged the Nicaraguan Sandinista government with attacking El Salvador by means of an arms flow to anti-government guerrillas in El Salvador, and that the Sandinistas denied the arms-flow charge. Recall also that the Bush administration has denied the charges of Venezuela's president, Hugo Chávez, that the United States is involved in efforts to overthrow him and his government. And recall that the Bush administration charged Iraq with illegal WMD possession and that the Iraqi government denied these charges as well. In each of these cases, and in many others not specifically addressed in this volume, the *New York Times* simply assessed such claims and counterclaims by heavily weighting US government claims with an assumption of accuracy and credibility—with disastrous results for its record of US foreign-policy coverage.

In each of these cases, the *Times* applied at best what could be called a "rational basis" standard of coverage. For example, it may have appeared rational for the Johnson administration to bomb PT-boat bases inside North Vietnam in response to reported North Vietnamese PT-boat attacks on US destroyers in the Tonkin Gulf. Or it may have appeared rational for the Reagan administration to initiate military and para-military attacks in and against Nicaragua in response to a reported Nicaraguan arms flow to Salvadoran guerrillas. And it may have seemed rational to invade Iraq to prevent that country from using its weapons of mass destruction against the United States and other countries, as we were told it would. However, in each of these cases, while the US government engaged in illegal military conduct under international law, it also misreported or lied about facts that it asserted to justify that conduct. Given these examples and others, a "rational basis" standard of review, which resembles the *Times'* "non-crusading" standard in the sense that it does not reflect the most rigorous standards of factual and legal scrutiny, has proven to be a deficient journalistic standard for assessing the facts and law pertaining to war and peace.

A strict scrutiny standard, on the other hand, that evaluated the legality of actions taken in response to reported facts, would improve both the factual and legal reporting of the press. For example, even though the *Times* could not confirm at the time that the *Maddox* and *Turner Joy* had been attacked on August 4, it could have confirmed that the US reprisal bombings of North Vietnam—even if the ships had been attacked as reported by Johnson and McNamara—could not be justified under international law. Likewise, strict scrutiny would have permitted the *Times* to demonstrate that US military and paramilitary attacks in and against Nicaragua in the 1980s were illegal under the circumstances as a response to a reported Sandinista arms flow to Salvadoran guerrillas. And strict scrutiny would have permitted the *Times* to confirm that a US invasion of Iraq would violate international law without Security Council authorization, even if Iraqi WMD possession were to be confirmed, which it never was. Finally, because even nuclear war and total environmental destruction can be made to appear rational by government propagandists, it is imperative that the press adopt a higher standard of journalistic review, as a practical matter, to cover the most important challenges facing the United States and the world today.

In the next volume we examine the *New York Times'* coverage of the Israeli–Palestinian conflict, of the cold-war and post-cold-war nuclear-weapons policies of the United States, and of the science and politics of global climate change to show that the failure of editorial policy at the *Times* is indeed pervasive and profound, and that the need to change course journalistically today in the United States is also great—because doing so only in retrospect might be too late.

NOTES

INTRODUCTION

1. See the privately circulated memorandum by the international law expert, Howard N. Meyer, "On Not Taking International Law Seriously," circulated by the author, June 2004, meyerlang@msn.com; see also the collection of writings on international law aspects of the Iraq war in a two-part forum of international law experts, "Agora: Future Implications of the Iraq Conflict," *American Journal of International Law* 97, nos 3 and 4, 2003, pp. 553–642 and 803–72.

2. The New York Times Company was named to the top 100 best corporate citizens by *Business Ethics* magazine in its Spring 2004 issue. It has also been ranked no. 1 for four consecutive years among publishing companies by *Fortune* in its annual list of America's Most Admired Companies. *New York Times Company News Release*, February 24 2004.

3. See the reference in note 1 to the Agora published in the *American Journal of International Law*; see also "Iraq: One Year After," American Society of International Law panel, April 2004, to be published in the ASIL annual volume of proceedings. For a helpful overview see Dominic McGlodrick, *From '9-11' to the Iraq War 2003: International Law in an Age of Complexity* (Portland, OR: Hart, 2004); see also C. G. Weeramantry, *Armageddon or Brave New World? Reflections on the Hostilities in Iraq* (Ratmalana, Sri Lanka: Weeramantry International Centre for Peace Education & Research, 2003).

4. Speech given by Prime Minister Blair justifying action in Iraq and warning of the continued threat of global terrorism, full text reproduced in the *Guardian* (UK), March 5 2004.

5. "Realism" when used in the setting of world politics is an outlook that regards world order and international stability as being based on the ways *power* is used by the main sovereign states; it is correspondingly skeptical about, if not dismissive of, the role of law and morality. Prominent recent realists include George Kennan, Henry Kissinger, and Hans Morgenthau.

6. George F. Kennan, *American Diplomacy 1900–1950* (Chicago: University of Chicago Press, 1951); Hans J. Morgenthau, *Politics Among Nations: The Struggle for Power and Peace,* revised by Kenneth W Thompson (New York: Knopf, 6th ed., 1985).

7. McNamara makes this assertion very clearly in the documentary film on his service as secretary of defense, *The Fog of War* (2003).

8. Often this debate was framed in terms of Machiavellian "realism" versus Wilsonian "idealism," the latter flawed by its allegedly naïve trust of international norms of behavior and by an unwarranted confidence in the capacity of international institutions. An influential formulation of this debate is to be found in Robert Osgood, *Ideals and Self-interest in America's Foreign Relations: The Great Transformation of the Twentieth Century* (Chicago: University of Chicago Press, 1953); for a more recent contention that the supposedly persisting American aversion to realist thinking prevents the US from pursuing a sensible foreign policy, see Henry A. Kissinger, *Diplomacy* (New York: Simon & Schuster, 1994).

9. On the former see Richard Falk, *The Great Terror War* (Northampton, MA: Olive Branch Press, 2003), pp. 82–128; on the latter see a group of eight books on encroachments on American liberties reviewed by Ethan Bronner in the *New York Times Book Review* of February 22 2004 under the heading "Collateral Damage: The effects of the war on terrorism and American freedom and privacy are not easy to assess."

10. "The Times and Iraq," *New York Times*, May 26 2004. See also, "Weapons of Mass Destruction? Or Mass Distraction?" *New York Times*, May 30 2004.

11. Or for that matter with respect to Japan's responsibility for waging aggressive war. For a still useful critical account see Richard H. Minear, *Victors' Justice: The Tokyo War Crimes Tribunal* (Princeton, NJ: Princeton University Press, 1971).

12. See the Resolution on the Definition of Aggression, General Assembly Res. 3314, adopted December 14 1974.

13. It is noteworthy that the US government boycotted the judicial proceedings in The Hague after it lost the jurisdictional phase of the proceedings, and then proceeded to withdraw altogether its acceptance of compulsory jurisdiction, indicating its refusal to be bound by the adverse ICJ outcome. Such a posture by the leading state in the world inflicted a body blow to the stature of international law, and the viability of judicial settlement of international disputes with respect to the most important subject-matter in international life, thereby making international law ineffectual in a smaller state's encounter with a stronger, larger state.

14. See John Hart Ely, *War and Responsibility: Constitutional Lessons of Vietnam and its Aftermath* (Princeton, NJ: Princeton University Press, 1993); also, Ely, *Democracy and Distrust: A Theory of Judicial Review* (Cambridge, MA: Harvard University Press, 1980). There is a big literature on various aspects of this argument, including a series of books written by former members of the CIA.

15. Had international law been adhered to, the two most glaring instances of American foreign-policy failure in the last half-century, the Vietnam War and the Iraq War, would both have been avoided with dramatically positive results with respect to both the realities of claims to provide leadership for the world and the sense of legitimacy of the governing process in the country.

16. John Lewis Gaddis, Council on Foreign Relations Interview, February 6 2004; see also Gaddis, *Surprise, Security, and the American Experience* (Cambridge, MA: Harvard University Press, 2004); the doctrine of preemptive attack is not even conditioned by clear standards or presumptions in its authoritative depiction as a centerpiece in the official document, "National Security Strategy of the United States of America," issued by the White House in September 2002.

I WITHOUT FACTS OR LAW

1. The Consultative Council of the Lawyers Committee on Vietnam, Richard Falk, chair, John HE Fried, Rapporteur. The other members of the consultative council were Richard J Barnet, John H Herz, Stanley Hoffmann, Wallace McClure, Saul H Mendlo-

vitz, Richard S Miller, Hans J Morgenthau, William G Rice, Burns H Weston, and Quincy Wright.

2. The Consultative Council of the Lawyers Committee on Vietnam, *Vietnam and International Law: An Analysis of International Law and the Use of Force, and the Precedent of Vietnam for Subsequent Interventions* (Northampton: Aletheia Press, 1990), pp. 93–4.

3. *This Week with George Stephanopoulos, ABC News,* July 6 2003.

4. "Report of the First Panel Established Pursuant to the Note by the President of the Security Council on 30 January 1999 (S/1999/100), Concerning Disarmament and Current and Future Ongoing Monitoring and Verification Issues," S/1999/356, 27 March 1999.

These itemized statements were written by Howard Friel and Richard Falk in March 2003, with assistance from John Burroughs, Marcelo G Kohen, David Krieger, Andrew Strauss, Peter Weiss, and Burns H Weston, and delivered in the form of a letter to Kofi Annan, Secretary-General of the United Nations, on March 10 2003, above the signatures of the following individuals: Richard Falk, Burns H Weston, Howard Friel, Jean Allain, Asli U Bali, John Burroughs, Joseph Camilleri, BS Chimni, Marcelo G Kohen, Smitu Kothari, David Krieger, Maivan Lam, Chandra Muzaffar, Roger Normand, Michael Ratner, Andrew Strauss, Majid Tehranian, Peter Weiss, and Sarah Zaidi.

5. Ibid.

6. http://www.iaea.org/worldatom/Programmes/ActionTeam/reports2.html.

7. The Status of Nuclear Inspections in Iraq, Statement to the United Nations Security Council, New York, January 27 2003, Mohamed ElBaradei, Director General, International Atomic Energy Agency.

8. "The Iraq Report," *New York Times,* January 28 2003.

9. The Status of Nuclear Inspections in Iraq: 14 February 2003 Update, by IAEA Director General Dr Mohamed ElBaradei.

10. "Disarming Iraq," *New York Times,* February 15 2003.

11. The Status of Nuclear Inspections in Iraq, Statement to the United Nations Security Council, New York, 27 January 2003, Mohamed ElBaradei, Director General, International Atomic Energy Agency.

12. The Status of Nuclear Inspections in Iraq: 14 February 2003 Update, by IAEA Director General Dr Mohamed ElBaradei.

13. *Associated Press,* January 24 2003.

14. "U.S. May Not Press U.N. for a Decision on Iraq for Weeks," *New York Times*, January 25 2003.

15. "The Iraq Report," *New York Times*, January 28 2003.

16. Briefing the Security Council, 19 December 2002: Inspections in Iraq and a Preliminary Assessment of Iraq's Weapons Declaration, Dr Hans Blix, Executive Chairman of UNMOVIC, 19 December 2002.

17. Briefing the Security Council, 9 January 2003: Inspections in Iraq and a Further Assessment of Iraq's Weapons Declaration, Dr Hans Blix, Executive Chairman.

18. Briefing of the Security Council, 27 January 2003: An Update on Inspections, Executive Chairman of UNMOVIC, Dr Hans Blix.

19. Ibid.

20. "U.N. Inspector Says Iraq Falls Short on Cooperation," *New York Times*, January 28 2003.

21. "The Iraq Report."

22. "Exclusive: The Defector's Secrets," *Newsweek*, March 3 2003.

23. "A Road Map for Iraq," *New York Times*, September 18 2002.

24. "The Exercise of American Power," *New York Times*, January 2 2003.

25. "Iraqi Stonewalling," *New York Times*, December 20 2002.

26. "The Iraq Dossier," *New York Times*, January 10 2003.

27. Status of Nuclear Inspections in Iraq—Update: Report Delivered by IAEA Director General to the Security Council, March 7 2003.

28. "Iraqi Stonewalling."

29. "The Iraq Dossier."

30. Status of Nuclear Inspections in Iraq—Update: Report Delivered by IAEA Director General to the Security Council, March 7 2003.

31. Ibid.

32. "Iraqi Stonewalling."

33. "The Iraq Dossier."

34. "President's State of the Union Message to Congress and Nation," *New York Times*, January 29 2003.

35. "The Nation, the President, the War," *New York Times*, January 29 2003.

36. "The Vanishing Uranium," *New York Times*, June 13 2003.

37. "Reviewing the Intelligence on Iraq," *New York Times*, May 26 2003.

38. "A Measured Pace on Iraq," *New York Times*, September 14 2002.

39. "A Nation Wary of War," *New York Times*, October 8 2002.

40. "In Bush's Words: On Iraq, U.N. Must Face Up to Its Founding Purpose," *New York Times*, September 13 2002.

41. "Bush Sees 'Urgent Duty' to Pre-empt Attack by Iraq," *New York Times*, October 8 2002.

42. "A Nation Wary of War."

43. "Lighting the Fuse on Iraq," *New York Times*, January 22 2003.

44. "Back to the United Nations," *New York Times*, February 13 2003.

45. "A Unified Message to Iraq," *New York Times*, November 9 2002.

46. "The Exercise of American Power," *New York Times*, January 2 2003.

47. "The Race to War," *New York Times*, January 26 2003.

48. "Endgame," *New York Times*, February 7 2003.

49. "Power and Leadership; The Real Meaning of Iraq," *New York Times*, February 23 2003.

50. "Saying No to War," *New York Times*, March 9 2003.

51. Ibid.

52. "How to Watch the War," *New York Times*, March 21 2003.

53. "Comment: L'Affaire Blair," *New Yorker*, May 26 2003.

54. "Tumult in the Newsroom," *New Yorker*, June 30 2003.

2 THE LIBERAL HAWKS ON IRAQ

1. Michael Ignatieff, "The American Empire: The Burden," *New York Times Magazine*, January 5 2003. "The American Empire: Get Used To It," was how Ignatieff's article was headlined in big letters on the magazine's cover.

2. Anne-Marie Slaughter, "Good Reasons for Going Around the U.N.," *New York Times*, March 18 2003.

3. Michael Glennon, "How War Left the Law Behind," *New York Times*, November 21 2002.

4. "Shift Toward the U.S. Stand on Iraq Is Noted in Council," *New York Times*, November 1 2002.

5. "Annan Says U.S. Will Violate Charter If it Acts Without Approval," *New York Times*, March 11 2003.

6. Bruce Ackerman, "The Legality of Using Force," *New York Times*, September 21 2002. Note that Professor Ackerman is known exclusively for his contribution to liberal theory and American constitutional law, and is not considered an expert in international law.

7. Kenneth Pollack, *The Threatening Storm: The Case for Invading Iraq* (New York: Random House, 2002).

8. Jack F Matlock, Jr, "Deterring the Undeterrable," *New York Times*, October 20 2002.

9. Richard Bernstein, "Making a Case for a U.S. Invasion of Iraq," *New York Times*, October 22 2002.

10. Bill Keller, "The I-Can't-Believe-I'm-a-Hawk Club," *New York Times*, February 8 2003.

11. Pollack, *The Threatening Storm*, p. 424.

12. Keller, "The I-Can't-Believe-I'm-a-Hawk Club."

13. Published at http://www.iaea.org/worldatom/Programmes/ActionTeam/reports2.html.

14. Pollack, *The Threatening Storm*, p. 174.

15. Kenneth M Pollack, "Why Iraq Can't Be Deterred," *New York Times*, September 26 2002.

16. Martin Indyk and Kenneth M Pollack, "How Bush Can Avoid the Inspections Trap," *New York Times*, January 27 2003.

17. Kenneth M Pollack, "A Last Chance to Stop Iraq," *New York Times*, February 21 2003.

18. Kenneth M Pollack, "Saddam's Bombs: We'll Find Them," *New York Times*, June 20 2003.

19. Ibid.

20. Ignatieff, "The American Empire: The Burden."

21. Ibid.

22. Ibid.

23. PJ O'Rourke, "We'll Run This Planet as We Please," *Wall Street Journal*, August 23 2001.

24. Robert L Bartley, "Engaging the Irritating Europeans," *Wall Street Journal*, April 22 2002.

25. Robert L Bartley, "World Law or Institutionalized Hypocrisy," *Wall Street Journal*, May 13 2002.

26. Editorial, *Wall Street Journal*, October 29 2002.

27. "Kofi's Patience," *Wall Street Journal*, November 15 2002.

28. Michael Ignatieff, "Why Are We In Iraq? And Liberia? And Afghanistan?" *New York Times Magazine*, September 7 2003.

29. Ibid.

30. Ibid.

31. "Legality of United States Participation in the Defense of Vietnam, Memorandum from the Department of State, Office of the Legal Adviser," March 4 1966.

32. Ibid.

33. Consultative Council of the Lawyers Committee on Vietnam,

Vietnam and International Law: An Analysis of International Law and the Use of Force, and the Precedent of Vietnam for Subsequent Interventions (Northampton: Aletheia Press, 1990), p. 22.

34. Ibid., p. 95.

35. "Legality of United States Participation in the Defense of Vietnam."

36. Lawyers Committee, *Vietnam and International Law*, p. 20.

37. Ibid.

38. Ibid.

39. "Legality of United States Participation in the Defense of Vietnam."

40. Lawyers Committee, *Vietnam and International Law*, pp. 21–2.

41. Lawyers Committee, *Vietnam and International Law*, p. 22. See also: "The Webster formulation of self-defense is often cited as authoritative customary law. It cannot be said that the formulation reflects state practice (which was understandably murky on this point when war was legal), but it is safe to say it reflects a widespread desire to restrict the right of self-defense when no attack has actually occurred"; Louis Henkin, Richard C Pugh, Oscar Schacter, and Hans Smit, *International Law: Cases and Materials*, 2nd ed. (St. Paul: West Publishing Co., 1987), p. 746. Furthermore, "Mr Webster's description of the permissible basis for self-defense was relied upon in the Nuremberg Judgment in the case against major German war criminals. This judgment was, of course, based upon pre-United Nations law and, in turn, was affirmed unanimously by the United Nations General Assembly at its first Session (Res.95(I))." Lawyers Committee, *Vietnam and International Law*, p. 22.

42. Lawyers Committee, *Vietnam and International Law*, p. 24.

43. "Iraq War Swells Al-Qaeda's Ranks, Report Says," *Reuters*, October 15 2003, citing a report by the International Institute for Strategic Studies; "Another Fine Mess," *Guardian*, September 11 2003, citing a report by the Oxford Research Group.

44. Ignatieff, "Why Are We In Iraq? And Liberia? And Afghanistan?"

45. Ibid.

46. Lawyers Committee, *Vietnam and International Law*, p. 24.

47. Independent International Commission on Kosovo, *The Kosovo Report*, available at www.reliefweb.int/library/documents/thekosovoreport.htm.

48. See chapter 6.

49. James Traub, "Who Needs the United Nations?" *New York Times Magazine*, November 17 2002.

50. Barry Bearak, "Scott Ritter's Iraq Complex," *New York Times Magazine*, November 24 2002.

51. Scott Ritter, "Is Iraq a True Threat to the US," *Boston Globe*, July 20 2002. See also, Scott Ritter, "The Case for Iraq's Qualitative Disarmament," *Arms Control Today*, June 2000.

52. Bearak, "Scott Ritter's Iraq Complex."

53. Ibid.

54. "Effects of the Gulf War on Infant and Child Mortality in Iraq," *New England Journal of Medicine*, September 24 1992.

55. "The Effect of Economic Sanctions on the Mortality of Iraqi Children Prior to the 1991 Persian Gulf War," *American Journal of Public Health*, April 2000.

56. "A Multivariate Method for Estimating Mortality Rates Among Children Under 5 Years From Health and Social Indicators in Iraq," *International Journal of Epidemiology*, June 29 2000.

57. "Sanctions and Childhood Mortality in Iraq," *Lancet*, May 27 2000.

58. George Packer, "The Liberal Quandary Over Iraq," *New York Times Magazine*, December 8 2002.

59. Quoted in Ibid.

60. Quoted in Ibid.

61. Ibid.

62. James Traub, "The Next Resolution," *New York Times Magazine*, April 13 2003.

63. Ibid.

64. Ibid.

65. "Bill Keller, Columnist, Is Selected as the Times's Executive Editor," *New York Times*, July 15 2003.

66. "The Sunshine Warrior," *New York Times Magazine*, September 22 2002.

67. "Reagan's Son," *New York Times Magazine*, January 26 2003.

68. Letter to President Bill Clinton on Iraq, January 26 1998. Those people who signed the letter were Elliott Abrams, Richard L Armitage, William J Bennett, Jeffrey Bergner, John Bolton, Paula Dobriansky, Francis Fukuyama, Robert Kagan, Zalmay Khalilzad, William Kristol, Richard Perle, Peter W Rodman, Donald Rumsfeld, William Schneider Jr., Vin Weber, Paul Wolfowitz, R. James Woolsey, Robert B Zoellick. The letter is posted at www.newamericancentury.org/iraqclintonletter.htm.

69. Keller, "Reagan's Son."

70. "Blueprint for a Mess: How the Bush Administration's Prewar Planners Bungled Postwar Iraq," *New York Times Magazine,* November 2 2003.

71. David Corn, *The Lies of George W Bush* (New York: Crown Publishers, 2003), p. 1.

72. Keller, "Reagan's Son."

73. Ibid.

74. Ibid.

75. Bob Woodward, *Bush at War* (New York: Simon & Schuster, 2002).

76. Bob Woodward, *Maestro* (New York: Simon & Schuster, 2000).

77. Keller, "Reagan's Son."

78. Ibid.

79. Ibid.

80. Keller, "The I–Can't–Believe–I'm–a–Hawk Club."

81. "Iraq's Weapons of Mass Destruction: The Assessment of the British Government," September 24 2002; "Iraq—Its Infrastructure of Concealment, Deception and Intimidation," February 3 2003.

82. "After Hutton, the Verdict: 51 Per Cent Say Blair Should Go," *Independent* (UK), February 7 2004; "PM in Peril After Hutton, Says Key Ally," *Guardian*, February 8 2004.

83. Keller, "The I–Can't–Believe–I'm–a–Hawk Club."

84. Francis A. Boyle, *The Bosnian People Charge Genocide: Proceedings at the International Court of Justice Concerning Bosnia v. Serbia on the Prevention and Punishment of the Crime of Genocide* (Northampton: Aletheia Press, 1996), p. 4.

85. Quoted in Ibid., p. xi.

86. UNICEF, "Child Maternal Mortality Survey, Preliminary Report," July 1999.

87. "UN Says Sanctions Have Killed Some 500,000 Iraqi Children," *Reuters*, July 21 2000.

88. "Sanctions and Childhood Mortality in Iraq," *Lancet*, May 27 2000.

89. Keller, "The Sunshine Warrior."

90. Keller, "The I–Can't–Believe–I'm–a–Hawk Club."

91. Ibid.

92. Ibid.

93. Ibid.

94. "Can Anything Stop Toyota?" *Business Week*, November 17 2003.

95. Cyde Prestowitz, *Rogue Nation: American Unilateralism and the Failure of Good Intentions* (New York: Basic Books, 2003).

96. Bill Keller, "Does Not Play Well With Others," *New York Times*, June 22 2003.

97. Ibid.

98. *New York Times Co. v. United States*, 403 U.S. 713 (1971).

99. "Annan Says U.S. Will Violate Charter If It Acts Without Approval," *New York Times*, March 11 2003.

100. "U.N. Resolutions Allow Attack on the Likes of Iraq," *New York Times*, February 5 1998.

101. "Muslims Protest Month-long Detention Without a Charge," *New York Times*, April 20 2003.

102. "Annan Says U.S. Will Violate Charter If It Acts Without Approval."

103. Ibid.

104. Ibid.

105. A few months earlier, the *Times* quoted Gardner: "We have the right to use force [against Iraq] because there has been a material breach" of past Council resolutions by Iraq, and "no administration is going to allow the French to take away from us a right we clearly have." "Shift Toward the U.S. Stand On Iraq Is Noted in Council," *New York Times*, November 1 2002.

106. "Annan Says U.S. Will Violate Charter If It Acts Without Approval."

107. "Powell Will Press U.S. Case in Security Council Next Week," *New York Times*, January 29 2003.

108. "How War Left the Law Behind," *New York Times*, November 21 2002.

109. "Good Reasons for Going Around the U.N.," *New York Times*, March 18 2002.

110. Ibid.

111. Ibid.

112. Independent International Commission on Kosovo, *The Kosovo Report*.

113. Ibid.

114. "Good Reasons for Going Around the U.N."

3   EDITORIAL POLICY AND IRAQ

1. Arthur Gelb, *City Room* (New York: A Marian Wood Book, 2003), pp. 138–9.

2. Ibid., p. 402.

3. Ibid., p. 544.
4. John L. Hess, *My Times: A Memoir of Dissent* (New York: Seven Stories Press, 2003), p. 29.
5. Gelb, *City Room*, p. 535.
6. Hess, *My Times*, p. 93.
7. *New York Times*, May 8 1935.
8. Gay Talese, *The Kingdom and the Power* (Cleveland: The New American Library, 1969), p. 6.
9. Ibid., pp. 6, 12.
10. Hess, *My Times*, p. 4.
11. Talese, *The Kingdom and the Power*, p. 6.
12. Ibid., pp. 6–7.
13. Gelb, *City Room*, p. 403.
14. Ibid., p. 8.
15. Ibid.
16. Ibid.
17. Ibid, p. 501.
18. Ibid., p. 502.
19. Ibid., p. 501.
20. Elvis Mitchell, "Triumph Tinged With Regret in Middle Earth," *New York Times*, December 16 2003.
21. Joe Morgenstern, "Now That's an Epic: Jackson Conjures Magical Ending to 'Lord of the Rings' Trilogy," *Wall Street Journal*, December 19 2003.
22. Mitchell, "Triumph Tinged With Regret in Middle Earth."
23. A Statement, *New York Times*, May 8 1935.
24. "The Failure to Find Iraqi Weapons," editorial, *New York Times*, September 26 2003.
25. *New York Times Co. v. United States*, 403 U.S. 713 (1971).
26. Report of the Committee on Safeguarding the Integrity of Our Journalism ("The Siegal Committee Report"), *New York Times*, July 28 2003, published at www.nytco.com/newsroomreports.
27. The Siegal Committee Report, p. 49.
28. "Correcting the Record; Times Reporter Who Resigned Leaves Long Trail of Deception," *New York Times*, May 11 2003.
29. Ibid.
30. "Bush Sees 'Urgent Duty' to Pre-empt Attack by Iraq," *New York Times*, October 8 2002.
31. "News Analysis; Stern Tones, Direct Appeal," *New York Times*, October 8 2003.

32. "A Nation Wary of War," *New York Times*, October 8 2003.

33. The Siegal Committee Report, p. 38.

34. http://www.iaea.org/worldatom/Programmes/ActionTeam/reports2.html.

35. "Iraq's Weapons of Mass Destruction: The Assessment of the British Government," Chapter Three, September 24 2002.

36. Briefing the Security Council, 19 December 2002: Inspections in Iraq and a Preliminary Assessment of Iraq's Weapons Declaration, Dr Hans Blix, Executive Chairman of UNMOVIC," 19 December 2002.

37. Report of the First Panel Established Pursuant to the Note by the President of the Security Council on 30 January 1999 (S/1999/100), Concerning Disarmament and Current and Future Ongoing Monitoring and Verification Issues, S/1999/356, 27 March 1999, para. 25.

38. "Ex Aide: Powell Misled Americans," *CBS News*, October 15 2003.

39. "The Case Against Iraq," editorial, *New York Times*, February 6 2003.

40. Scott Ritter, "Is Iraq a True Threat to the US," *Boston Globe*, July 20 2002.

41. Scott Ritter, "The Case for Iraq's Qualitative Disarmament," *Arms Control Today*, Arms Control Association, June 2000.

42. "Powell, Foreign Minister Moussa on Iraq, Mideast Peace, U.S.-Egypt Ties," *Washington File*, U.S. Department of State, International Information Programs, February 24 2001, published at http://usinfo.state.gov/topical/pol/arms/stories/01022453.htm.

43. "Bush Aides Set Strategy to Sell Policy on Iraq," *New York Times*, September 7 2002.

44. "Threats and Responses: The Iraqis; U.S. Says Hussein Intensifies Quest for A-Bomb Parts," *New York Times*, September 8 2002.

45. "Bush Aides Set Strategy to Sell Policy on Iraq."

46. "Iraq Said To Buy Antidote Against Nerve Gas," *New York Times*, November 12 2002.

47. "C.I.A. Hunts Iraq Tie to Soviet Smallpox," *New York Times*, December 3 2002.

48. "Defectors Bolster U.S. Case Against Iraq, Officials Say," *New York Times*, January 24 2003.

49. "Team of Experts to Hunt Iraq Arms," *New York Times*, March 19 2003.

50. "WMD in Iraq: Evidence and Implications," Carnegie Endowment for International Peace, January 2004, p. 7. The Carnegie report stated: "It is unlikely that Iraq could have destroyed, hidden, or sent out of the country the hundreds of tons of chemical and biological weapons, dozens of Scud missiles and facilities engaged in the ongoing production of chemical and biological weapons that officials claimed were present without the United States detecting some sign of this activity before, during, or after the major combat period of the war."

51. "Blix Says He Saw Nothing to Prompt a War," *New York Times*, January 31 2003.

52. The Siegal Committee Report, p. 27.

53. Ibid., pp. 11, 27–8.

54. "Illicit Arms Kept Till Eve of War, An Iraqi Scientist Is Said to Assert," *New York Times*, April 21 2003.

55. Ibid.

56. Ibid.

57. Ibid.

58. "Focus Shifts from Weapons to the People Behind Them," *New York Times*, April 23 2003.

59. "U.S. Aides Say Iraqi Truck Could Be a Germ-War Lab," *New York Times*, May 8 2003; "Trailer Is a Mobile Lab Capable of Turning Out Bioweapons, a Team Says," *New York Times*, May 11 2003; "U.S. Analysts Link Iraq Labs to Germ Arms," *New York Times*, May 21 2003.

60. "U.S. Aides Say Iraqi Truck Could Be a Germ-War Lab."

61. Ibid.

62. Ibid.

63. "Trailer Is a Mobile Lab Capable of Turning Out Bioweapons, a Team Says."

64. Ibid.

65. "Iraqi Mobile Labs Nothing To Do With Germ Warfare, Report Finds," *Observer* (UK), June 15 2003.

66. "Ex-Inspector Says C.I.A. Missed Disarray in Iraqi Arms Program," *New York Times*, January 26 2004.

67. "Trailer Is a Mobile Lab Capable of Turning Out Bioweapons, a Team Says."

68. "U.S. Analysts Link Iraq Labs To Germ Arms," *New York Times*, May 21 2003.

69. Ibid.

70. "Intra-Times Battle Over Iraqi Weapons," *Washington Post*, May 26 2003.

71. Ibid.

72. Letter to President Bill Clinton on Iraq, January 26 1998. Posted at www.newamericancentury.org/iraqclintonletter.htm.

73. Letter to Speaker of the House Newt Gingrich and Senate Majority Leader Trent Lott, May 29 1998. Posted at www. newamericancentury.org/iraqletter1998.htm.

74. Public Law 105–338—October 31 1998.

75. "Even U.S. Sees Iraqi Opposition as Faint Hope," *New York Times*, November 19 1998.

76. "A Special Report: Defector Describes Iraq's Atom Bomb Push," *New York Times*, August 15 1998.

77. "Truth, War and Consequences," *PBS Frontline*, October 9 2003.

78. Jane Mayer, "The Manipulator," *New Yorker*, June 7 2004, pp. 66, 58.

79. Ibid., p. 58.

80. Bob Woodward, *Bush at War* (New York: Simon & Schuster, 2002), p. 49.

81. "Plans for Iraq Attack Began on 9/11," *CBS News*, September 4 2002.

82. Woodward, *Bush at War*, p. 49.

83. "Selective Intelligence," *New Yorker*, May 12 2003.

84. Ibid.

85. "Iraqi Tells of Renovations at Sites for Chemical and Nuclear Arms," *New York Times*, December 20 2001.

86. Hersh, "Selective Intelligence."

87. "US Paid $1M for 'Useless Intelligence' From Chalabi," *Independent* (UK), September 30 2003.

88. "Agency Belittles Information Given By Iraq Defectors," *New York Times*, September 29 2003.

89. "Threats and Responses: The Iraqis; U.S. Says Hussein Intensifies Quest for A-Bomb Parts."

4 A CRIME AGAINST PEACE

1. "Civilian Death Toll Rises in Iraq," *Agence France Press*, April 1 2003.

2. Ibid.

3. "Children Killed and Maimed in Cluster Bomb Attack on Town," *Independent*, April 2 2003.

4. Ibid.

5. "Iraq: Use of Cluster Bombs—Civilians Pay the Price, *Amnesty International*, April 2 2003.

6. "Cluster Bombs Liberate Iraqi Children," *Asian Times*, April 3 2003.

7. "Wailing Children, the Wounded, the Dead: Victims of the Day Cluster Bombs Rained on Babylon," *Independent*, April 3 2003.

8. "Civilian Casualties 'Horrifying': Truck Delivered Dismembered Women, Children," *Canadian Press*, April 4 2003.

9. "Widespread Use of Cluster Bombs Sparks Outrage," *Financial Times* (UK), April 4 2003.

10. "Iraq: Civilians Under Fire," Amnesty International, April 8 2003.

11. "Iraq Shows Casualties in Hospitals," *New York Times*, April 3 2003.

12. Ibid.

13. "A Nation at War: A Capital's Plight," *New York Times*, April 4 2003.

14. "A Nation at War: Mideast Coverage; Arab Media Portray War as Killing Field," *New York Times*, April 4 2003. A week earlier, Sachs reported in the *Times*: "Since the war began, nearly all the Arab news media, reflecting their audiences' concern for the welfare of ordinary Iraqis, have concentrated heavily on recounting civilian casualties and damage to Iraqi cities. Many also embroidered their reports, labeling the Iraqis victims of 'American war crimes' or 'murder' by coalition troops." "A Nation at War: The Arab World; Commentators See Dangers in Distorted News Coverage," *New York Times*, March 28 2003.

15. *New York Times*, March 26 2003.

16. Ibid.

17. Ibid.

18. Ibid.

19. Ibid.

20. *New York Times*, March 28 2003.

21. Ibid.

22. Ibid.

23. *New York Times*, March 29 2003.

24. "Conservatives Tailor Their Tone to Fit Course of the War," *New York Times*, March 28 2003.

25. "A Tough Fight, a Retreat and a Look Ahead," *New York Times*, March 28 2003.

26. "Military Analysis; New Reality, Hard Choices," *New York Times*, March 28 2003.

27. "The Attack; Airstrikes Continue as Allies Consider Timing of a Thrust," *New York Times*, March 29 2003.

28. "A Nation at War: Combat; 2 U.S. Columns Are Advancing on Baghdad Defenses," *New York Times*, April 1 2003.

29. "A Nation at War: In the Field; 101st Airborne Division; Under a Blizzard of Bullets, a Battle Inches On," *New York Times*, April 1 2003.

30. Ibid.

31. "A Nation at War: In the Field; First Marine Division; Marines Move Into 'Bad Guy' Land," *New York Times*, April 1 2003.

32. Ibid.

33. "Questions Linger About Hillah Battle That Left Hundreds of Civilian Casualties," *Associated Press*, May 15 2003.

34. Ibid.

35. "Iraq Blames U.S. For Market Blast That Killed Civilians in Baghdad," *New York Times*, March 29 2003.

36. Ibid.

37. "Iraq Blames U.S. For Market Blast That Killed Civilians in Baghdad," *New York Times*, March 29 2003.

38. Ibid.

39. Ibid.

40. "In Baghdad, Blood and Bandages for the Innocent," *Independent*, March 30 2003.

41. "The Proof: Marketplace Deaths Were Caused By a US Missile," *Independent*, April 2 2003.

42. "Iraq Blames U.S. For Market Blast That Killed Civilians in Baghdad."

43. "In Baghdad, Blood and Bandages for the Innocent."

44. "Poor Pay With Their Lives In Baghdad's Cratered Suburbia," *Observer*, April 3 2003.

45. Ibid.

46. "Witnesses Say U.S. Bombs Hit Iraqi Hospital," *Reuters*, April 2 2003. On April 3 2003 the International Federation of Red Cross and Red Crescent Societies reported: "An Iraqi Red Crescent (IRCS) maternity hospital in the al-Mansour district of Baghdad was damaged on 2 April in an attack by American and British

forces on a nearby building. Three passers-by were killed and 27 injured as a result of the bombing. The bombs hit a building opposite the hospital, and the blast was so strong it damaged nearby buildings. The windows of the maternity hospital were broken and its roof collapsed. The maternity hospital is part of a Red Crescent compound that also includes the IRCS headquarters and a surgical hospital. No casualties were reported from the hospitals, as they had been evacuated some days previously."

47. "Where Were the Panicked Crowds? Where Were the Food Queues? Where Were the Empty Streets?" *Independent*, April 5 2003.

48. "A Morally Hollow Victory," *Observer*, April 6 2003.

49. "Red Cross: Iraq Casualties Too High to Count," *Associated Press*, April 6 2003.

50. "The Twisted Language of War That Is Used To Justify the Unjustifiable," *Independent*, April 7 2003.

51. "Amid Allied Jubilation, a Child Lies in Agony, Clothes Soaked in Blood," *Independent*, April 8 2003.

52. "Final Proof That War Is About the Failure of the Human Spirit," *Independent*, April 10 2003.

53. "Frenzy Over Ali, But There Are Thousands of Children Like Him," *Independent*, April 12 2003.

54. "A Burden Too Heavy to Put Down," *New York Times*, November 4 2003.

55. "America and the U.N., Together Again?" *New York Times*, August 3 2003.

56. "The Lessons of a Quagmire," *New York Times*, November 16 2003.

57. "Who Says We Never Strike First?" *New York Times*, October 4 2002; "A War For Oil? Not This Time," *New York Times*, February 13 2003; "The Nation. Sparing Civilians, Buildings and Even the Enemy," *New York Times,* March 30 2003; "The Back Page; A How-To Manual: A Century of Small Wars Shows They Can Be Won," *New York Times*, July 6 2003; "America and the U.N., Together Again?" *New York Times*, August 3 2003; "A Soldier First," *New York Times*, September 7 2003; "The Lessons of a Quagmire," *New York Times*, November 16 2003; "What the Dreadnoughts Did," *New York Times*, November 23 2003; "Human Rights As Victims of Politics," *New York Times*, December 30 2003; "Soft Power and Hard, and Perhaps Compromise," *New York Times*, February 25 2004.

58. "The New York Times Appoints a Columnist," *New York Times*, July 25 2003.

59. "A Nation at War: The Casualties; Delicate Calculus of Casualties and Public Opinion," *New York Times*, March 27 2003.

60. "A Nation at War: Military Analysis; The Goal Is Baghdad, But At What Cost?" *New York Times*, March 25 2003.

61. "A Nation at War: Military Technology; Digital Links Are Giving Old Weapons New Power," *New York Times*, April 7 2003.

62. "After Effects: Medical Care; In a Functioning Hospital, Scenes of Chaos and Horror," *New York Times*, April 27 2003.

63. "A Nation at War: An Overview: April 7, 2003, Bomb Attack on Hussein, a Bush-Blair Meeting, and Protests at Home," *New York Times*, April 8 2003.

64. "A Nation at War: Combat; U.S. Ground Forces Sweep Toward Baghdad," *New York Times*, April 3 2003.

65. "U.S. Under Fire For Use of Cluster Bombs in Iraq," *San Francisco Chronicle*, May 15 2003.

66. "A Nation at War: In the Field, First Marine Division; Little Resistance Encountered as Troops Reach Baghdad," *New York Times*, April 5 2003.

67. "U.S. Use of Cluster Bombs in Baghdad Condemned," Human Rights Watch, April 16 2003.

68. "Grisly Results of U.S. Cluster Bombs," *New York Newsday*, April 15 2003.

69. Ibid.

70. Ibid.

71. *Associated Press*, April 12 2003, cited in "How Many Civilians Were Killed By Cluster Bombs?" May 6 2003, Iraq Body Count (www.iraqbodycount.net).

72. "A Nation at War: News Analysis; Bush's War Message: Strong and Clear," *New York Times*, April 9 2003.

73. "A Nation at War: News Analysis: A High Point in 2 Decades of U.S. Might," *New York Times*, April 10 2003.

74. Ibid.

75. *New York Times*, April 4 2003.

76. *New York Times*, April 1 2003.

77. *New York Times*, April 2 2003.

78. Ibid.

79. Ibid.

80. *New York Times*, April 3 2003.

81. *New York Times*, April 9 2003.
82. *New York Times*, April 10 2003.
83. *New York Times*, April 15 2003.
84. *New York Times*, April 7 2003.
85. *New York Times*, April 12 2003.
86. *New York Times*, April 27 2003.
87. *New York Times*, April 13 2003.
88. *New York Times*, April 9 2003.
89. *New York Times*, April 20 2003.
90. *New York Times*, April 25 2003.
91. *New York Times*, May 2 2003.
92. "A Nation at War: The Casualties; U.S. Military Has No Count of Iraqi Dead In Fighting," *New York Times*, April 2 2003; "A Nation at War: The Casualties; Number of Iraqis Killed May Never Be Determined," *New York Times*, April 10 2003.
93. "Aftereffects: News Analysis: Cold Truths Behind the Pomp," *New York Times*, May 2 2003.
94. "Family Dreads Telling Father That Three Daughters Are Dead," *New York Times*, April 14 2003.
95. Ibid.
96. "Civilian Deaths in 'Noble' Iraq Mission Pass 10,000," Iraq Body Count (www.iraqbodycount.net), February 7 2004.
97. United Nations General Assembly Resolution 3314 (XXIX). Definition of Aggression, December 14 1974.
98. Principles of the Nuremberg Tribunal, 1950, published in *Report of the International Law Commission Covering Its Second Session*, June 5–29 1950.
99. London Agreement of August 8 1945.
100. Charter of the International Military Tribunal, October 6 1945, Article 6(a).
101. Indictment of the German Major War Criminals: Nazi Conspiracy and Aggression, Volume 1, Chapter 3; October 6 1945.
102. Indictment of the German Major War Criminals, October 6 1945.
103. Judgment of the International Military Tribunal, September 30 1946.
104. United Nations General Assembly Resolution 177 (II), "Formulation of the Principles Recognized in the Charter of the Nurnberg Tribunal and in the Judgment of the Tribunal," November 21 1947.

105. *Report of the International Law Commission Covering its Second Session.*

106. "As U.S. Detains Iraqis, Families Plead For News," *New York Times*, March 7 2003.

107. The Rome Statute of the International Criminal Court, July 17 1998, Part 2, Article 7: Crimes against humanity include "the arrest, detention or abduction of persons ... followed by a refusal to acknowledge that deprivation of freedom or to give information on the fate or whereabouts of those persons, with the intention of removing them from the protection of the law for a prolonged period of time."

108. Todd Purdum and the Staff of the New York Times, *A Time of Our Choosing: America's War in Iraq* (New York: Times Books, 2003).

5   THE TORTURE OVERTURE

1. Michael Ignatieff, "Lesser Evils," *New York Times Magazine*, May 2 2004.

2. "Abuse of Iraqi POWs by GIs Probed," *60 Minutes II*, April 28 2004.

3. Susan Sontag, "Regarding the Torture of Others," *New York Times Magazine*, May 23 2004.

4. Michael Ignatieff, "Mirage in the Desert," *New York Times Magazine*, June 27 2004.

5. Judgment of the International Military Tribunal, September 30 1946.

6. "The American Empire: The Burden," *New York Times Magazine*, January 5 2003.

7. Rome Statute of the International Criminal Court, Part 2. Jurisdiction, Admissibility and Applicable Law, Article 7(1)(f), Article 8(2)(a)(ii), July 17 1998.

8. "The American Empire: The Burden."

9. "Why Are We in Iraq? And Liberia? And Afghanistan?" *New York Times Magazine*, September 7 2003.

10. Association of the Bar of the City of New York; Committee on International Human Rights; Committee on Military Affairs and Justice, "Human Rights Standards Applicable to the United States' Interrogation of Detainees," April 2004, p. 6.

11. Ibid.

12. "Report of the High Commissioner For Human Rights: The Present Situation of Human Rights in Iraq," June 4 2004.

13. "Regarding the Torture of Others."
14. "Bush Says Only Lawful Questioning Authorized," *Reuters*, June 10 2004.
15. "Ashcroft Says the White House Never Authorized Tactics Breaking Laws on Torture," *New York Times*, June 9 2004.
16. Ignatieff, "Mirage in the Desert."
17. "Harsh C.I.A. Methods Cited in Top Qaeda Interrogations," *New York Times*, May 13 2004; "General Took Guantánamo Rules to Iraq for Handling of Prisoners," *New York Times*, May 13 2004; "Earlier Jail Seen as Incubator for Abuses in Iraq," *New York Times*, May 15 2004; "Some Iraqis Held Outside Purview of U.S. Command," *New York Times*, May 17 2004; "Military Police Got Instructions at Iraqi Prison," *New York Times*, May 18 2004; "Officer Says Army Tried to Curb Red Cross Visits to Prison in Iraq," *New York Times*, May 19 2004; "Officers Say U.S. Colonel at Abu Ghraib Prison Felt Intense Pressure to Get Inmates to Talk," *New York Times*, May 19 2004; "Afghan Policies on Questioning Taken to Iraq," *New York Times*, May 21 2004; "Justice Memo Explained How to Skip Prisoner Rights," *New York Times*, May 21 2004; "Dogs and Other Harsh Tactics Linked to Military Intelligence," *New York Times*, May 22 2004; "Handful of Soldiers Spoke Out, As Many Kept Quiet on Abuse," *New York Times*, May 22 2004; "Testimony From Abu Ghraib Prisoners Describes a Center of Violence and Fear," *New York Times*, May 22 2004; "Afghan Deaths Linked to Unit at Iraq Prison," *New York Times*, May 24 2004; "General Says Sanchez Rejected Her Offer to Give Address to Iraqis About Abuses," *New York Times*, May 24 2004; "Pentagon Is Replacing Sanchez as the U.S. Commander in Iraq," *New York Times*, May 25 2004; "G.I.'s Prison Abuse More Widespread, Says Army Survey," *New York Times*, May 26 2004; "Lawyers Decided Bans on Torture Didn't Bind Bush," *New York Times*, June 8 2004; "Forced Nudity of Iraqi Prisoners Is Seen as a Pervasive Pattern, Not Isolated Incidents," *New York Times*, June 8 2004; "Ashcroft Says the White House Never Authorized Tactics Breaking Laws on Torture," *New York Times*, June 9 2004; "Higher Ranking Officer Is Sought to Lead Inquiry Over Abu Ghraib," *New York Times*, June 10 2004; "Army Policy Bars Interrogations by Private Contractors," *New York Times*, June 12 2004; "Unit Says It Gave Earlier Warning of Abuse in Iraq," *New York Times*, June 14 2004; "Rumsfeld Issued an Order to Hide

Detainee in Iraq," *New York Times*, June 17 2004; "Rumsfeld Admits He Told Jailers to Keep Detainee in Iraq Out of Red Cross View," *New York Times*, June 18 2004; "Documents Are Said to Show Earlier Abuse at Iraq Prison," *New York Times*, June 19 2004; "Exaggeration Seen on Value of Guantánamo Detainees," *New York Times*, June 21 2004; "Top Commanders Face Questioning on Prison Abuse," New York Times, June 22 2004; "Legal Scholars Criticize Torture Memos," *New York Times*, June 25 2004; "Abu Ghraib, Stonewalled," *New York Times*, June 30 2004.

6 INTERVENTIONISM AND DUE DILIGENCE

1. "Hugo Chávez Departs," *New York Times*, April 13 2002.
2. "Venezuela's Political Turbulence," *New York Times*, April 16 2002.
3. "Bush Officials Met With Venezuelans Who Ousted Leader," *New York Times*, April 16 2002.
4. "U.S. Cautioned Leader of Plot Against Chávez," *New York Times*, April 17 2002.
5. "U.S. Bankrolling Is Under Scrutiny for Ties to Chávez Ouster," *New York Times*, April 25 2002.
6. "Out With the Old, In With the Old: Events in Venezuela that forced President Hugo Chávez from power, then reinstated him," *New York Times*, April 20 2002.
7. "World Briefing: Americas: Venezuela: Politician Seeks Asylum," *New York Times*, May 24 2002; "World Briefing: Americas: Colombia: Safe Haven for Venezuelan," *New York Times*, May 30 2002.
8. "Uprising in Venezuela: Latin America; Fear of Loss of Democracy Led Neighbors to Aid Return," *New York Times*, April 15 2002.
9. Charter of the Organization of American States, December 13 1951, and as amended.
10. Inter-American Democratic Charter, September 11 2001.
11. "Bush Bypasses Senate on 2 More Nominees," *New York Times*, January 12 2002.
12. The National Security Archive (at www.nsarchive.org/NSAEBB/ NSAEBB40) states that a staff report by the US House Foreign Affairs Committee (Staff Report, State Department and Intelli-

gence Community Involvement in Domestic Activities Related to the Iran/Contra Affair, September 7 1988) "summarized various investigations of Mr. Reich's office." The staff report concluded that "senior CIA officials with backgrounds in covert operations, as well as military intelligence and psychological operations specialists from the Department of Defense, were deeply involved in establishing and participating in a domestic political and propaganda operation run through an obscure bureau in the Department of State which reported directly to the National Security Council rather than through the normal State Department channels. ... Through irregular sole-source, no-bid contracts, S/LPD [headed by Reich] established and maintained a private network of individuals and organizations whose activities were coordinated with, and sometimes directed by, Col. Oliver North as well as officials of the NSC and S/LPD. These private individuals and organizations raised and spent funds for the purpose of influencing Congressional votes and U.S. domestic news media. This network raised and funneled money to off-shore bank accounts in the Cayman Islands or to the secret Lake Resources bank account in Switzerland for disbursement at the direction of Oliver North. Almost all of these activities were hidden from public view and many of the key individuals involved were never questioned or interviewed by the Iran/Contra Committees."

13. "Bush Bypasses Senate on 2 More Nominees." The *Times* reported: "In the mid-1980's, Mr. Reich led a covert program to generate public support in the United States for the anti-Sandinista rebels, or contras, in Nicaragua. As the Iran-contra affair became known, a government investigation concluded that Mr. Reich's office had engaged in prohibited acts of domestic propaganda. Mr. Reich's defenders have denounced the inquiry as flawed and note that no charges were filed against him."

14. "U.S. Cautioned Leader of Plot Against Chávez." "U.S. Revises Report of Venezuelan Contacts," *New York Times*, April 18 2002.

15. "Venezuelan Opposition Files to Seek Referendum on Chávez," *New York Times*, August 21 2002.

16. "Will Calgary Be the Next Kuwait," *New York Times*, August 14 2003.

17. "Hugo Chávez Departs," *New York Times*, April 13 2002.

18. "A Review of U.S. Policy Toward Venezuela: November 2001–April 2002," United States Department of State and the Broad-

casting Board of Governors Office of Inspector General, Report Number 02-OIG-003, July 2002, Redacted For Public Release, Unclassified. Hereinafter, all references to the Inspector General's report in our text below refer to this document.

19. "State Dept. Issues Report on U.S. Actions During Venezuelan Coup," U.S. Department of State, Office of International Information Programs, 30 July 2002; "State Dept. Issues Report on U.S. Actions During Venezuela Coup (Inspector General Finds U.S. Officials Acted Properly During Coup)," Embassy of the United States, Caracas, Venezuela, Public Affairs Office, Press Release (undated).

20. "Bush Official Met With Venezuelans Who Ousted Leader," *New York Times*, April 16 2002; "U.S. Cautioned Leader of Plot Against Chávez," *New York Times*, April 17 2002; "Man in the News: Combative Point Man on Latin Policy—Otto J. Reich," *New York Times*, April 18 2002; "U.S. Revises Report of Venezuela Contacts," *New York Times*, April 18 2002; "U.S. Bankrolling Is Under Scrutiny for Ties to Chávez Ouster," *New York Times*, April 25 2002.

21. "U.S. Bankrolling Is Under Scrutiny for Ties to Chávez Ouster."

22. "Bush Officials Met With Venezuelans Who Ousted Leader."

23. "U.S. Bankrolling Is Under Scrutiny for Ties to Chávez Ouster."

24. "IRI President Folsom Praises Venezuelan Civil Society's Defense of Democracy," *PR Newswire Association*, April 12 2002.

25. "U.S. Bankrolling Is Under Scrutiny for Ties to Chávez Ouster."

26. "Venezuela Inquiry Clears U.S. Aides," *New York Times*, July 30 2002.

27. "US Revealed To Be Secretly Funding Opponents of Chavez," *Independent*, March 13 2004.

28. "Chávez Says U.S. Is Fueling His Enemies," *New York Times*, March 11 2004.

29. Ibid.

7 A DODGY DISSENT

1. Case Concerning Military and Paramilitary Activities In and Against Nicaragua (*Nicaragua v. United States of America*), Merits, International Court of Justice, June 27 1986, para. 292.

2. "America's Guilt—or Default," *New York Times*, July 1 1986.

3. "U.S. Voids Role of World Court on Latin Policy," *New York Times*, April 9 1984.

4. Statute of the International Court of Justice, Article 53.

5. *Nicaragua v. United States of America*, Merits, International Court of Justice, June 27 1986, para. 31.

6. Letter to the Honorable Jack Brooks, Chairman, Committee on Government Operations, U.S. House of Representatives, and the Honorable Dante B. Fascell, Chairman, Committee on Foreign Affairs, U.S. House of Representatives, from the Comptroller General of the United States, September 30, 1987 (B-229069). The Comptroller General reported: "S/LPD engaged in prohibited, covert propaganda activities designed to influence the media and the public to support the [Reagan] Administration's policies. The use of appropriated funds for these activities constitutes a violation of a restriction on the State Department annual appropriations prohibiting the use of federal funds for publicity or propaganda purposes not authorized by the Congress."

7. *Nicaragua v. United States of America*, Merits, International Court of Justice, June 27 1986, para. 73.

8. Ibid.

9. Ibid., para. 93.

10. Ibid.

11. Ibid.

12. Ibid., para. 94.

13. Ibid.

14. Ibid.

15. Ibid.

16. *Nicaragua v. United States of America*, Edgar Chamorro, affidavit, September 11 1985.

17. Bob Woodward, *Veil: The Secret Wars of the CIA, 1981–1987* (New York: Simon and Schuster, 1987), p. 113.

18. *Report of the Congressional Committees Investigating the Iran–Contra Affair*, 100th Congress, 1st Session (Washington: U.S. Government Printing Office, 1987), p. 27.

19. *Nicaragua v. United States of America*, Merits, International Court of Justice, June 27 1986, paras. 102, 108.

20. *Nicaragua v. United States of America*, Edgar Chamorro, affidavit, September 11 1985.

21. *Nicaragua v. United States of America*, Merits, International Court of Justice, June 27 1986, para. 104.

22. Ibid., para. 108.
23. Ibid., para. 113.
24. Ibid., para. 116.
25. Ibid.
26. Ibid.
27. Ibid., para. 117.
28. Ibid., para. 118.
29. Ibid., para. 122.
30. Ibid., para. 95.
31. Ibid., para. 99.
32. Ibid., para. 78.
33. Ibid., para. 79.
34. The government of Nicaragua accused the United States of the following attacks: (a) September 8 1983: An attack on Sandino International Airport by a Cessna aircraft, which was shot down; (b) September 13 1983: An attack on an underwater oil pipeline and part of the oil terminal at Puerto Sandino; (c) October 2 1983: An attack on oil storage facilities at Benjamin Zeledon on the Atlantic coast, causing the loss of a large quantity of fuel; (d) October 10 1983: An attack by air and sea on the port of Corinto, involving the destruction of five oil storage tanks, the loss of millions of gallons of fuel, and the evacuation of large numbers of the local population; (e) October 14 1983: An attack on the underwater pipeline at Puerto Sandino for the second time; (f) January 4/5 1984: An attack by speedboat and helicopters using rockets against the Potosi Naval Base; (g) February 24/25 1984: The explosion of a US-made mine at El Bluff; (h) March 7 1984: An attack on an oil and storage facility at San Juan del Sur by speedboats and helicopters; (i) March 28/30 1984: Clashes at Puerto Sandino between speedboats during mine-laying operations and Nicaragua patrol boats; (j) April 9 1984: A helicopter allegedly launched from a mother ship in international waters provided fire support for an ARDE attack on San Juan del Norte. *Nicaragua v. United States of America*, Merits, International Court of Justice, June 27 1986, para. 81.
35. *Nicaragua v. United States of America*, Merits, International Court of Justice, June 27 1986, para. 85.
36. Woodward, *Veil*, pp. 271–2.
37. *Nicaragua v. United States of America*, Merits, International Court of Justice, June 27 1986, para. 85.

38. Ibid., para. 86.
39. Ibid., para. 87.
40. Ibid., para. 88.
41. Ibid.
42. Ibid., para. 91.
43. Ibid.
44. Ibid.
45. Ibid., para. 125.
46. "Merits," as in the merits phase of a court case, is defined as "the substantive considerations to be taken into account in deciding a case, as opposed to extraneous or technical points, esp. of procedure." *Black's Law Dictionary: Seventh Edition* (St. Paul: West Group, 1999), p. 1003.
47. *Nicaragua v. United States of America*, Merits, International Court of Justice, June 27 1986, para. 292.
48. Ibid.
49. Ibid.
50. Ibid.
51. *Nicaragua v. United States of America*, Merits, International Court of Justice, June 27 1986, para. 292.
52. Ibid.
53. "America's Guilt—or Default," *New York Times*, July 1 1986.
54. *Nicaragua v. United States of America*, Declaration of Intervention by the Republic of El Salvador, August 15 1984.
55. Ibid.
56. *Nicaragua v. United States of America*, Declaration of Intervention of the Republic of El Salvador, Order, October 4 1984; *Nicaragua v. United States*, Jurisdiction of the Court and Admissibility of the Application, November 26 1984, paras. 6, 74.
57. Case Concerning Military and Paramilitary Activities In and Against Nicaragua (*Nicaragua v. United States of America*), Dissenting Opinion of Judge Schwebel, International Court of Justice, June 27 1986, paras. 112–13.
58. *Nicaragua v. United States of America*, Declaration of Intervention by the Republic of El Salvador, August 15 1984.
59. *Nicaragua v. United States of America*, Merits, International Court of Justice, June 27 1986, para. 133.
60. Ibid., para. 127.
61. *Nicaragua v. United States of America*, Edgar Chamorro, affidavit, September 11 1985.

62. Ibid.
63. *Nicaragua v. United States of America*, David MacMichael, testimony, September 16 1985.
64. Ibid.
65. Ibid.
66. Ibid.
67. Ibid.
68. *Nicaragua v. United States of America*, Edgar Chamorro, affidavit, September 11 1985.
69. *Nicaragua v. United States of America*, Dissenting Opinion of Judge Schwebel, June 27 1986, para. 28.
70. Ibid., para. 2. Schwebel stated: "[T]he differences between the Court's views and mine turn particularly on the facts. The facts are in fundamental controversy. I find the Court's statement of the facts to be inadequate, in that it sufficiently sets out the facts which have led it to reach conclusions of law adverse to the United States, while it insufficiently sets out the facts which should have led it to reach conclusions of law adverse to Nicaragua. In such a situation, where the Parties differ profoundly on what the facts are, and where the Court has arrived at one evaluation of them and I another, I believe that it is my obligation to present the factual support for the conclusions which I have reached."
71. UN Charter Article 39 gives the Security Council authority to determine threats to the peace and measures to address them. Article 51 requires any state taking individual or collective self-defense measures to report such measures to the Security Council.
72. *Nicaragua v. United States of America*, Dissenting Opinion of Judge Schwebel, June 27 1986, para. 183.
73. Ibid., para. 191.
74. *Nicaragua v. United States of America*, Dissenting Opinion of Judge Schwebel, Factual Appendix, June 27 1986, para. 20.
75. Ibid., para. 179.
76. Ibid., para. 20.
77. Ibid., para. 19. Judge Schwebel footnoted this statement by citing State Department documents as his sources for refuting the press criticisms as follows: "Department of State, 'Response to Stories Published in the Wall Street Journal and the Washington Post about Special Report No. 80', 17 June 1981, and 'Revolution Beyond Our Borders', p. 5, note 2, which maintains that: 'The

authenticity of these documents ... have since been corroborated by new intelligence sources and defectors.' "

78. Jonathan Kwitny, "Apparent Errors Cloud U.S. White Paper on El Salvador," *Wall Street Journal*, June 8 1981.

79. Ibid.

80. Ibid.

81. Robert G Kaiser, "White Paper on El Salvador is Faulty," *Washington Post*, June 9 1981.

82. Ibid.

83. Ibid.

84. Ibid.

85. *Nicaragua v. United States of America*, Dissenting Opinion of Judge Schwebel, Factual Appendix, June 27 1986, para. 19.

86. Christopher Dickey, *With the Contras: A Reporter in the Wilds of Nicaragua* (New York: Simon and Schuster, 1985), p. 281.

87. *Nicaragua v. United States of America*, Dissenting Opinion of Judge Schwebel, June 27 1986, para. 32.

88. Dickey, *With the Contras*, p. 75, 281.

89. Ibid., p. 75.

90. *Nicaragua v. United States of America*, Dissenting Opinion of Judge Schwebel, June 27 1986, para. 32.

91. Dickey, *With the Contras*, p. 133.

92. *Nicaragua v. United States*, Merits, June 27 1986, para. 63.

93. Raymond Bonner, *Weakness and Deceit: U.S. Policy and El Salvador* (New York: Times Books, 1984), p. 255.

94. Ibid., pp. 256–7.

95. Robert F. Turner, *Nicaragua v. United States: A Look at the Facts* (Cambridge: Institute for Foreign Policy Analysis, Inc., 1987).

96. Ibid., p. vii.

97. *Nicaragua v. United States of America*, Dissenting Opinion of Judge Schwebel, Factual Appendix, June 27 1986, para. 19.

98. Ibid.

99. Turner, *Nicaragua v. United States: A Look at the Facts*, pp. xii–xiv.

100. *Nicaragua v. United States of America*, Dissenting Opinion of Judge Schwebel, Factual Appendix, June 27 1986, paras. 28–188.

101. Letter to the Honorable Jack Brooks, Chairman, Committee on Government Operations, U.S. House of Representatives, and the Honorable Dante B. Fascell, Chairman, Committee on Foreign Affairs, U.S. House of Representatives, from the Comptroller General of the United States, September 30 1987 (B-229069).

102. Ibid.
103. Robert Parry and Peter Kornbluh, "Reagan's Pro-Contra Propaganda Machine," *Washington Post*, September 4 1988.
104. Ibid.
105. *Nicaragua v. United States of America*, Dissenting Opinion of Judge Schwebel, Factual Appendix, June 27 1986, para. 179.
106. Morris Morley and James Petras, *The Reagan Administration and Nicaragua: How Washington Constructs Its Case For Counterrevolution in Central America* (New York: Institute for Media Analysis, 1987), p. 33.
107. Ibid., p.41.
108. Clifford Krauss and Robert S. Greenberger, "Despite Fears of U.S., Soviet Aid to Nicaragua Appears to Be Limited—White House Still Will Push To Aid Contras to Lessen Risk of Region Revolution—Managua Shuns Puppet Role," *Wall Street Journal*, April 3 1985.
109. Ibid.
110. *Nicaragua v. United States of America*, Dissenting Opinion of Judge Schwebel, June 27 1986, para. 30.
111. *Nicaragua v. United States of America*, Dissenting Opinion of Judge Schwebel, Factual Appendix, June 27 1986, para. 98.
112. "Captive Recants Salvador Story, to U.S. Dismay," *New York Times*, March 13 1982.
113. "Contra Chief Says North Arranged For Payments," *New York Times*, February 21 1987; "Notes From North Describe Meeting on Contra Support," *New York Times*, July 15 1987.
114. *Nicaragua v. United States of America*, Dissenting Opinion of Judge Schwebel, Factual Appendix, June 27 1986, para. 143.
115. Ibid.
116. Ibid., para. 149.
117. Ibid.
118. Woodward, *Veil*, p. 229.
119. *Nicaragua v. United States of America*, David MacMichael, testimony, September 16 1985.
120. The Boland Amendment of December 1982 prohibited the Reagan administration from providing military support to the contras for the purpose of overthrowing the Government of Nicaragua.
121. *Report of the Congressional Committees Investigating the Iran–Contra Affair*, p. 31.

122. Ibid.

123. Ibid., p. 12.

124. *U.S. Intelligence Performance on Central America: Achievements and Selected Instances of Concern: Staff Report, Subcommittee on Oversight and Evaluation: Permanent Select Committee on Intelligence* (Washington DC: US Government Printing Office, 1982).

125. Ibid., pp. 8–9.

126. Ibid., pp. 15–16.

127. *Nicaragua v. United States*, Merits, June 27 1986, para. 230.

128. *Nicaragua v. United States of America*, Dissenting Opinion of Judge Schwebel, June 27 1986, para. 157.

129. Ian Brownlie, *International Law and the Use of Force By States* (Oxford: Clarendon Press, 1963), p. 278.

130. *Nicaragua v. United States*, Merits, June 27 1986, para. 160.

131. Ibid., para. 230.

8   THE VIETNAM SYNDROME

1. "The President's Address," *New York Times*, August 5 1964.

2. "2 Carriers Used: McNamara Reports on Aerial Strikes and Reinforcements," *New York Times*, August 5 1964.

3. *New York Times*, August 5 1964. (Note: While today the front page of the *New York Times* has six columns across the front page, in 1964 it had eight columns.)

4. "Forces Enlarged: Stevenson to Appeal for Action by U.N. on 'Open Aggression,' " *New York Times*, August 4 1964.

5. "2 Carriers Used: McNamara Reports on Aerial Strikes and Reinforcements."

6. "Reds Driven Off: Two Torpedo Vessels Believed Sunk in Gulf of Tonkin," *New York Times*, August 4 1964.

7. "The President Acts," *New York Times*, August 5 1964.

8. Ibid.

9. "Vast Review of War Took a Year," *New York Times*, June 13 1971.

10. See Daniel Ellsberg, *Secrets: A Memoir of Vietnam and the Pentagon Papers* (New York: Viking 2002); David Rudenstine, *The Day the Presses Stopped: A History of the Pentagon Papers Case* (Berkeley: University of California Press, 1996).

11. "Vietnam Archive: Pentagon Study Traces 3 Decades of Growing U.S. Involvement," *New York Times*, June 13 1971.

12. Ibid.

13. Separate Opinion of Justice Hugo Black, *New York Times Co. v. United States*, 403 U.S. 713 (1971).

14. Separate Opinion of Justice Potter Stewart, *New York Times Co. v. United States*, 403 U.S. 713 (1971).

15. Gulf of Tonkin Resolution, Joint Resolution of Congress, HJ RES 1145 August 7 1964.

16. Associated Press report, untitled, *New York Times*, August 5 1964.

17. "Peking Condemns U.S. 'Aggression,' " *New York Times*, August 6 1964.

18. "Texts of Addresses by Stephenson and Morozov Before U.N. Security Council," *New York Times*, August 6 1964.

19. Ellsberg, *Secrets*, p. 7.

20. Ibid., p. 9.

21. Ibid., pp. 9–10.

22. Ibid., p. 10.

23. Ibid., p. 10.

24. Ibid.

25. Ibid.

26. Robert S McNamara, James G Blight, and Robert K Brigham, *Argument Without End: In Search of Answers to the Vietnam Tragedy* (New York: Public Affairs, 1999), p. 202.

27. Ibid.

28. Robert S McNamara with Brian VanDeMark, *In Retrospect: The Tragedy and Lessons of Vietnam* (New York: Times Books, 1995), p. 128.

29. McNamara et al., *Argument Without End*, p. xi.

30. Ibid., pp. 202–3.

31. Ibid., p. 215.

32. Ibid., pp. 202–3.

33. Ibid., p. 158.

34. Ibid.

35. The Consultative Council of the Lawyers Committee on American Policy Toward Vietnam, Richard Falk, Chair, John HE Fried, Rapporteur, *Vietnam and International Law* (Northampton: Aletheia Press, 1990), p. 57.

36. Quoted in Ibid.

37. Ibid., pp. 57–8.

38. Ibid., p. 58.

39. Ibid., p. 119.

40. "376 Americans Killed in Vietnam Since 1961," *New York Times*, February 8 1965.

41. Ibid.

42. Noam Chomsky and Edward S Herman, *The Political Economy of Human Rights, Volume II: After the Cataclysm: Postwar Indochina and the Reconstruction of Imperial Ideology* (Boston: South End Press, 1979), p. 13. Chomsky and Herman report "the slaughter of over 150,000 South Vietnamese by 1965" (p. 13). Furthermore, AJ Langguth reports that in a meeting with "an array of military advisers" on July 22 1965, President Johnson, while distinguishing between "Vietcong" and "South Vietnamese," itemized the number of casualties in South Vietnam up to that point: "The Vietcong dead is running at a rate of 25,000 a year. At least 15,000 have been killed by air—half of those are not part of what we call Vietcong. Since 1961, a total of 89,000 have been killed. The South Vietnamese are being killed at a rate of 12,000 a year." This accounting appears to indicate that the US had been killing people in South Vietnam at a rate of 37,000 a year by 1965. AJ Langguth, *Our Vietnam: The War, 1954–1975* (New York: Simon & Schuster, 2000), p. 380.

43. "Seven G.I.'s Slain in Vietcong Raid; 80 Are Wounded," *New York Times*, February 7 1965.

44. "Capital Is Tense: But President Asserts Nation Still Opposes Widening of War," *New York Times*, February 8 1965.

45. Ibid.

46. Ibid.

47. McNamara et al., *Argument Without End*, p. 173.

48. "Reprisal in Vietnam," *New York Times*, February 8 1965.

49. "2 Carriers Used: McNamara Reports on Aerial Strikes and Reinforcements."

50. "4 Bases Bombed: Oil Depot Also Target of 5-Hour Attack—2 Planes Lost," *New York Times*, August 6 1964.

51. Ibid.

52. "Patrol Ended Sunday," *New York Times*, August 14 1964.

53. "Warning to Hanoi," *New York Times*, August 4 1964.

54. Lawyers Committee, *Vietnam and International Law*, p. 59.

55. "Comments on U.S. Action in Vietnam," *New York Times*, February 17 1965.

56. "U.S. Widens Basis For Retaliation: Aides Say Strikes at Saigon Forces May Bring Raids," *New York Times*, February 10 1965.

57. "What Price Vietnam," *New York Times*, February 10 1965.

58. "Vietnam Archive: Pentagon Study Traces 3 Decades of Growing U.S. Involvement," *New York Times*, June 13 1971.

59. Ibid.

60. "Washington: The Undeclared and Unexplained War," *New York Times*, February 14 1965.

61. McNamara et al., *Argument Without End*, p. 173.

62. Final Declaration of the Geneva Conference, July 21 1954.

63. Quoted in Lawyers Committee, *Vietnam and International Law*, p. 167.

64. Ibid., p. 41.

65. "New Victory For Reds," *New York Times*, July 21 1954.

66. "Truce in Indochina," *New York Times*, July 21 1954.

67. David Rudenstine, *The Day the Presses Stopped: A History of the Pentagon Papers Case* (Berkeley: University of California Press, 1996), p. 28.

68. Lawyers Committee, *Vietnam and International Law*, p. 43.

69. Final Declaration of the Geneva Conference, July 20 1954, Article 6.

70. Lawyers Committee, *Vietnam and International Law*, pp. 43, 47.

71. Dwight D. Eisenhower, *The White House Years: Mandate For Change, 1953–1956* (New York: Doubleday & Company, 1963), p. 372.

72. Lawyers Committee, *Vietnam and International Law*, p. 49.

73. Ibid., pp. 49–50.

74. Rudenstine, *The Day the Presses Stopped*, p. 55.

75. Ibid., p. 92.

76. Ibid., p. 99.

77. Ibid., pp. 99–100.

78. *New York Times Company v. United States*, 403 U.S. 713 (1971).

79. Rudenstine, *The Day the Presses Stopped*, pp. 302–4.

80. Ibid., p. 305.

81. Separate Opinion of Justice Hugo Black, with Justice Douglas Concurring, *New York Times Co. v. United States*, 403 U.S. 713 (1971).

CONCLUSION: STRICT SCRUTINY

1. Robert S. McNamara, *In Retrospect: The Tragedy and Lessons of Vietnam* (New York: Times Books, 1995), p. 328.

2. Ibid.

3. Ibid., p. 128.

4. John L. Hess, *My Times: A Memoir of Dissent* (New York: Seven Stories Press, 2003), p. 29.

5. Arthur Gelb, *City Room* (New York: A Marian Wood Book, 2003), p. 8.

INDEX